Building legislation and historic buildings

A guide to the application of the Building Regulations, the Public Health Acts, the Fire Precautions Act, the Housing Act and other legislation relevant to historic buildings

Alan C. Parnell, FRIBA, FSIAD, PI Fire E, Dip TP

The Architectural Press: London

First published in 1987 by The Architectural Press Ltd,
9 Queen Anne's Gate, London SW1H 9BY, for the
Historic Buildings and Monuments Commission for
England.

British Library Cataloguing in Publication Data
Parnell, Alan
Building legislation and historic buildings: a guide to the application of the Building Regulations, the Public Health Act, the Fire Precautions Act, the Housing Act and other legislation relevant to historic buildings.
1. Historic buildings – Law and legislation – England 2. Historic buildings – Conservation and restoration – England
I. Title
344.204'94 KD3740
ISBN 0-85139-790-5

Typeset by Crawley Composition Ltd, Stephenson Way, Three Bridges, Crawley, Sussex

Printed in Great Britain at the University Press, Cambridge

This publication is based on a report prepared by the author with the assistance of Anthony Ferguson MSc, BArch, RIAS, for the Historic Buildings and Monuments Commission for England.

Contents

Foreword

This study has been the subject of extensive consultation with those responsible for the legislation relevant to historic buildings. But interpretation of their requirements varies so much from authority to authority and from case to case that it is not possible to give prescriptive guidance. Instead, the study discusses the issues and provides a wealth of examples carefully cross-referenced to the narrative text showing solutions which have been accepted in specific instances.

During the 1980s there have been considerable advances in our knowledge of the causes and effects of deterioration and damage to buildings, particularly the effects of fire. There have also been changes in our attitude towards the purpose and effectiveness of building control, resulting in a radical revision of the legislation. These developments are discussed in the text and reflected in the case studies, which cover a broad time span.

The purpose of this study is to aid the architect in tackling his own design problems and support him in his negotiations with the various controlling authorities.

Acknowledgements

The author has been assisted in the preparation of this study by so many organisations and individuals that it is impossible to acknowledge them all here by name. We would like to thank historic building owners who have allowed us to visit their property or told us about their experiences, and architects and surveyors who have provided information, drawings and guidance tours of historic buildings. Many local authorities provided valuable information at interviews or in answering questionnaires. Specific mention should be made of the help that conservation and amenity societies gave in finding relevant case studies and making contact with conservation specialists.

The following organisations were invited to comment on those sections most relevant to their areas of responsibility, and we would like to thank them for their cooperation:

The Directorate of Ancient Monuments and Historic Buildings, the Housing Directorates and the Development Control and Building Regulations Divisions, Department of the Environment;
The Department of Education and Science;
Her Majesty's Inspector of Fire Services, Home Office;
The Health and Safety Executive;
The Fire Branch of the Directorate of Architectural Services, Property Services Agency;
The Fire Research Station, Building Research Establishment;
The Building Regulation and Historic Buildings Division, Greater London Council;
The Council for the Care of Churches.

Every effort has been made to ensure that their observations have been taken into account.

Opinions expressed in this report are those of the author and do not necessarily represent the views of English Heritage, any Government department or official body. *Author's comments are printed in italics.*

Original use	*Existing and proposed uses*
Town houses:	Residential/hostels/ hotels, etc
Civic buildings:	Town halls/guildhalls
Shops:	Shops/offices/small workshops/restaurants
Shops with mixed uses and tenancies:	Multi-purpose uses generally
Warehouses and mills:	All uses
Churches:	Residential
Victorian villas:	Residential
Country houses:	Residential/offices/ educational/tourist
Country cottages:	Housing/old people's residential/holiday uses
Hotels and public houses:	Hotels/offices/ residential/tourist uses
University buildings:	Educational and extramural holiday uses
Schools:	Educational and holiday uses

General introduction

Appreciation of the cultural value of historic buildings in post-war years has been reflected in protective legislation and the criteria for inclusion within this protective framework. The first major step was the Listing of Buildings of Architectural or Historic Interest under the Town and Country Planning Acts. The first round of listing was completed in 1969, by which time the statutory lists for the whole of England included about 120,000 buildings. The second round, due to be completed in 1987, will increase this number to about 460,000.

New legislation in 1967 enabled local authorities to designate conservation areas. The aim was to preserve and enhance the character of these areas. We have no estimate of the number of buildings which can be regarded as contributing to the character of conservation areas, but the number must be large as there are well over 5,500 such areas, some covering virtually a whole town centre and its environs. Few towns lack at least one designated area and some 3,000 villages are also covered by designation.

The accent now is on repair and, where appropriate, finding new uses for those buildings which no longer fulfil their original purpose.

As a result of the extension of protection to whole areas, allied to the shift in favour of keeping old buildings, we can expect an increasing number of historic buildings to be the subject of applications for change of use, alteration, extension and sub-division. It is at this stage that the problems of complying with a whole range of statutory controls will be encountered.

Controls were originally designed for buildings with specific, designated uses; major difficulties occur when they are applied to historic buildings which are to be altered or extended or where a change of use is proposed. This is because such buildings vary enormously in construction, materials, and in internal and external layout, resulting in a bewildering range of individual problems for which there are few guidelines.

To date, this problem has sometimes been met by waiving standards or, in individual cases, exempting buildings from normal requirements. This course is recommended for consideration in DOE Circular 8/87, following the earlier Circulars 53/67, 91/73, 23/77 and 92/81.

We have therefore to reconcile a variety of objectives: to provide for modern use and comfort, to comply with acceptable standards of safety, health and neighbourliness, and to retain the historic integrity and visual character of the building. The value of such a reconciliation will be more apparent when it is remembered that the objectives of preservation and modern use are interdependent; and further, that modern use and preservation will both be more fully guaranteed if the building is made structurally sound, hygienic, pleasant and convenient by adhering as far as possible to desirable standards of daylighting, ventilation, damp-proofing, insulation, fire safety, etc.

The book intends to examine the question of balancing these varied objectives and to relate this balance to the range of statutory and other controls normally applicable in given situations. We attempt to do this by:

— reviewing the statutory controls exercised in England and Wales, including London, by local authorities over historic buildings in use, and when alterations or a change of use are proposed;
— indicating the impact of such controls on the character and environment of historic buildings, outlining the main problems that result, and showing how far and in what ways they can be resolved;
— considering the case for relaxing some buildings from control in the interests of conservation of historic character;
— examining the possibility of improving the application of the various administrative procedures to historic buildings; and
— increasing understanding of the problems of the continuing use of historic buildings and the current standards for safety and amenity and recommending ways in which this understanding can best be promoted.

This has involved investigating the effects of statutory controls on the building types in the table opposite. A selection of these have been included as case studies to illustrate general points discussed in the text.

1

The legislation before the Building Regulations 1985

1.1 Introduction

This chapter reviews the statutory controls exercised over historic buildings in England up to 1984. The new Building Regulations have proved to be a watershed in building control and their effect is considered in Chapter 4.

Statutory controls have not been designed specifically for historic buildings, but they affect them in various ways, depending on their use, the ways in which these uses change, and the alterations which historic buildings undergo. The controls are summarised in Table 1 (p. 41).

Later chapters consider the ways in which statutory controls affect the character and environment of historic buildings.

1.2 The Public Health Acts

1.2.1 Dangerous structures

Under S.25 of the 1961 Act, a local authority had powers to take immediate steps to protect the public from the danger of the complete or partial collapse of a building, after having attempted to contact the owner.

Under S.58 of the 1963 Act (as amended by S.24 of the 1961 Act to include the safety of people in an adjoining street), the local authority could obtain a court order requiring a building owner to make good defects if it considered a building to be 'in such a condition or is used to carry such loads, as to be dangerous'. The order could restrict the use of the building until the defect was corrected, the local authority could shore up or fence off a dangerous building, and an owner receiving an S.58 notice could elect to demolish the building rather than carry out the work.

Section 25(1) gave the surveyor of a local authority the power to act without first having to consult his authority. The potential conflict with listed building legislation which resulted from this power is discussed in Chapter 2.

1.2.2 Sanitary fittings

Section 33(1)(b) of the 1961 Act empowered the local authority to reject plans deposited for consideration of any conversion of a building into a house or dwelling if they did not show that each dwelling had a bathroom with a fixed bath or shower having a hot and cold supply.

1.2.3 Means of escape

The local authority is enabled by S.59 of the 1936 Act as amended by the Local Government (Miscellaneous Provisions) Act 1982 to make requirements for suitable means of ingress and egress from certain assembly buildings. 'Assembly' is interpreted in the broadest sense to mean places to which there is public access.

Section 59 is a 'long stop' in means of escape legislation and would only be used where none of the licensing or entertainment provisions applied. We have found no examples.

Section 60 of the 1963 Act empowered the local authority to make means of escape requirements for buildings of more than two storeys, in which people slept, on floor levels more than 6 m above ground level. The section referred to lettable dwellings, residential schools, children's homes 'and the like'. It did not apply in Inner London and some Local Acts amended its powers and scope. Also, it did not apply to owner-occupied dwellings. The requirements were not codified, but were generally interpreted as being restricted to the provision of a protected escape route or routes. Means of safeguarding that route, warning systems and fire fighting equipment were not covered by the Section. Escape routes had to be provided to the outside at ground level. A common application in historic buildings was to caretakers' flats.

There was provision for an appeal to a magistrate's court against any requirements made by the local authority.

1.3 The Building Regulations 1976

The original 1976 Regulations were made under the Public Health Act to protect the health and safety of building users and to promote energy conservation. Changes since 1984 are discussed in Chapter 4.

1.3.1 Scope

The following is a list of matters which were controlled by the Regulations affecting historic buildings:
— fitness of materials;
— exclusion of damp;
— protection against some of the damaging effects of water penetration;
— structural stability and the calculation of applied loads;
— fire resistance of elements of structure;
— sub-division of buildings with fire resisting walls and/or floors to control fire spread and fire size;
— separation of buildings to control fire spread between different buildings and between parts of one building that are put to different uses;
— control of openings in fire resisting walls (and floors) including the performance of fire resisting doors, to control fire spread;
— provision of fire barriers in concealed cavities to prevent fire spread in them;
— restriction on the use of combustible material on the external faces of buildings used for assembly purposes;
— restrictions on the materials to be used in stairways to prevent them contributing to a fire;
— control of the surface flame spread properties of walls and ceilings in circulation areas and rooms;
— restrictions on the use of roofing materials with poor resistance to ignition or penetration by fire from the outside;
— the design of stairs, handrails and landings;
— provisions for ventilating habitable rooms;
— restrictions on the use of materials in flues, fireplaces and hearths.

This is not a complete list of the topics covered by the Regulations since we have excluded items which are not likely to have any relevance to or detrimental effect on historic buildings.

1.3.2 Application to historic buildings

A. Totally exempt buildings

The application of the Regulations depends on the circumstances of the case; Crown buildings and maintained schools, for example, are exempt from them altogether.
Schools. Fire precautions in existing maintained schools have been controlled by Standards for school premises regulations and the DES Building Bulletin 7, and it appears to be up to the education authority to decide whether, and by how much, to upgrade fire precautions in existing maintained schools.
Crown buildings. Although the Crown is not obliged to obtain consent under Building Regulations, it is usual to do so. Private architects, commissioned to work on Crown properties, normally follow the ordinary building control procedure. The Property Services Agency has its own regulations system incorporating the Regulations, which runs in parallel with that of the local authority and has its own relaxations procedure, as well as means of escape provisions.

B. Partially exempt buildings

There were also some types of buildings which were 'partially exempt' from the Regulations. They were divided into eight classes, of which classes 2, 4, 5 and 8 were unlikely to include historic buildings. The other classes and the principal exceptions were as follows:
Class 1. Detached buildings of not more than 30 m^2 in private daytime recreational use or for storage. Compliance with Part E was required unless its volume was less than 30 m^3 and it was more than 2 m from any residential building on the same property.
Class 3. A Scheduled Ancient Monument did not have to comply with Part E, which dealt with fire precautions.
Class 6. Compliance with Part E (except E15) was not required for a single-storey detached building for accommodating materials, products, livestock or plant, and in which people were employed only to supervise and remove the contents stored there.
Class 7. A detached greenhouse used for agriculture without retail sales and sufficiently far from any building containing dwelling accommodation to satisfy Regulation E7 did not have to comply with Part E (except E7), or any other Regulation.

C. New work and maintenance

New work, if not affected by one of these exemptions, had to comply with the Regulations, whereas maintenance work to replace like with like without any alterations or modification did not. Regulations A7 and A9 concerned the application of Regulations when alterations or extensions were to be made to an existing building, or where a change of use occurred.

Under A7, parts of the existing building affected by the new work had to comply so far as was necessary to prevent the finished job from contravening Regulations to a greater extent than had been the case before, and from contravening Regulations which did not apply before. The problem for the building inspector was to decide what was 'affected'. His decision could have a significant effect on the work, as is illustrated in the case studies.

D. Change of use

Regulation A9 defined four cases of 'material change of use' which required some of the Building Regulations to be applied to an existing building. For example, Case A concerned the change of use of a building, or part of a building, into a house, and specified the Regulations that applied. If the change of use proposed did not involve any work to the building, the Regulations specified by the appropriate case were applied as though the building were new. This was also done when the proposals included alteration or extension work, but in this case A7 could be invoked to make additional requirements for the pre-existing parts of the building to prevent there being a greater contravention of any Regulations, in the finished job, than there had been before it was done.

The significance of this was that, as a result of a change of use, alterations could be required to be made to an historic building even though no works were originally proposed by its owner. For example, if a shop in a narrow medieval street was converted into an office, the requirements for fire resistance of external walls (E7) could be imposed and might have affected the sizes of windows or the construction of the walls.

1.3.3 Determination, relaxation and dispensation

Where the local authority and the applicant could not agree on the interpretation of a regulation (i.e. on whether a proposal did or did not comply with the Regulation), they could agree to apply to the Minister for a determination of the point in question. This was done in the case of Brocket Hall (see Case Study 9A).

See Case Study 9A, pp. 117-19

Where an applicant considered that the effect of a Regulation was too onerous in the circumstances, he could apply for a relaxation of a specific or performance requirement or a dispensation of a functional requirement of any of the Regulations listed in A13. If the building was owned by the local authority they had to apply to the Minister for a relaxation or dispensation.

Relaxations and dispensations of Part E of the Regulations had to be referred to the Minister in any case where the building's volume exceeded 7,000 m^3 or, in the case of multi-occupied premises, including shopping facilities, if the floor area exceeded 4,000 m^2.

1.3.4 Administration and powers

The Building Regulations are enforced at district local authority level. The 1976 Regulations did not apply to Inner London, where the London Building Acts were used. Charges are made for the examination of plans and for the inspection of work on site, unless the value of the relevant work is less than £1,000.

The local authority has five weeks, which may be extended to eight with the applicant's agreement, in which to consider and give a decision on a plan. If it fails to do so and the plans are later found to be defective, its scope for enforcement action is prejudiced. Work can legally start on site once plans and a notice of intent have been submitted, but an authority can serve a notice to stop unauthorised or defective work and can have openings made to inspect hidden work.

A decision on an application for a relaxation or dispensation must be given within two months if handled by a local authority. If it is refused, the applicant may appeal to the Secretary of State.

1.3.5 Deemed to satisfy and British Standards

Quite frequently the Building Regulations refer to specifications (e.g. the Schedule No. 6 on timber joints referred to by Regulation D12), or to British Standards or Codes of Practice (e.g. CP 3 chapter IV, part 3, for means of escape from office buildings). If the deposited plans complied with these specifications, etc, they were deemed to satisfy the Regulation (Regulation D8 in the case of the example above on timber joists, and E22 in the case of the code on means of escape).

The designer was not obliged to use the quoted code or whatever, and could use any means he thought fit to achieve the stated aim of the Regulation. He had to be able to demonstrate compliance to the satisfaction of the authority.

1.4 The London Building Acts and Constructional By-laws

In the Inner London area, the London Building Acts 1930–78 and Constructional By-laws applied until 1986 instead of the National Building Regulations. The details of the 1986 changes are given in Chapter 4.

1.4.1 Scope

The by-laws covered constructional matters under the following headings:

A materials of construction;
B(i) sites of buildings, excavations, foundations, voids beneath floors and the prevention of damp;
B(ii) roofs and roof coverings, external enclosures and cladding and projections from buildings;
C(i) walls and piers;
C(ii) the structural use of steel;
C(iii) the structural use of reinforced concrete, prestressed concrete and precast concrete;
C(iv) the structural use of timber;
C(v) dead, imposed and wind loads;
D(i) fire resistance of elements of construction and separation between buildings;
D(ii) flues, chimneys, hearths, ducts and chimney shafts;
D(iii) oil-burning appliances and the associated storage of oil-fuel; and
E lighting, ventilation and height of rooms.

It can be seen from this list that proportionately more attention was given to structural matters than in the Building Regulations. Further fire precautions provisions were contained in Section 35 of the London Building (Amendment) Act 1939, requiring improvement to means of escape in a wide range of building types.

Section 20 of the Act concerned large or tall buildings and gave the building authority power to make requirements about fire precautions, means of escape, smoke ventilation and assistance to the fire brigade.

Section 26 concerned 'public' buildings, the construction of which was left entirely to the satisfaction of the district surveyor, but the control over the means of escape from such buildings was the same as for other non-public buildings.

1.4.2 Application to historic buildings

Section 132 provided that, where part of a building of historic interest was taken down as part of the process of repair, it could be rebuilt in the manner of the original in the interests of preservation, even though not conforming to the by-laws.

The special problems of historic buildings were considered entirely on their merits, the administrative system and arrangements for modifications or waivers allowing considerable flexibility.

1.4.3 Modifications and waivers

During the application procedure for approval, the GLC professional officers were in a position to discuss details on the drawings or specification which did not appear to conform: in the case of major proposals, they could suggest meetings with the appropriate officers to resolve the matter. These decisions would then be incorporated in the letter of consent with any subsequent conditions (e.g. 'to the approval of the council').

If need be, a modification or waiver of the by-laws could be negotiated under Section 9 of the 1935 Act.

Although the district surveyor received a copy of the approval documents, he could also question the use of constructional systems or materials during the course of the work. Some decisions made in direct discussions would be referred back to the GLC for ratification. In the event of a disagreement with the district surveyor, an appeal could in many cases be made to the council for a determination. If still aggrieved, the owner could usually appeal to a tribunal for an ultimate decision.

1.4.4 Administration

The superintending architect (Building Regulation division) was responsible for means of escape requirements and was the principal authority for granting by-law waivers and consents, etc, under the London Building Acts. The approval of plans was administered by the Building Regulation division of the GLC Department of Architecture and Civic Design. The enforcement of the Acts and by-laws on site was carried out by the district surveyors, who were entirely independent from the Inner London boroughs.

1.4.5 Codes and Standards

The GLC produced Codes of Practice on means of escape in case of fire and on special requirements for large or tall 'Section 20' buildings. These documents were intended for the guidance of designers and were intended to make the complex legislative process as clear and comprehensible as possible. They were not binding on either the designer or the authority, which was in a position to demand a higher standard if circumstances required it.

1.5 The Fire Precautions Act

When occupied buildings are put to a use or uses designated under the Fire Precautions Act 1971, as amended by the Health and Safety at Work etc Act 1974,* the fire precautions are controlled by a certification procedure. Proposed amendments are described in Chapter 4.

* With respect to premises previously subject to fire precautions control under the Factories Act 1961 and the Offices, Shops and Railway Premises Act 1963.

1.5.1 Scope

The Act enables the Secretary of State to designate a wide range of building occupancies, and those designated so far comprise hotels, boarding houses, factories, offices, shops and railway premises.

Certain buildings do not require certificates:

— hotels and boarding houses where there are no more than six people (staff and guests) sleeping and where their bedrooms are confined to the ground and first floors (see para 2.4.5);
— certain factories, offices, shops and railway premises in which no more than twenty persons are employed to work or not more than ten persons are so employed elsewhere than on the ground floor;
— premises appropriated to and used solely or mainly for public religious worship, houses that are single private dwellings, houses that are in multiple occupation (but see para 1.6 on the Housing Acts); prisons and similar penal establishments and premises occupied solely for the purpose of the armed forces.

Crown premises are not exempt from certification. However, the responsibility for this rests not with the fire authority but with the Home Office Fire Service Inspectorate.

An important provision concerning the scope of the Act is contained in Section 10. This enables a fire authority to apply for a court order so that it may take immediate steps to deal with a serious fire risk even though no designating order may have been made concerning that type of use.

1.5.2 The content of a fire certificate

Under Section 6(1) of the Act a certificate must specify:

— the use or uses of the premises;
— the means of escape;
— the means for ensuring that the means of escape can be safely used at all relevant times;
— the means by which the occupants may fight a fire; and
— the means for giving warning to the occupants in case of fire.

At the discretion of the fire authority the certificate may also include provisions for:

— the maintenance of the means of escape (including keeping it free of obstruction);
— maintenance of other fire precautions specified in the certificate;
— training staff and keeping records of training;
— limiting the number of occupants at any one time; and
— other relevant fire precautions.

The certificate and any drawings included in it must be kept on the premises. The fire authority is entitled to make periodic surveys of the premises and the inspecting officer may ask for the certificate. The certificate may cite an individual as being responsible for complying with its requirements.

1.5.3 Procedure and administration

It is the responsibility of the occupier or owner to apply to the fire authority for a certificate. If the building is let to several tenants, the owner must apply.

The fire authority will usually ask for drawings of the premises and, in due course, will make an inspection. If they consider that the fire precautions are satisfactory, a certificate will be issued. In any other case the applicant will be sent a notice and a schedule of requirements for alterations to be made before a certificate can be issued. The notice will specify a period of time for the completion of the work. Failure to issue a certificate within this period (which the authority may extend) is deemed to be a refusal to issue the certificate and continued use of the building then becomes illegal.

Because the fire authority has a duty to inspect the building it cannot provide a 'final' set of requirements on the basis of drawings of proposed alterations or a change of use. Equally, although it is a very good idea to arrange for the fire officer to visit a building where changes to a designated use are proposed so that his views on fire precautions may be taken into account, the fire authority will not be bound by such comments. The certificate is issued for the building, not for proposals or drawings. This can cause additional expense and delay, etc, if further requirements are made after completion of the work.

1.5.4 Relationship to other legislation

Building Regulations. Where a building is to be put to a designated use under the Fire Protection Act 1971 and is one to which Building Regulations on means of escape apply, the fire authority may not make further requirements for means of escape work as a condition of issuing of a fire certificate other than for matters such as exit signs and fire fighting equipment which are not part of the Regulations.

Factories Act and OSR Act certificates. Only the fire safety provision of these Acts has been transferred to the Fire Precautions Act. If a building already has a fire certificate granted under the Offices, Shops and Railway Premises Act or Factories Act, this will continue in force the use or layout of the premises.

Special fire or explosion hazards, etc. A building where there are special process hazards or hazardous materials could come within the scope of Health and Safety Fire Certificates (Special Premises) Regulations S.1 1976, No. 2003. In this case the fire certificate would be issued by the Health and Safety Executive which is linked to the Department of Employment.

1.5.5 Consultation

The fire authority must consult the local authority before issuing a schedule of requirements. The local authority must consult the fire authority if it receives an application for Building Regulations approval in respect of any building which is to be put to a designated use, and before relaxing or dispensing with any requirements as to structural fire precautions in any premises.

In Fire Service Circular 14/1972 it is stated that under Section 43 of the Act, the fire authority may not make requirements which would conflict with any legislation directed towards the preservation of historic buildings. *We have found no instances of this interpretation being cited as a reason for modifying or withdrawing requirements made under the Fire Precautions Act.*

1.5.6 The maintenance of certificate conditions

The occupier is normally the person responsible for seeing that the conditions of a fire certificate are maintained. If there is a need to make alterations or extensions, including any material changes to the internal layout or changes in furniture or equipment, Section 8(2) requires that the fire authority be notified in advance. There must similarly be notification of any intention to keep prescribed explosive or highly inflammable material on certified premises. The authority may then either endorse the changes on the certificate or require improvements to be made before altering or reissuing a certificate.

1.5.7 Appeals

An aggrieved applicant has twenty-one days to appeal to a magistrate's court.

In the first instance, an applicant who is dissatisfied with the outcome of discussions with a fire officer over certification requirements would be well advised to take the matter up with a senior member of the fire prevention branch of the fire service.

1.5.8 Guidance to the Act

The Home Office has produced three booklets on the application of the Act and the rights and duties of the various parties involved. These guidance documents also describe the basis on which the fire authority will assess the adequacy of existing fire precautions and make any requirements for improvements to them. The booklets are: 'No. 1 Hotels and Boarding Houses', 1972; 'No. 2 Factories', 1977; and 'No. 3 Offices, Shops and Railway Premises', 1977, and are published by HMSO.

1.6 The Housing Acts

Details of the recent Consolidation Act are given in Chapter 4.

1.6.1 Houses in multiple occupation

Schedule 24 of the 1980 Act enables local authorities to make requirements for the improvement or provision of means of escape in a 'house which is occupied by people who do not form a single household' or is let in lodgings. The local authority is obliged to consult the fire authority before issuing any requirements. In Greater London and Greater Manchester the fire authorities have published guidance on the application of the statutory provision and, by following it, the local authority is deemed to have consulted. Some other fire authorities, such as South Glamorgan, have also produced guidance notes. Local authorities can, within the provisions of the 1980 Act, pay grants towards the cost of work undertaken pursuant to a notice served under Schedule 24.

The interpretation of the definition of a house in multiple occupation varies widely. This is discussed in para 3.6.4. A case study concerned with Schedule 24 of the Housing Act 1980 is 57 The Close, Norwich (No. 3A). An important court case involving Hull University and Schedule 24 is also discussed in para 5.3.

See Case Study 3A, pp. 49-51

Under S.22 of the 1961 Act (as amended by S.64 of the 1969 Act) a local authority could make a scheme for the registration of houses in multiple occupation.

1.6.2 Housing fitness standards

Section 9 of the 1957 Housing Act enabled a local authority to require the repair of a house that they judged to be unfit for human habitation. There was a proviso that the necessary works were capable of being done at 'reasonable cost'. If they could not, the house had to be demolished or, in certain circumstances – such as where it was listed – closed.

For the purpose of assessing the fitness of a dwelling in relation to this Act the following matters were taken into account:

— repair;

— stability;
— freedom from damp;
— internal arrangement;
— natural lighting;
— ventilation;
— water supply;
— drainage and sanitary conveniences;
— facilities for preparation and cooking of food; and for the disposal of water.

The house was deemed to be unfit for human habitation if it was so far defective in one or more of the above aspects that it was not reasonably suitable for occupation.

S.15 of the 1961 Act contained a list for houses in multiple occupation which omitted the first four items and added artificial lighting and heating installations.

1.6.3 Improvement grants

Section 56 of the 1974 Housing Act (as amended by the Housing Act 1980) empowers the local authority to give grants for home improvement and defines four types of grant. The 'improvement grant', which is the type most relevant to this study, is available at the discretion of the authority if the house after improvement:

— has the standard basic amenities (bath/shower, WC, etc) for the exclusive use of the occupants;
— is in reasonable repair considering its age and locality;
— conforms to such requirements as to construction standards, physical condition and the provision of services and amenities as the Secretary of State may specify;* and
— is likely to provide satisfactory housing for at least thirty years.

See Case Studies 11A, B, pp. 141-4

Section 61 allowed the authority to dispense with the first three conditions to such an extent as they thought fit if it was not practicable to fulfil them. They could also reduce the standard in the fourth but not to less than ten years.

Improvement grants were available also for conversion schemes. In addition, there were three other types of grant:

— intermediate grants were for the provision of standard amenities, where they were missing, together with associated repairs. They were available provided the qualifying conditions were met;
— repairs grants were available for repairs of a substantial and structural nature to dwellings erected before 1 January 1919;
— special grants applicable to houses in multiple occupation were available for the provision of standard amenities and means of escape from fire. If standard amenities or means of escape from fire were being installed, the grant could also cover work needed to put the house into a reasonable state of repair.

* The requirements specified by the Secretary of State are set out in para 5, Appendix A of DOE Circular 21/80. These constitute the 'ten point standard'.

1.7 Other Legislation

1.7.1 The Education Act 1944 and Amendments

By virtue of S.10, the Secretary of State may make Regulations concerning standards for school premises. Regulations were made in 1981 and include, in Section 24, a duty on the local education authority to ensure that all parts of their school premises are designed and constructed to ensure the health, safety and the safe escape of the occupants in case of fire. The Department of Education and Science has produced Building Bulletin No. 7 for the guidance of authorities on fire safety.

Under Section 63 of the Act, schools subject to approval by the Secretary of State – virtually all maintained schools – are exempt from Building Regulations.

Maintained further education establishments have a similar set of Standards and Regulations but they are not exempt from Building Regulations.

Independent schools have to comply with Building Regulations. They also have to register with the DES (Section 70 of the Act). Before accepting a school for registration, the DES obtains a report from the appropriate fire service on the standard of fire precautions and on aspects of environmental health and fitness of construction, layout, etc.

The Inner London Education Authority has been obliged to conform to the London Building Acts, but S.63(2) of the Education Act would enable the Secretary of State to set aside the provision of the London Building Acts in a specific case.

School buildings are considered in more detail in Case Study No. 11 A, B.

1.7.2 The Health and Safety at Work etc Act 1974

This Act places a duty of care on employers and employees to guard against injury and hazards at the place of work and to protect the public against any danger emanating from the place of work, such as the release of toxic material.

Employers are obliged to set up an organisation to allow staff representation on health and safety matters and they have to be able to demonstrate that they are fulfilling their responsibilities.

Enforcement is mainly through the Health and Safety Executive which is linked to the Department of Employment. Their inspectors include specialists on all aspects of industrial safety, hygiene and environmental health. The day-to-day application of the Act is the employer's responsibility. The inspectors carry out spot-checks and may serve notices preventing the operation of a hazardous process or procedure, or may require corrective measures to be put into effect within a given period.

Although this Act has been mentioned as the reason for altering an historic building, we have come across no cases of notices being served under the Act. Mills are the only class of historic building repeatedly subject to considerations of health or safety.

1.7.3 The Licensing Act 1964

The Act set up licensing authorities with powers to regulate the planning, management, structure, and fire precautions of any premises in which intoxicating liquor is sold, as a condition of the issue of a licence.

The licensing authority must consult the police and fire authorities over relevant matters. An aggrieved applicant has fourteen days to lodge an appeal against a refusal or any conditions attached to a licence. There is no published guidance on the Act for building owners or designers.

1.7.4 Entertainment and theatre licensing

The Cinematograph Acts, the Gaming Act and the Theatres Act were until 1983 the only national legislation concerned with entertainments licensing. Other facets of entertainments licensing, such as music and dancing licences needed for any kind of musical performance or boxing and wrestling licences, were the subject of local Acts. On 1 January 1983 the Licensing of Public Entertainments provisions of the Local Government (Miscellaneous Provisions) Act 1982 came into force, and introduced a uniform code of licensing of such entertainments to cover the whole of England (outside Greater London) and Wales. In Greater London these entertainments have been controlled under the London Government Act 1963. The administrative procedures have since been raised and details are given in Chapter 4.

A range of historic building types can be affected by entertainments licensing, including country houses where occasional recitals are given. It is quite common for new uses to be proposed for historic buildings which would require a licence, such as community centres and meeting halls. Relevant buildings include Thaxted Guildhall (Case Study No. 4B) and Kenwood House (Case Study No. 9B).

1.7.5 Personal social services care establishment legislation

We refer here to the following legislation:

— the National Assistance Act 1948 (residential homes for the elderly);
— the Nurseries and Childminders Regulation Act 1948;
— the Nursing Homes Act 1975 (private and local authority nursing homes);
— the Child Care Act 1980;
— the Children and Young Persons Act 1969;
— the Mental Health Act 1959; and
— the Nursing Homes and Mental Nursing Homes Regulations 1981.

Buildings serving these functions are subject to licensing by district authorities. In a similar way to entertainments licensing, the authority consults the fire authority before registering or licensing the establishment.

Crown property of the National Health Service is exempt from all building legislation save the Fire Precautions Act and Health and Safety at Work etc Act.

Guidance on the application of these Acts is contained in Home Office circulars and the draft guides for fire precautions in hospitals and residential care premises, 1982 and 1983.*

1.7.6 The Highways Act 1980

The Act defines the various responsibilities of the Minister and county highway authorities. Local authorities are empowered to improve highways under S.62, and Part V of the Act specifies a number of types of improvement, including widening of roads, the provision of footways and the cutting of corners to improve visibility. The authority can require adjoining owners to alter or remove walls, fences and planting which it considers obstructs visibility, although under Sections 78 and 79 this does not apply to walls of 'a permanent edifice' such as a building.

Each authority determines the standards to be applied and the technical solutions. The Department of Transport has issued codes for the guidance of authorities, and technical memoranda and circulars. A number of highway authorities have written their own highway design guides. For the design of street lighting, BS 5489: Parts 1 and 2 and CP 1004: Parts 1–9 are available for the authorities' guidance.

* 'Draft Guide to Fire Precautions in Hospitals', September 1982, and 'Draft Guide to Fire Precautions in Existing Residential Care Premises', January 1983. Home Office Fire Department, 50 Queen Anne's Gate, London SW1H 9AT.

See Case Studies 4B and 9B, pp. 55-6 and 120-23

Case Study 1: Shops with mixed uses and tenancies

We have found relatively few historic buildings that are used solely as shops, it being more usual to combine them with other uses on the upper floors. Table 2 (p. 47) shows that Building Regulations and the Fire Precautions Act are the two most influential pieces of legislation for this category of building. The need to compartment different types of occupancy from one another – no matter how small the building – is the most obvious effect of the Regulations. The designation of offices and shops accounts for the influence of the Fire Precautions Act, although very small premises are to a great extent exempted from its full application.

A. Nos. 5-10 Kingsmead Square, Bath

Nos. 5–10 form one side of this Georgian square near the centre of Bath. They are of four storeys, and three of the houses also have basements.

The terrace is constructed of Bath stone, ashlar faced, with timber floors. In common with many Georgian buildings in the city, the original standard of construction was low and, through a combination of settlement, damp-induced rot and structural movement, this terrace had reached a potentially dangerous state when the present owner bought it. He proposed to alter and renovate the buildings to provide offices, shops and a wine bar in the basement.

Architect: Derek Stollar of Hugh Roberts, Graham and Stollar

Listed Grade II

Legislation involved

Structural remedial work was discussed with building control but was considered to be outside the scope of the Regulations in this case. The fire legislation involved was contained in the Building Regulations 1976, the Fire Precautions Act and the Offices, Shops and Railway Premises Act.

Walls

Some rooms were found to contain timber panelling worthy of retention. Where these are full height, the local authority required a fire retardant treatment to reduce flame spread (the material used is not visible). Dado height panelling did not have to be treated. One full height panelled partition separated a shop from the ground floor exit corridor serving the offices above. Its fire resistance was regarded as inadequate but the architect felt that its appearance should be changed as little as possible and there was very little scope for increasing its overall thickness. A half-inch sheet of fire resisting material was applied to the corridor side and the dado rail was re-planted on this to give much of the original effect. As there was an alternative route from the staircase, a fire resisting self-closing door was fitted at ground level between the corridor and the stair to protect it.

Doors

Several panelled doors were rebuilt to incorporate fire resisting interlayers within their thickness at 'weak' points around the perimeter of raised panels. The detail was similar to that used by the same architects in Marshal Wade's House (Case Study No. 1C).

Means of escape

None of the offices on the upper floors has access to more than one stairway, there is no lobbying to protect the stairs, most offices open directly on to the stair via a half-hour closing door, and there are some inner offices with travel distances slightly in excess of those given in the guidance notes to the Fire Precautions Act. Automatic fire detection using ionisation-type detectors was required by the fire authority in all the escape stairs. There is also an electric alarm system but it does not extend beyond the stairway, except where the owner has installed a separate detection system in one of the shops which deals with electronic equipment.

The absence of two-door protection to the stairs highlights one of the differences between guidance booklets on the implementation of the Fire Precautions Act and on the Offices, Shops and Railway Premises Act. Under the latter, the lobbying of a single stair in offices of this height was not advocated, whereas under the Fire Precautions Act it is.

Structural problems and solutions

It was necessary to tie back the front elevation in places. The basic technique was the commonly adopted one of fixing long stainless steel tie bars into the cross walls with resin anchors with retaining plates on the outer surface of the exterior wall. In this case the plates were disguised as fixings for rainwater down pipes.

Some parts of the top floor have very long joist spans, which could not provide support for the floor loads likely to be imposed by the new office use. An application for relaxation of Part D of the 1976 Regulations was discussed but the local authority considered that it was not applicable. A steel structure with channel section hangers was designed to transfer the floor loads up to bearing points on the external walls at eaves level.

References: Paras 2.2.12B and 3.3.1

Nos. 5 to 10 Kingsmead Square, Bath Approximate scale 1:200

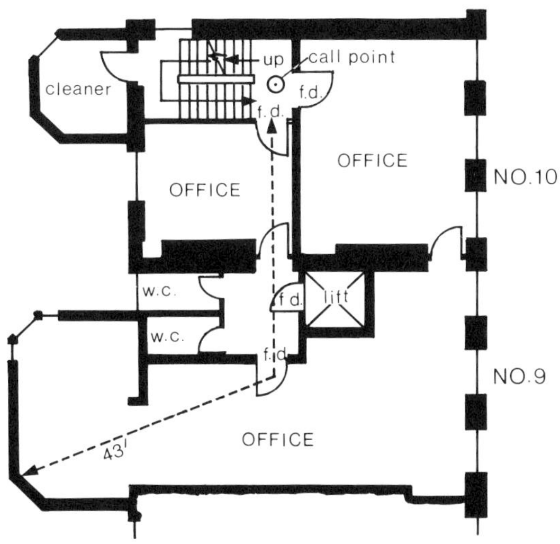

Second floor plan of nos. 9 and 10

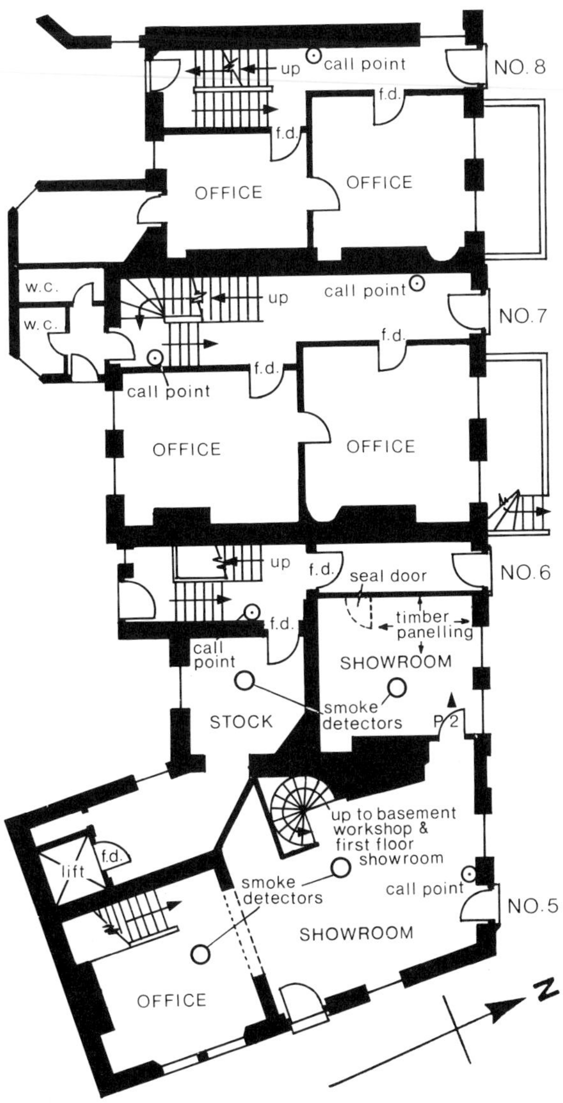

Ground floor plan of nos. 5 to 8

B. No. 76 Low Petergate, York

This building is a fairly extreme example of the problems of small scale coupled with mixed use which were solved with ingenuity and by close liaison with the local authority.

Architect: Noel Hutchinson

Listed Grade II

Before the alterations were made the upper floors of this three-storey building were unused. The new proprietor wanted to convert the top floor and part of the first floor for his own residential use. The building is in the heart of medieval York and, despite a tiny courtyard, there was no possibility of extending the accommodation.

The building is timber-framed with a jetted street elevation and a fairly massive brick chimney stack dividing the floors front and back. The ceiling heights were all less than the 2.3 m required for habitable rooms, part of the first and second floors being barely 1.8 m. The conversion used the first floor back room as a bedroom where headroom was adequate, and the top floor living room's ceiling was raised by putting the ceiling above the main beams. The other rooms were not 'habitable' ones and so the headroom was not controlled.

The public health officer's requirements for daylight involved enlarging the bedroom window to the maximum extent allowed by the structural timbers, putting a new – second – window into the street elevation for the top floor and forming a rooflight and light shaft over the top floor kitchen. The ratio of window to floor area in the two habitable rooms was increased to about 1:20.

The bathroom was accommodated at first floor level off the bedroom in such a way that the shower room formed the ventilated lobby which the public health authority required between the WC compartment and the bedroom. A new window was made to the courtyard to light and ventilate the WC compartment.

The domestic areas did not need to be compartmented from the shop, and the stair is not protected. The large opening in the first floor makes it more a gallery to the ground floor. Those people to whom we spoke on this project felt that the authority was sympathetic with the need to have the upper storeys occupied. As the proprietor was the occupant of the whole building, there is no control over means of escape under current legislation except possibly for S.10 of the Fire Precautions Act.

Reference: Para 3.3.1

The shop at first floor level

No. 76 Low Petergate, York Approximate scale 1:200

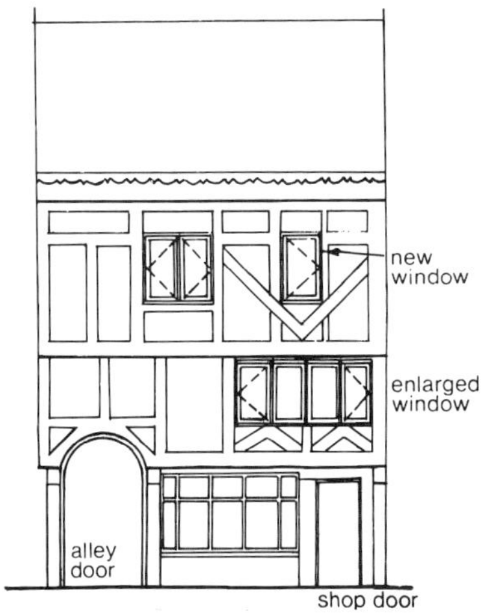

Street elevation

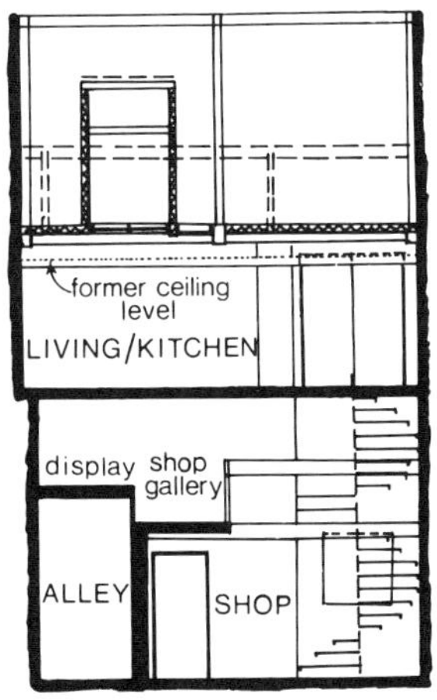

Section B-B Street elevation

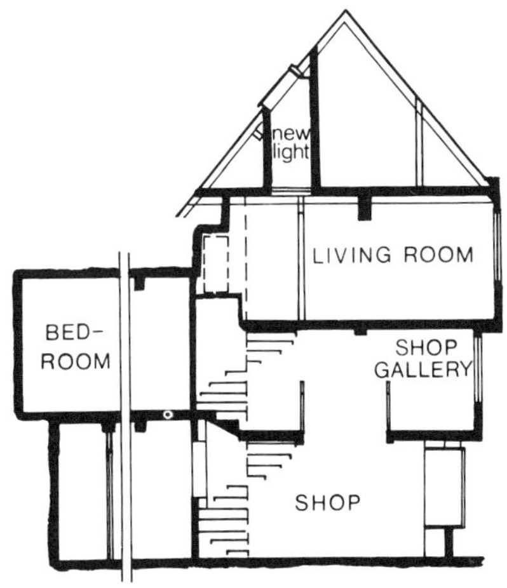

Section A-A

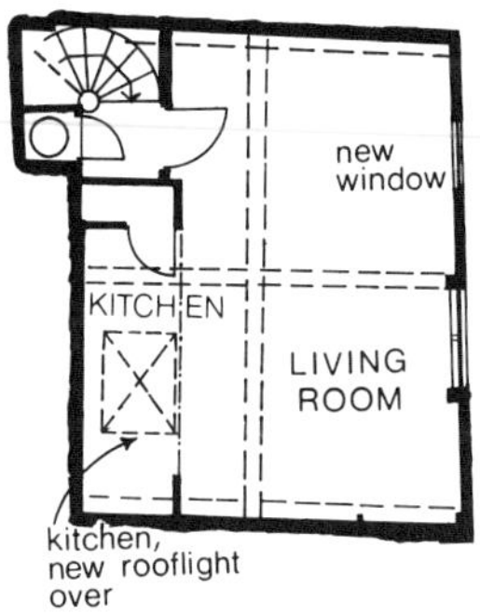

Second floor plan

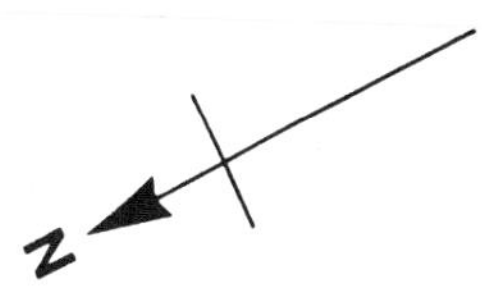

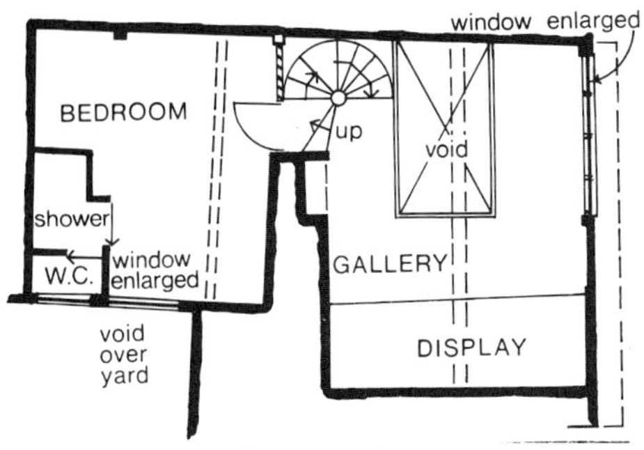

First floor plan

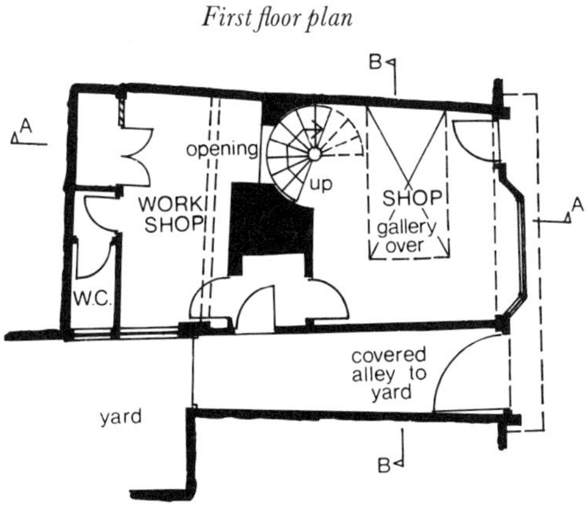

Ground floor plan

C. Marshal Wade's House, Bath

This is a Georgian town house of four storeys and a basement built in about 1700 on the north side of the Abbey precinct, which is now a pedestrian area. Before the most recent alterations it had become a shop and a photographer's studio and was in a poor state of repair. The authorities displayed both expertise and a sympathetic attitude to the historic building aspects of the project.

Architects: David Brain and Hugh Stollar

Listed Grade I

Construction

The building's main elevation is in Bath stone, ashlar with pilasters, cornice and other classical decoration. The floors are of timber with good elm boards, and second floor rooms have raised and fielded panelling and the ceiling and plasterwork details generally at first floor level are of good quality.

Legislation

Listed building consent and Building Regulations approval were sought for a change of use to a shop on the basement, ground and first floors and a maisonette above. The maisonette was to be let by the Landmark Trust and it was therefore subject to Section 60 of the Public Health Act for means of escape.

Building Regulations

The provision of E5 of the 1976 Regulations requiring a one-hour fire resisting compartment floor between the shop and maisonette was relaxed because the applicant wished to leave both the elm flooring and decorative ceiling exposed. Building control officers inspected the ceiling and were satisfied that it would give adequate fire resistance.

Means of escape

The stair serving the maisonette already had a separate street entrance. It was closed off from the shop at first floor level, where there had been a door. The fire authority objected to the provision of a cupboard off the stair for a refuse bin at ground level and asked for automatic fire detection to be installed to protect the means of escape. Ionisation-type detectors were installed in the stair to the maisonette and in the ground and basement levels of the shop. The alarm system operates sounders throughout the building.

Under the Building Regulations 1976, the requirement was the stair to the basement had to be separated from the rest of the shop by half-hour fire resisting construction. New open stairs were constructed between ground and first floors as part of the alterations and the basement stair was incorporated beneath these, with a fire resisting self-closing door to the basement stair in the spandrel. The basement is not a public area and the provision of a door has not been onerous.

The handrail to the new stair to the first floor had to comply with Part H of the 1976 Regulations and the architect felt that its height was out of scale with the interior.

The architect suggested forming a rooftop escape route to an adjoining building, but the fire authority actively discouraged this proposal.

Doors

Doors in the maisonette on to the stair were replaced with half-hour fire resisting self-closing doors. The raised and fielded pattern of the original were reproduced but the overall thickness was increased so that the main part of the panel was 44 mm thick. Timber doors of this thickness are generally accepted as meeting the half-hour fire resistance standard. In the fielded part of the panel the thickness is, of course, reduced. This 'weak' area is protected by incorporating a fillet of fire resistant material in the centre of the panel that overlaps sufficiently into the styles and rails and beyond the fielded area into the panel.

References: Paras 2.2.10D and 2.3.3, Case Study No. 1A

Marshal Wade's House, Bath Approximate scale 1:200

SCALE 1:200 approx

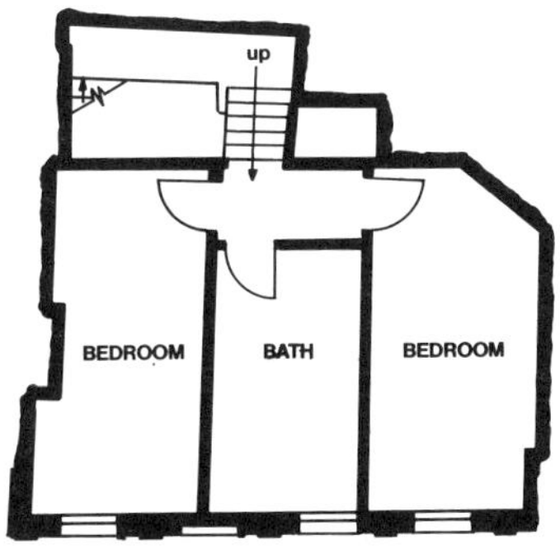

Third floor before

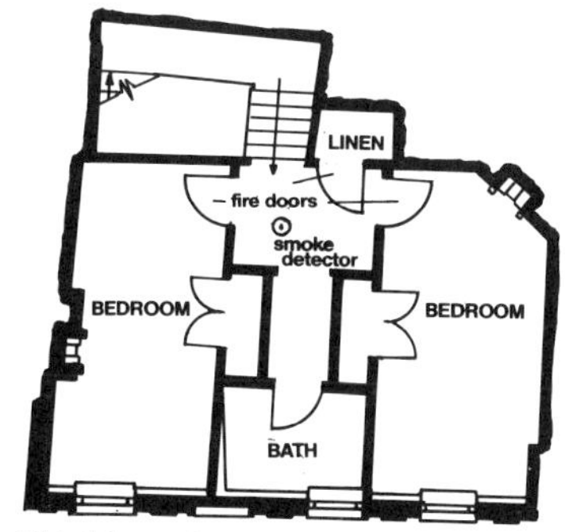

Third floor after

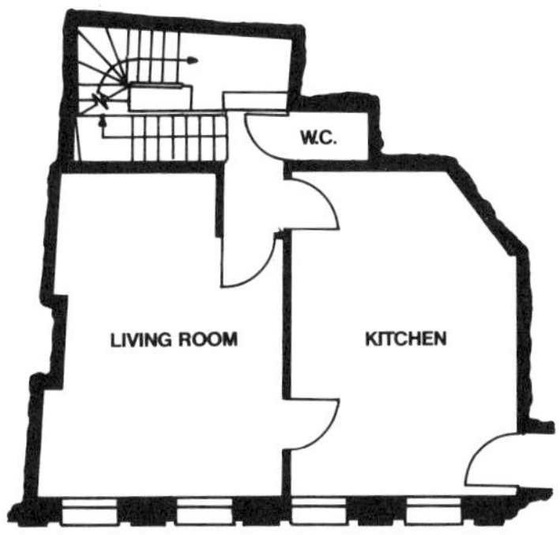

Second floor before

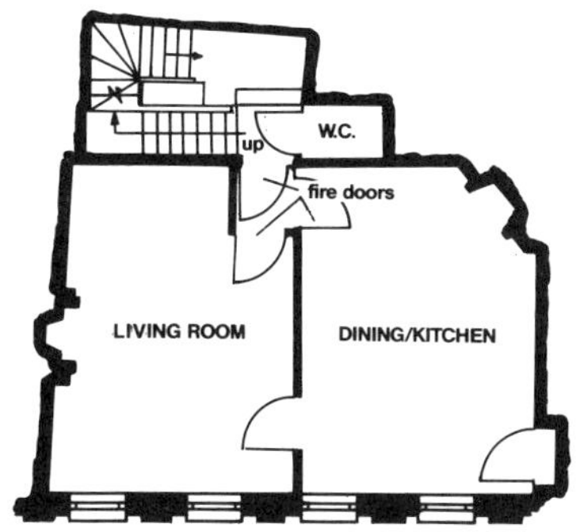

Second floor after

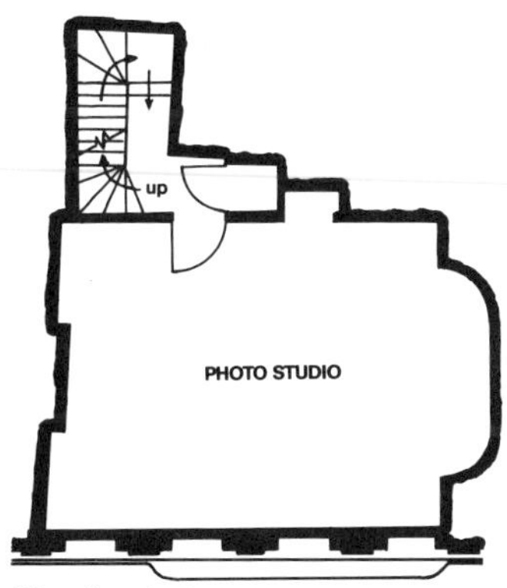

First floor before

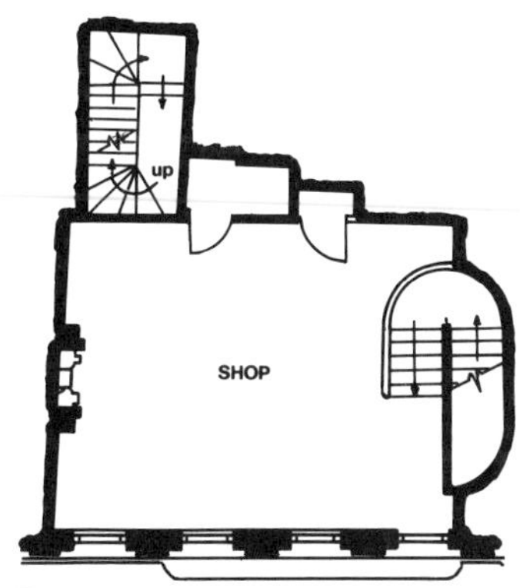

First floor after

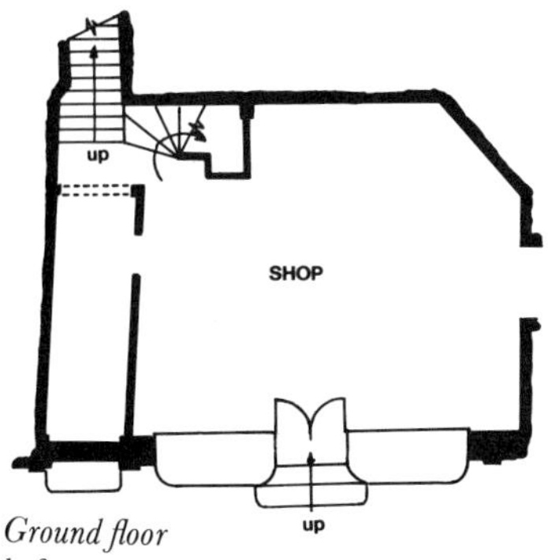

Ground floor before

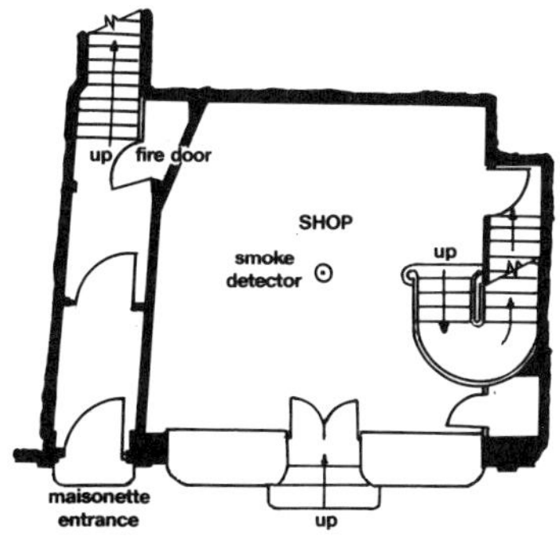

Ground floor after

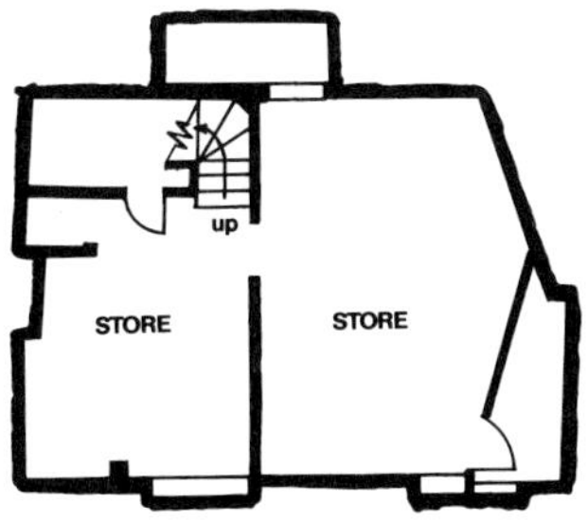

Basement before

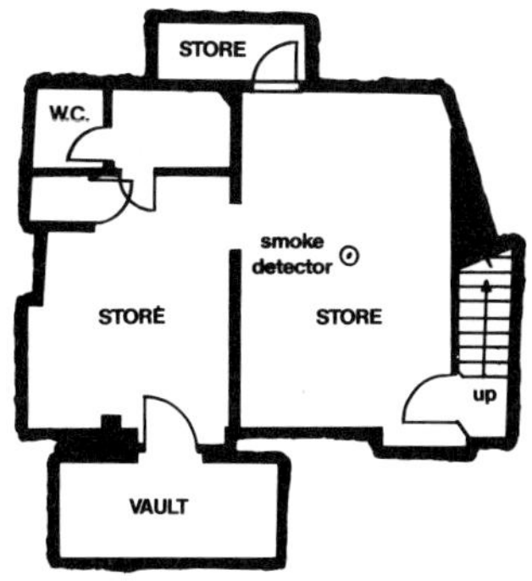

Basement after

Case Study 2: Warehouses and Mills

Generally, warehouses are attractive to those who need cheap space, and they are relatively easy to convert to a wide variety of uses, because there is little existing internal subdivision and the structure is usually capable of taking modern floor loadings. Their location in run-down industrial or commercial urban areas has been a disincentive to their re-use. In some instances a sympathetic attitude by the local authority anxious to revive these areas has helped to smooth a path through some of the legislative requirements.

On the other hand, the strong character of the interior of many warehouses can very easily be lost by covering up the exposed joists, iron columns and rough finishes. Legislation can require alterations of this sort to be made. Mills are attractive chiefly in terms of industrial archaeology; it is important for some of them to be preserved as they were when in commercial use. It is also important for them to be accessible to the public, and conflicts arise over public safety. Because of some of these fundamental contradictions, we have found that the attitude of the enforcement authorities is all-important.

A. No. 35 King Street, Bristol

Front elevation of 35 King Street

This building of four storeys and a basement was built in about 1800 and originally used as a cork warehouse and factory. An ornamental brick façade was added in the latter part of the nineteenth century. It was subsequently owned by the council and lay empty for some time. It was then acquired by a company that was formed to convert and run it as offices, mainly for self-employed individuals in the design business. The ground floor was to be converted into an art gallery with provision for occasional public performances, poetry readings, etc, and approval was obtained to convert the basement into a café. The planning and building control officers were sympathetic to the development, which was seen as a pilot study for the re-use of a number of similar buildings in the city's dock area.

Architects: Keith Hallet and others

Listed Grade II

Building Regulations

Compartmentation was needed between the ground and the first floors because they were different purpose groups. The floors are of timber boards about 32 mm thick, most of which are joined to one another by metal tongues. The exposed joists rest on very substantial timber beams and these are carried in iron shoes on cast-iron columns. Because of the size and uses of the two compartments, the 1976 Regulations called for a modified one-hour standard of fire resistance for the first floor – that is, one hour for the main beams and half an hour for the floor and joists, etc.

The developers did not want to conceal the joists, beams or columns and the authority accepted an intumescent treatment to the timber and cast iron instead of encasement with brick, etc. This treatment is invisible from the floor below. The building control officer did not require the protection of any of the other upper floors.

The original stairs were retained. They did not conform to the Building Regulations 1976 for timber construction and with a low handrail (being too steep), but were exempted because they did not conflict with the Regulations any more than they did before.

Fire Precautions Act

Over forty people worked in the building and, since the majority of them were self-employed, the managing company considered the possibility of the rest of them becoming self-employed to take the building out of the full scope of the designation order. But the fire authority could still have invoked Section 10 of the Act and the occupants therefore decided to proceed with a certification application in the normal way.

The single stair was accepted as the means of escape with a half-hour protective enclosure and a new exit door direct to the outside at ground level. It was accepted that the doors to the stair could open into the office area rather than on to the stair in the direction of escape because space in the enclosure was limited and the swings would have obstructed people on the stairway. There are fire resisting glazed openings into the stair from the offices, *which we consider would expose people on the stair to more radiation from a fire in an office than seems reasonable, in view of the narrowness of the stair enclosure,* but it was accepted by the authorities. Timberwork in the stair was treated with a surface flame spread retardant.

A fire alarm system with automatic detection using ionisation-type smoke detectors was required to compensate for the limitation of a single stair.

References: Paras 2.2.7 and 2.2.8

No. 35 King Street, Bristol Approximate scale 1:200

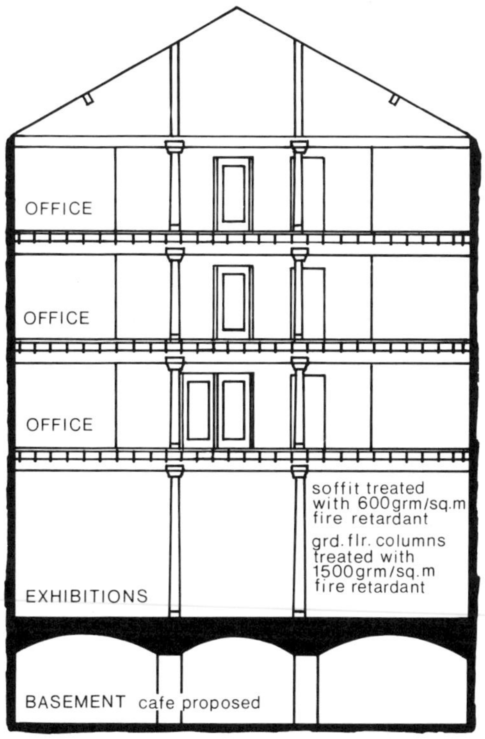

Section A-A

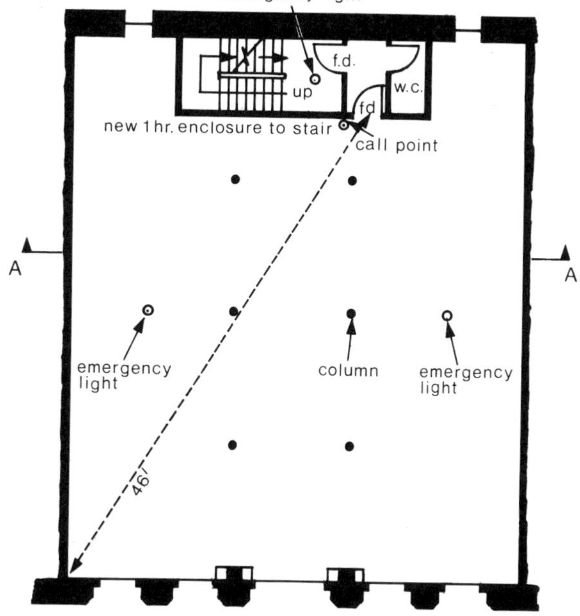

Typical upper floor

B. The Great Warehouse, Coalbrookdale, Shropshire

This warehouse was part of the Coalbrookdale Ironworks established in the eighteenth century by the Darby family. The works were the first to use coal (coke) in the smelting of iron, and the use of cast iron in the construction of the Great Warehouse of *c.* 1838 is one of its most interesting features. The warehouse is three storeys high and, being intended for the storage of iron products, was immensely strongly built.

Telford Development Corporation acquired the derelict building and decided to restore it to house a museum of iron where the public could learn about the history of iron working and the role of the Shropshire ironmasters in the Industrial Revolution.

Architects: Severn Gorge Development Group under L. Sparks for Telford New Town Development Corporation.

Listed Grade II

Construction

The external walls of the three-storey building are brick and carry the heavy trussed roof and cast-iron clock tower as well as the outer ends of the main oak floor beams, the other ends being carried on cast-iron columns. The beams are about 356 mm square, the floor joists about 279 × 76 mm and the boards about 31 mm thick with connecting iron tongues 19 × 20 mm.

Fire requirements

Preliminary discussions with the fire authority, who were approached for 'goodwill' advice, suggested that there would be no difficulty in accommodating reasonable safety measures. Two new stairs were planned, one of which was to be fully enclosed, and an application for approval under the 1976 Building Regulations was made.

The local authority interpreted the application as a change of use to Purpose Group VII. The applicants were advised to apply for a relaxation of the structural fire resistance provision of E5 and E13 of the 1976 Regulations. Part I of the Table E5 gave a modified one-hour requirement for a building less than 15 m in height and 300 m^3 in volume, under which non-compartment floors needed only a half-hour's resistance, while the beams and columns required the full one-hour's resistance. Although the applicant proposed to add 19 mm floorboards on top of the existing 38 mm boards, the authority were not satisfied with the overall fire performance of the structure.

Timber stair treads in dense hardwood 51 × 305 mm were proposed to keep in character with the interior. The relaxation of E13 was needed because the stair construction was not non-combustible.

The fire authority advised that a number of measures should be taken. The joists, beams and columns should be treated with 'an intumescent paint... to the manufacturer's specification', though no specific fire resistance period was given. The non-enclosed stair should be enclosed up to and including first-floor level, to a half-hour standard with self-closing doors, and glazing to this enclosure should be fire resisting. An automatic fire detection and alarm system, including a direct line to the fire brigade, should also, they considered, be installed, and an additional exit should be provided by the foot of the main stair. These measures were subsequently applied.

The product used to 'protect' columns and beams, etc, was one of two alternatives which a fire officer apparently suggested at an earlier meeting. It is actually a surface spread of flame retardant *and we do not consider that it would materially affect the fire resisting performance of the timber or of the cast-iron columns.*

The applicant's architect had the impression that relaxation would only be given if the fire authority's advice was taken. Much of this advice was concerned with means of escape and was outside the scope of the legislation being enforced. The advice apparently also contained measures which were not suggested when the original approach for 'goodwill' advice was made to the fire authority. The additional cost of automatic detection and structural fire 'protection' was about £8,000. As the main stair is part of the circulation route between the floors of the exhibition area, it was agreed with the fire authority that the doors could be held open on magnetic automatic catches released by the alarm system.

Single-swing double-leaf doors with rebated meeting styles were used and selector devices fitted to give the proper closing action.

Structural requirements

When the local authority responded to the Regulations application they asked for further information to show that the floor would support the proposed loading in accordance with Regulation D8, which was the basic requirement for stability of the structure above the foundation level.

Because the beams did not conform to C P 112 (the deemed to satisfy code for timber structures) the local authority was still not satisfied, and so the development corporation agreed to carry out load tests. During the tests the structure was, by mistake, subjected to a load 30 per cent greater than planned but, despite this, behaved quite adequately.

On the information made available to us it is our impression that the local authority were particularly onerous in their approach to this project, and we would question the applicability of Part D of the Regulations in these circumstances.

References: Paras 2.2.8, 3.3.1 and 3.4.2

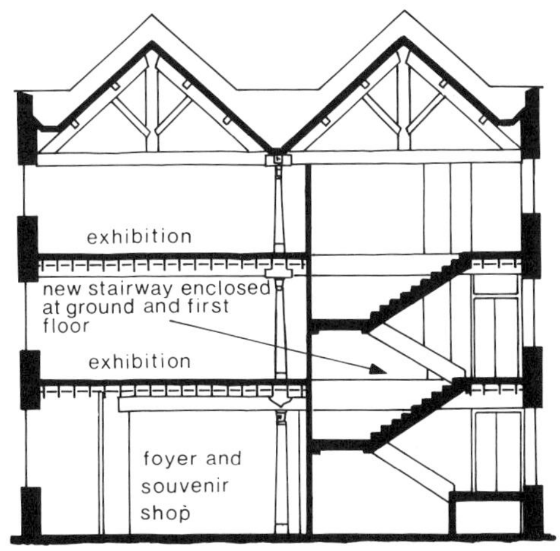

The Great Warehouse, Coalbrookdale, Shropshire Approximate scale 1:200

Section A-A

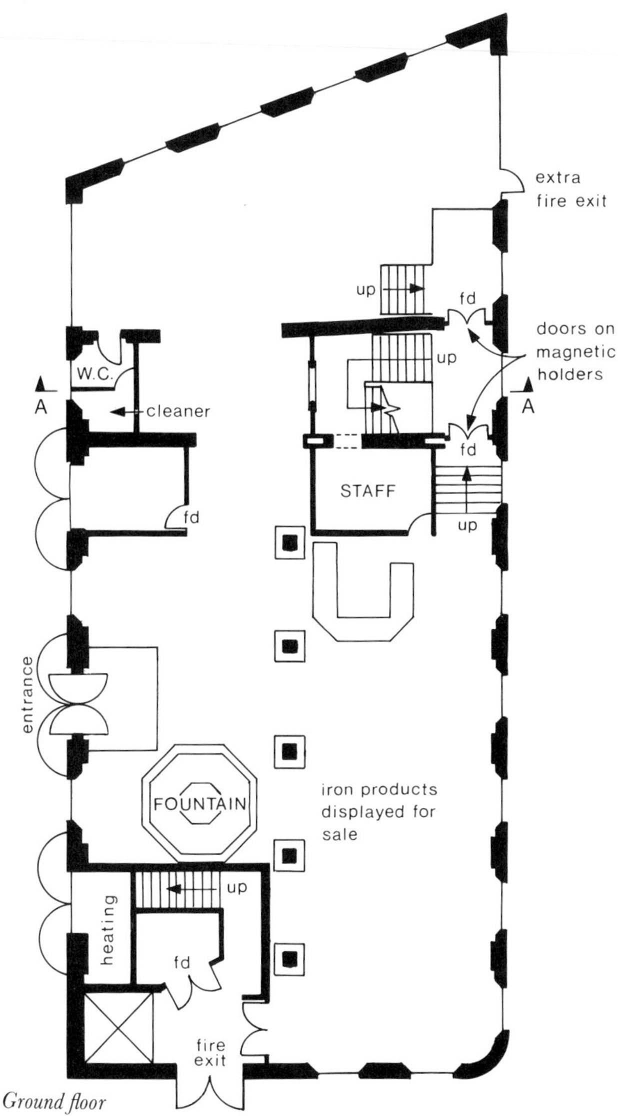

Ground floor

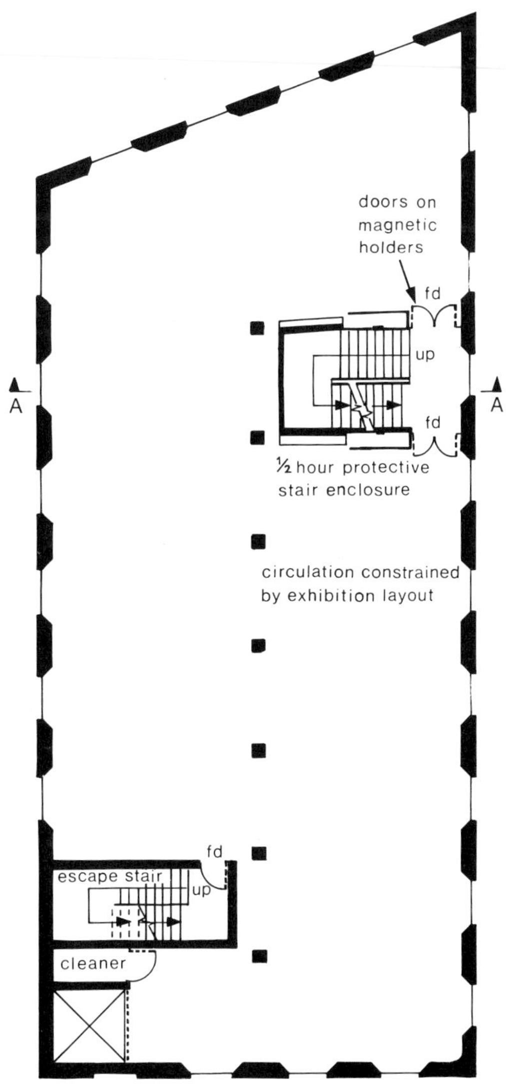

First floor

C. The No. 2 Mill, Shardlow, Derbyshire

This four-storey warehouse was built astride a canal inlet and served as a trans-shipment point between narrow boats of the inland canal system and wider vessels using the Trent Navigation. Brindley may have been the designer.

The building has brick external load-bearing walls with a heavy timber frame and floor structure. The floor-to-floor heights are not more than 2.13 m, and the soffit of some beams is about 1.52 m above floor level. There is an opening in the middle of the upper floors through which goods were hoisted from boats in the canal beneath.

Architect (for the scheme design but not its implementation): Desmond Thornhill

Listed Grade II

Legislation

When purchased by the developer, the building had fallen into dereliction and the canal inlet had been filled in. Proposals were made to restore the fabric and convert the warehouse into a tourist centre having a shop, café, museum of canal life and a maisonette for the caretaker. Structural fire precautions were required under the Building Regulations 1976 by the local authority and means of escape requirements were imposed under Section 60 of the Public Health Act on the maisonette, whose bedrooms are on the top floor.

Compartmentation and fire resistance

The building control officer's interpretation of the use of the building was that compartment walls and/or floors were required between the shop, café, museum and maisonette. The authority called for one-hour's fire resistance which, between the café, maisonette, and shop, threatened to change the character of floorboards on exposed joists. The owner wanted to keep the joists exposed and eventually the authority accepted a construction which allowed this and which was certified by a fire expert to have the necessary fire resistance. This consisted of 12.7 mm plasterboard fixed between the joists to 50 mm deep battens attached to their sides, above which was a 50 mm layer of mineral wool and then a proprietary asbestos board laid across the top of the joists beneath the boards of the floor itself.

East elevation

The No. 2 Mill, Shardlow, Derbyshire Approximate scale 1:200

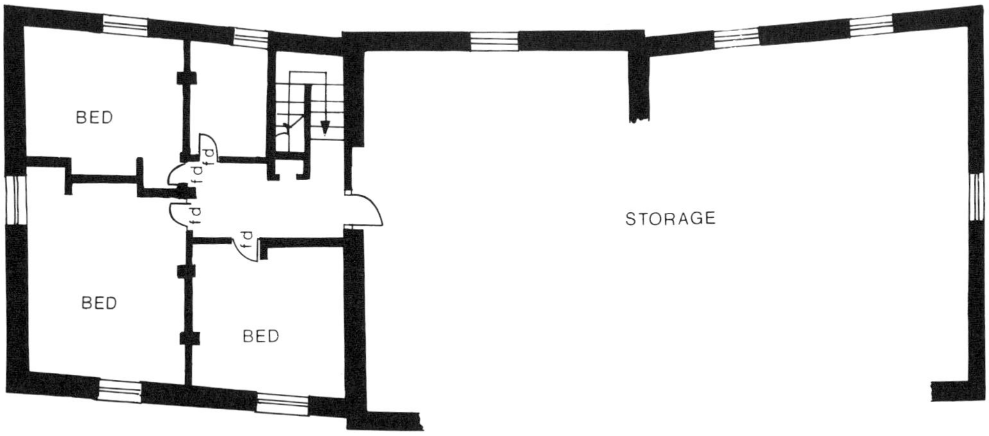

Third floor

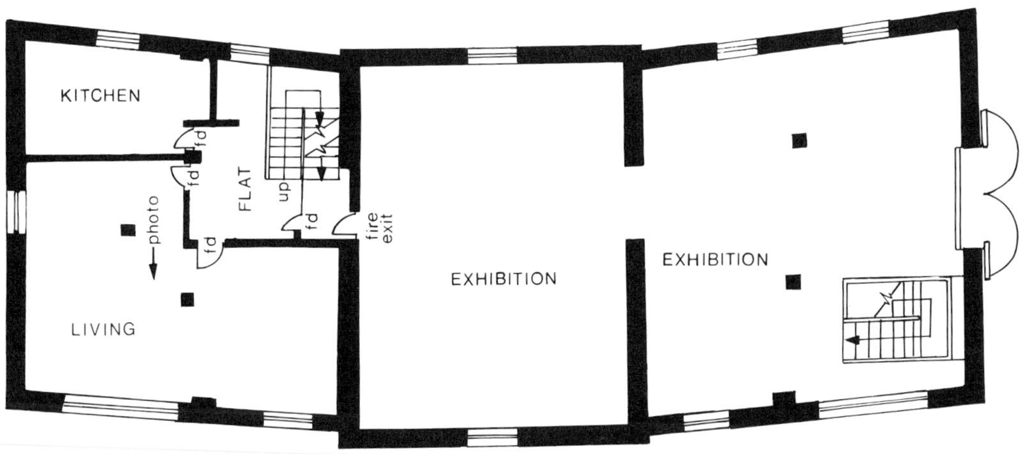

Second floor

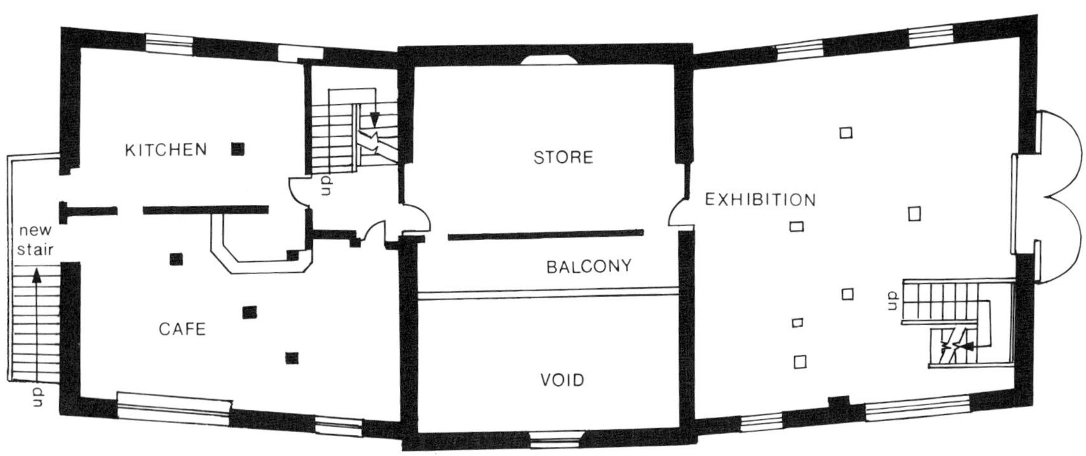

First floor

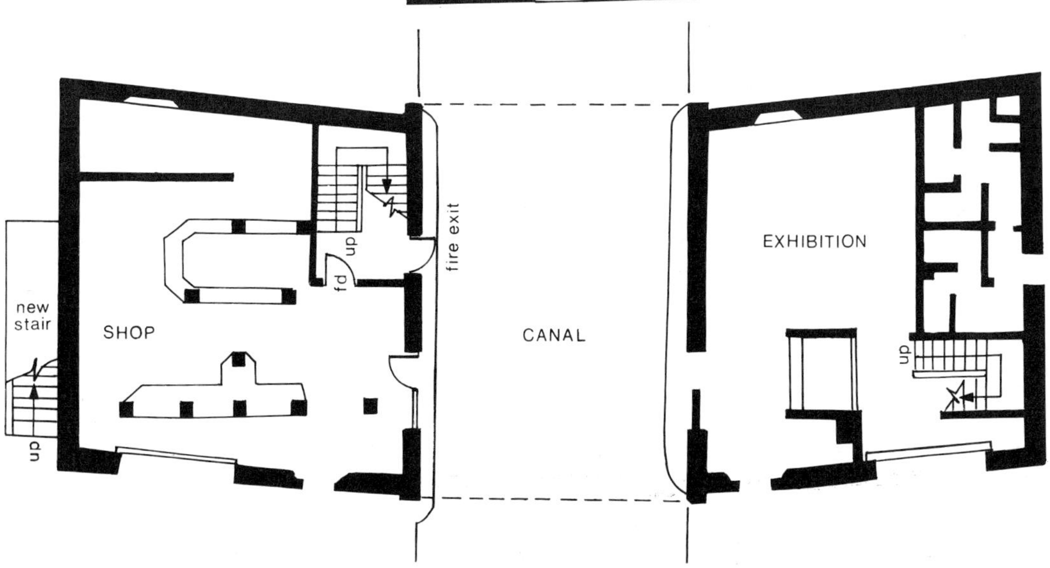

Ground floor

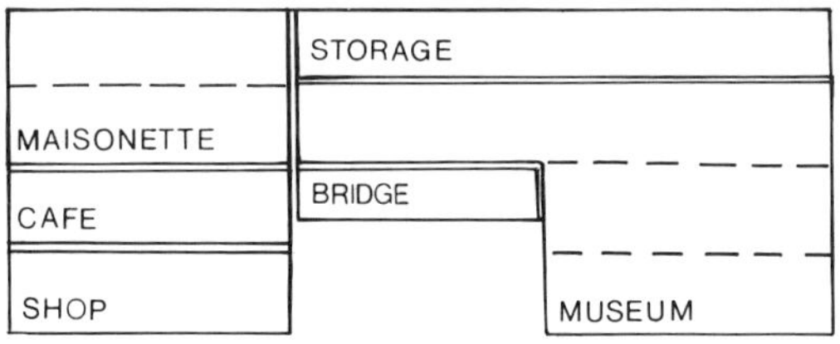

Section showing compartmentation for fire resistance purposes Approximate scale 1:400

A rough-textured plaster finish was applied to the soffit of the plasterboard and the exposed joists were given an intumescent surface flame-spread retarding treatment.

An application for a relaxation of the one-hour standard was then made for those remaining parts of the structure which were considered, on the charring rates in BS 5268: Part 4, not to have a full one-hour's resistance. This, however, was refused, so the owner decided to install a sprinkler system throughout the building and applied for a relaxation of Part E5 of the 1976 Regulations, which was given on the basis that the sprinklers could be expected to reduce fire severity. But they have proved unsightly. Compartmentation in the vertical plane was quite easily achieved on the line of the existing and new masonry walls by the addition of fire doors in the openings.

Relaxation was given from some very low beams in the maisonette. Similar beams in the museum were exempt because they are not in a habitable room.

Internal construction showing the underside of joists

Means of escape

By providing two internal stairs to replace steep ladders in the original, one of which

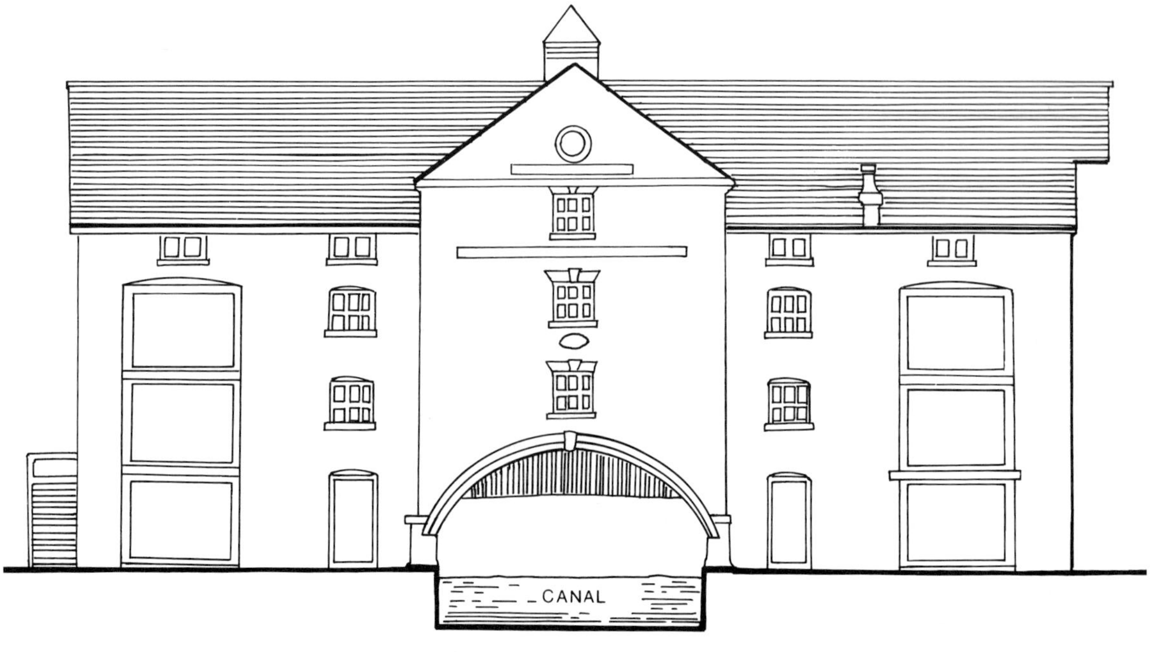

East elevation

serves the museum half of the building and the other principally providing access to the maisonette, it was possible to provide alternative means of escape from every floor. The stair to the maisonette is fully enclosed and constructed of concrete. Because of the limitations imposed by the existing structure, the headroom and width of the timber stair is restricted in places and conflicted with the 1976 Regulations, but a relaxation was given.

Planning and highways

One of the requirements for planning permission was that a new access road should be made. As the main road was classified as a trunk road, the new access had to be moved away from another existing junction. To satisfy these design standards, the owner had to purchase more land and demolish a cottage.

Enforcement action was threatened at one stage against unauthorised advertising signs because the owner put back the original canal sign reading 'Navigation from the Trent to the Mersey', but was withdrawn when the historical basis for it was established.

References: Paras 2.2.7, 2.3.3, 2.4.1A, 2.4.3B, 2.6.4C and 3.3.1

2

Problems and conflicts

2.1 Introduction

This chapter deals with the physical effects of the legislation as applied to historic buildings. The information on which the chapter is based comes from correspondence, meetings and site visits with building owners, local authorities at district and county levels, government departments, architects, amenity and conservation groups and the Fire Research Station of the Building Research Establishment. As part of the information gathering operation, a questionnaire was published in the *Architects' Journal*. The same questionnaire was also sent to individuals and organisations who were known or thought to be involved with the conservation or development of historic buildings. The Fire Services Inspectorate of the Home Office was most helpful in obtaining reports from fire services throughout the country on their recent dealings with historic buildings.

Replies to questionnaires were received concerning 147 historic buildings, from which the case studies in this report have been selected. The information received has been set out in tabular form. Most cases concerned more than one piece of legislation or more than one type of problem, hence the total number of problems reported and the incidence of all the legislation far exceed the number of buildings involved.

General Questionnaire

The following questionnaire was used to obtain basic information for the study on which this book has been based. It was published in *The Architects' Journal* (14.5.80) and, prior to that, had been sent to 116 individuals or organisations concerned with 192 buildings that were thought to be possible cases of interest. The results are given below in the summary of replies. Promising responses were followed up to obtain more detailed information for the case studies.

The following points should be noted:

Question No. 7: in simplifying the nature of the problems down to six headings, some variations in interpretation have occurred. Where the information in a reply, or from a later follow-up, suggested that a problem concerned more than one of these headings, we entered it under all the appropriate 'problem' headings in the table. For example, the substitution of a new fire door for an old door would be described both as affecting the architectural character and as a loss of the original fabric.

'Structural problem' included both physical difficulties in making the building (or part) stable and the interpretative or enforcement problems of agreeing what constituted 'adequate stability'.

'Dimensional problem' included headroom, insufficient window to floor area ratio for daylight or ventilation, stairways and any problem of fitting new measures into an existing building where physical dimensions were a constraint.

'Architectural or historic character' referred to the introduction of new elements or the removal or covering up of old ones, and referred to spatial matters as well as details.

'Inconvenience' referred mainly to fire precautions, such as extra self-closing doors on circulation routes.

'Additional cost' included both the direct costs of meeting the requirements and any indirect costs due to the delay or disruption of programmes, etc.

The heading 'Blight' was added to the table, although it did not appear in the questionnaire, as it was obvious from some responses that the inability to make full use of a building for one reason or another was a category that ought to be included.

Although Improvement Grants are made under the Housing Act, the work has also to comply with the Building Regulations. Relevant cases in the table have therefore been entered under both pieces of legislation.

Summary of replies to the general questionnaire (and their relationship to the case studies)

There have been two facets to the research on which this book is based: the study of the legislation itself and the collection of reports on its application. The latter has depended almost entirely on the active cooperation of authorities, owners and architects. In most cases these have been interested parties to the cases under study and this has affected the information on which the work has been based.

The brief gave eleven categories of historic building that were to be given particular attention. These are indicated under the heading 'Building Types' in the table, and some of these have been included as case studies throughout this report, to illustrate points in the main text. The cases selected include both good and bad examples of the application of legislation; some illustrate typical problems that arise with a particular type of historic building, and some are intended to show the effects of different approaches to the legislation on similar buildings. Sometimes the choice of group for a particular building has had to be rather arbitrary. The original form or use of a building may have become obscure: a 'country house' may have been swallowed up by an expanding town, a 'town house' may have

SURVEY

This feature has been based on the experiences of only a few architects and there are, no doubt, more sides to the story.
A two-year research contract has been awarded by the Historic Areas Conservation Division of the Department of the Environment to Alan C. Parnell, to investigate the impact of legislation on historic buildings. An important part of the study depends on information from the profession, building owners and those who enforce the legislation about their experiences in this field.
Anyone who has had experiences, good or bad, of legislative barriers to be overcome on historic building jobs is invited to complete the following questionnaire and send it to:

Alan C. Parnell FRIBA, FSIAD, FIFE,
6 Welbeck Street,
London W1
or to telephone his office on 01-935 3534/5.

INFORMATION RECEIVED FROM

ORGANISATION ....
ADDRESS ....
....
....

SIGNATURE ....
DATE ....

1 THE BUILDING (name or title, address and use): ....

2 IN WHAT CAPACITY WERE YOU INVOLVED?
OWNER OR OWNER'S REPRESENTATIVE a☐
OCCUPIER b☐
ARCHITECT c☐
ENFORCING OFFICER (please specify authority, eg public health, etc) d☐
OTHER (please specify).. e☐

3 WHEN WERE THE LEGISLATIVE REQUIREMENTS MADE OR NEGOTIATIONS HELD?

4 WHEN WERE THE REQUIREMENTS SATISFIED OR PROBLEMS RESOLVED?

5 IS THE BUILDING (circle as appropriate):
a LISTED I b LISTED II* c LISTED II d IN CONSERVATION AREA

6 PLEASE LIST THE LEGISLATION UNDER WHICH PROBLEMATIC REQUIREMENTS WERE MADE, GIVING THE SECTION OR REGULATION NUMBER, ETC, WHERE APPROPRIATE (see table I pp960-961 for a list of legislation. Where more than one piece of legislation or section of a particular Act was involved, please list each on a separate line ie a, b, c, etc):

a ....
b ....
c ....
d ....
e ....
f ....
g ....

Please include any requirements that were the subject of relaxation applications whether they were granted or not (see also question 8).

7 WHAT WAS THE NATURE OF THE PROBLEM? (Please tick one or more appropriate boxes. The column headings: a, b, c etc refer to the list of regulations or sections in question 6.)

	THE LEGISLATION						
	a	b	c	d	e	f	g
STRUCTURAL PROBLEM							
DIMENSIONAL PROBLEM							
ARCHITECTURAL OR HISTORIC CHARACTER AFFECTED							
LOSS OF ORIGINAL FABRIC OR FINISH							
USER INCONVENIENCE							
ADDITIONAL COST							

If you feel further elaboration is necessary please explain the circumstances on a separate sheet.

undergone many changes and is now an hotel.

We would like to emphasise here how grateful we are to the many owners, architects, authorities and their staff for the assistance given with the case studies.

We believe the outcome of one or two cases may have been changed simply because of our investigation. If there appeared to be an anomaly in the account of one of the parties to some negotiation, we have had to decide whether to report it as such, and risk misinterpreting the situation, or to contact the other party and risk influencing their opinion. For example, in one or two cases when authorities had made a 'lenient' interpretation, it was felt that close questioning of their reasoning for a DOE Research Report might cause them to change their attitude and make more stringent requirements which would perhaps have had serious consequences for the buildings and

8 HOW WAS THE PROBLEM RESOLVED? (Please mention any relaxations, waivers or appeals. Please explain on a separate sheet, indicating corresponding legislative letter ie a, b, c, etc.)

9 DO YOU THINK THAT THE FINAL OUTCOME WAS REASONABLE IN THE CIRCUMSTANCES?

	a		b		c		d		e		f		g	
	yes	no	yes	no	yes	no	yes	no	yes	no	yes	no	yes	no
HISTORICALLY														
VISUALLY														
FUNCTIONALLY														
FINANCIALLY														

10 WHICH OF THE FOLLOWING MEASURES WOULD BE USEFUL, SO FAR AS THE RELATIONSHIP BETWEEN LISTED BUILDINGS AND STATUTORY CONTROLS IS CONCERNED? (Mark appropriate boxes.)

EXTEND THE CATEGORIES OF EXEMPT OR PARTIALLY EXEMPT BUILDINGS IN BUILDING REGULATIONS ☐
INTRODUCE 'DEEMED TO SATISFY' CODES OF PRACTICE FOR LISTED BUILDINGS GOVERNING ASPECTS OF PUBLIC HEALTH, BUILDING REGULATIONS AND FIRE PRECAUTIONS ☐
PROVIDE MORE GUIDANCE ON THE AIMS OF LEGISLATION AND ITS INTERPRETATION ☐
SIMPLIFY AND CONSOLIDATE LEGISLATION ☐
REDUCE THE NUMBER OF ENFORCING AUTHORITIES ☐
NONE ☐
OTHER (please specify): ....
....

11 HAVE YOU ANY OTHER COMMENTS OR SUGGESTIONS TO MAKE ABOUT ANY ASPECT OF LISTED BUILDINGS AND THEIR RELATIONSHIP TO LEGISLATION?
....
....
....
....
....
....

12 IF YOU HAVE NO OBJECTION, WE WOULD LIKE TO CONTACT ANY OTHER PARTIES INVOLVED IN THIS JOB (eg building control, fire officer, public health, etc). WE WOULD BE GRATEFUL IF YOU COULD PROVIDE NAMES AND ADDRESSES AND TELEPHONE NUMBERS OF ANY SUCH PARTIES:

1 ....
....
....
....
....

2 ....
....
....
....
....

3 ....
....
....
....
....

their owners.

Feelings sometimes run high in the conservation lobby at the 'scandalous' treatment of historic buildings. Our research has shown very few cases justifying such a description.

In addition, twenty-four local authorities were sent a detailed questionnaire concerned with engineering, planning, Section 16 of the 1961 Housing Act and Home Improvement Grants.

Legislation	Town houses & public buildings	Shops	Mixed use, e.g. offices above shops	Warehouses or mills	Churches	Victorian villas	Country houses	Country cottages	Hotels or inns	University buildings	Schools	*Total: Incidence of each Act*	Structural problem	Dimensional problem	Architectural or historic character	Loss of fabric	Inconvenience	Cost	'Blight'	*Total: 'Problems' of each Act*
Building Regulations	10	2	9	13	5	1	12	17	4		2	*75*	29	34	51	37	7	35		*193*
Public Health Acts	3	1	2	2			7	4				*19*	3	6	13	4	2	6		*34*
Fire Precautions Act	7	2	3	2			8		16			*38*	10	11	22	16	11	20		*90*
Housing Acts	4					1	1	14				*20*	3	9	13	11		9		*45*
Licensing Act	1						5		4			*10*	4		4	2	1	4		*15*
Entertainment Licensing	2						1					*3*		3	3	2	1	1		*10*
Theatres Licensing Act			1								1	*2*		1	2			2		*5*
Private Places of Entertainment Act							1					*1*			1					*1*
Town & Country Planning Act	1		1	2	3		1		2			*10*	1	1	4	1		3	4	*14*
ditto (Listed Building & ... Conservation Area) Regs	2		2		1		3			2	1	*11*	1		8	4	1	3	1	*18*
ditto (General Development Order) 1977							2					*2*			1			2		*3*
Historic Buildings & Ancient Monuments Act							1					*1*			1		1			*2*
Education Act 1944	1						3				5	*9*	1		6	4	1	4		*16*
Mental Health Act							1					*1*	1				1	1		*3*
Conduct of Nursing Homes Regulations	1											*1*			1	1	1			*3*
Food & Drugs Act 1955				2					1			*3*			1	2		1	1	*5*
Local Government Act							1					*1*							1	*1*
Local Acts	1						3					*4*	1	2	1	1	1	3	1	*10*
Offices, Shops & Railway Premises Act	2		1									*3*		1	1	2	1			*5*
Factories Act	1											*1*					1			*1*
Highways Act	2+ 3D			2D	1		4		1+ 1D			*14*		3	2	3+ 5D		4	2	*19*
Health & Safety at Work, etc, Act				4								*4*			5	1		2		*8*
Total: Incidence all Acts by building type	*41*	*5*	*19*	*27*	*10*	*2*	*54*	*35*	*29*	*2*	*9*								*Total 'problems'*	*50*

Detailed Questionnaire

A: Engineering – roads, traffic engineering and street lighting

A1: How is responsibility for road layout design, traffic control schemes and street lighting design, divided between the county and the local authority in your area?

A2: What Codes or guidance documents do your engineers use when planning or assessing road layout (for sight lines, widths, radii, etc)?

A3: When historic buildings (i.e. listed buildings or ones in conservation areas) may be affected by road alterations or traffic routing schemes:
a. Is there a standard procedure for informal consultation with the planning authority at county or district level?
b. Would consideration be given to departing from the normal design standard in the interests of the historic or aesthetic importance of the building?

A4: Have any historic buildings been altered or demolished in your area in the last three years as a part of road improvements or traffic control schemes? (Please give the address of any such building, if possible.)

A5: If the answer to A4 was 'yes': why was alteration or demolition necessary?

A6: What Codes or Standards do your lighting engineers use when designing street lighting schemes?

A7: Has it been considered necessary or desirable to depart from these Codes, etc, when designing lighting schemes in conservation areas or in the vicinity of historic buildings?

B: Planning and historic buildings

B1: Has the county planning authority issued a design guide which includes reference to alteration or development to listed buildings and buildings in conservation areas?

B2: Does your authority employ conservation, or historic buildings officers and, if so, how many and what are their professional backgrounds (architect, planner, etc)?

B3: Are you aware of any conflict between:
a. Land-use zoning and the development or alteration of historic buildings (i.e. listed or in conservation areas)?
b. Density controls and the development or alteration of historic buildings?
(It would be helpful to give a reference to any recent case that you consider illustrates either of these problems, if they do occur.)

B4: a. Is there a county standard or policy for the amount of car parking to be provided on the site of developments or do any of the districts have such a standard?
b. In considering applications for development or change of use of an historic building, would a relaxation of the standard (if one exists) be contemplated if it could only be met to the detriment of the historic or architectural or aesthetic appeal of the building?

C: Housing Act 1961, Section 16 – means of escape from houses in multiple occupation

C1: Is the administration and enforcement of Section 16 handled at county or district level?

C2: How does the authority interpret the term 'multiple occupation' in Section 16 of the Housing Act 1961 (as amended by the Acts of 1964 and 1969)?

C3: Do staff of the authority inspect residential property to implement the provisions of Section 16?

C4: If the answer to C3 is 'yes': on what basis are premises selected for inspection?

C5: When an application for Building Regulations approval is received that concerns a house in multiple occupation, do the building control staff consider whether requirements should be made under Section 16 of the Housing Act and, if so, to whom is the matter referred?

C6: Are any special arrangements made for consultation with the conservation or historic buildings officer before requirements under Section 16 are served, when a listed building or building in a conservation area is involved?

C7: Are means of escape requirements based on a written Code? (If so, we would be very grateful to be lent a copy, or referred to any published work.)

C8: To what extent are the requirements influenced by the statutory consultation with the fire authority?

C9: What training in fire safety do the staff dealing with Section 16 have?

CC: Home improvement grants

CC1: Are home improvement grants administered at county or district level?

CC2: When application for improvement grant is made for an historic building (i.e. one listed or in a conservation area) what standards of 'fitness' (in Housing Act/environmental health terms) are applied in assessing the adequacy of the scheme? (If they are to be found in a published document, please give the reference. If you have produced your own Code we would very much like to borrow a copy.)

CC3: Are these standards ever relaxed in the interests of the historical importance of a building in accordance with Section 61(3) of the Housing Act 1974? (A reference to a specific instance that we could follow up later would be most useful.)

CC4: Have discretionary grants been given specifically to allow the quality or character of a listed building undergoing improvement to be maintained?

CC5: Are there procedures for consultation with the planning authority's staff when an historic building is involved in an improvement grant application?

CC6: Are there any recurring problems with improvement grants for historic buildings in your area (e.g. dampness of a traditional form of wall construction, etc)?

2.2 The Building Regulations 1976

The application of the Act to change of use for historic premises was found in the questionnaire to be the most onerous part of the Building Regulations, although the authorities sometimes invoked parallel requirements in other Acts. These are summarised in Table 3 (p. 58). All parts of the Building Regulations were found to be applicable to historic buildings as a special building type, except for Parts J, H and P, which relate to refuse disposal, drainage, private sewers, cesspools and sanitary conveniences.

2.2.1 Part A: Interpretation and administration

Details of Regulation A7, which was concerned with maintaining comparable standards in an extension to an existing building, and A9, which was concerned with defining 'material change of use', are given in para 1.3.2D. Since they relate to administrative matters, they are discussed further in Chapter 3.

2.2.2 Part B: Fitness of material

We have found that most designers and clients are sympathetic to using materials which are compatible with the original building.

2.2.3 Part C: Preparation of site and resistance to moisture

The problem of change was frequently mentioned in the questionnaire, largely in connection with housing improvement grants. Under the part of A7 concerned with alterations, ground floor damp-proofing could not be a Building Regulation requirement unless a change of use under Cases A or D was involved and where the lack of damp-proofing was a pre-existing contravention of Part C. The most important type of change of use, as far as historic buildings were concerned, proved to be Case A, the conversion of a house into some other occupancy group.

The physical problems of damp-proofing vary with the type of construction. Clay lump and similar constructions shrink and crumble if dried out, so that a new inner wall lining is needed to act as a moisture barrier.

Chemical injection is probably the least visually disruptive damp-proof treatment for solid walls, but with thick rubble masonry it may not be effective and a slate or felt DPC may therefore be necessary, although the latter process can cause damage if not skilfully executed.

Although the damp-proofing of floors causes disruption during the work, it is unlikely to cause any damage, except to the tiles or slates of a decorative and brittle floor. The cost can be considerable, especially if it involves changes of level or alterations to steps, skirtings, etc. Damp-proofing was an important improvement grant condition in the case of Nos. 5 and 8 St John's Square, Wilton (Case Study No. 10A). *See Case Study 10A, pp. 130-31*

It has been suggested that, in buildings with high internal humidity, the insulation of external walls and roof space may lead to damage from interstitial condensation. This would obviously be detrimental to historic buildings if damage were caused to finishes, or if fungal destruction of timbers occurred.

2.2.4 Part D: Structural stability

Structural stability requirements, whether to satisfy Part D of the Regulations, or when the possibility of a dangerous structures notice arose under Section 58 of the Public Health Acts 1961 and 1936, were, and still are, far from being a straightforward matter in an old building, and need checking for various reasons:

See Case Studies 2A, 2C and 4B, pp. 16-17, 20-23 and 55-56

— the dead loading can change with alterations in the fabric of the building or with settlement and consequent load transfer;
— changes may set up eccentric loadings, and the vibration of heavy road or rail traffic may induce unexpected live load conditions;
— some modern uses can impose far greater floor loads than, say, an eighteenth-century domestic use would have done;
— the structural movement of joints and the way loads are transmitted can be difficult to assess; and
— decay in timber or brickwork, or the lack of homogeneity in cast iron make the strength of old materials unreliable.

For example, a reroofing operation at 25 Beaumont Street, Oxford, led to structural changes and the owners opted to replace the original timber with mild steel purlins. The size of the timbers which would have been required if the 'deemed to satisfy' Code of Practice had been applied would have restricted the headroom at the top of the stairs. The roof was therefore considered as being of new construction, requiring alterations to the pitch of the roof and the position of the ridge.

Many engineers are unhappy to outline new and old materials because their structural action is different and will consequently set up new forces which could cause further changes within the combined structure.

2.2.5 Part E: Fire

In our experience the section of the Building Regulations of 1976 which caused most of the problems in work to historic buildings was that relating to fire precautions.

2.2.6 The fire protection of structural elements

The structural elements were required to have a prescribed standard of fire resistance which was defined by means of laboratory tests set out in B.S. 476: Part 8, 1972. The Standards were also dependent on the use of the premises, the number of storeys, and the height, floor area and volume of the building. Under certain circumstances, roofs could be omitted from these controls.

See Case Studies 2A, 2B and 8C, pp. 16-17, 18-19 and 107-10

2.2.7 Timber structures

Timber structures can be assessed for fire resistance on the basis of their accepted 'sacrificial charring rate' figures for different grades of hardwood and softwood (BS 5268: Part 3: Section 4.1: 1978). By this method the amount of charred timber remaining after the required period is estimated, and the structural adequacy of the remaining section is assessed. As timber members in historic buildings are very often oversized they are therefore acceptable, *and we have not found cases of radical alterations being required to obtain sufficient fire resistance.* Relevant case studies: Thaxted Guildhall (Case Study No. 4B), 35 King Street, Bristol (Case Study No. 2A), and especially No. 2 Mill, Shardlow (Case Study No. 2C).

2.2.8 Metal structures

Metal structures in historic buildings generally comprise cast iron or, occasionally, wrought iron. They are not usually considered to have any significant fire resistance. Any assessment should take into consideration the mass and surface area of the section, although there are often uncertainties as cast iron is not as homogeneous a material as modern structural steel and the thickness of the walls of a hollow section often varies.

Although cast iron retains its working strength to higher temperatures than mild steel, cast-iron structures which had been 'heat soaked' for days during the Second World War tended to shatter when suddenly cooled by water jets. Even though this does not occur in ordinary fires (such as the Alexandra Palace fire of 1980), many fire officers recommend protection.

The common remedial treatments all have some effect on the appearance of the metalwork. It can be encased, which conceals it completely, or sprayed with a thick mineral fibre of cementitious coating, which obliterates all details and leaves an object of different proportions and surface, or a thinner intumescent coating can be applied which, at 6 mm thickness or thereabouts, can still hide fine details but gives reasonably inconspicuous protection.

Hollow iron sections can be filled with concrete to improve fire resistance, but no instances of this in historic buildings have come to our notice. Encasing and intumescent coatings can be removed to expose the metalwork unharmed, should a change in circumstances allow it. The other spray treatments are more difficult to remove completely and details might suffer from abrasion in the process. (See Case Studies Nos. 2A, 2B and 8C: No. 35 King Street, Bristol, The Great Warehouse, Coalbrookdale, and the Central Market Building, Covent Garden.)

2.2.9 Compartmentation

Problems relating to the interpretation of the Regulations were found to be of two types: where the building control officers considered that there were various 'purpose groups' within the building (an example of this problem is given in Case Study No. 9A, Brocket Hall, Hertfordshire), or where the fire resistance of the floors, ceilings and walls of the existing structure had to be upgraded to meet the Regulation requirements.

2.2.10 Ceilings and floors

A. Fire resistance

Building Regulations can impose requirements for fire resistance on ceiling/floor structures as a result of alterations or a change of use. All floors in residential institutions for the care of the sick, the young or old and those which separate flats or maisonettes may be required to be compartment floors.

B. Floors

Floor structures of one hour's fire resistance or more may also need to be non-combustible. As the majority of floors in historic buildings are of timber this can have serious consequences if a relaxation application is refused. Timber floor finishes do not conflict with the non-combustible requirement.

C. Exposed structures

The BRE Digest 108 (new edition 1980) is widely used in assessing the suitability of existing arrangements or proposals for upgrading a floor's fire resistance. Difficulties arise where there is no ceiling and the joists and underside of floorboards are exposed, as in warehouses, mills and industrial buildings. To add a protective layer of plaster beneath the joists to such a ceiling may completely change the character of an interior. Acceptability not only depends on the proposed use, but also on the historical importance of the interior.

D. Decorative ceilings

Another problem is presented by a decorative ceiling which cannot be underdrawn without damaging or hiding the decoration. It is possible to apply adequate protection within the depth of the floor by working from above, but this is expensive, and undesirable if the floor surface is of high quality, as was the case at Marshal Wade's House, Bath (Case Study No. 1C). All the treatments recommended by the BRE which are applied from above involve placing hardboard or plywood on top of the floor surface, unless the latter is of well-fitting tongued and grooved boards (see also Case Study No. 3A, 57 The Close, Norwich).

See Case Study 1C, pp. 14-15

See Case Study 3A, pp. 49-51

Cavities within floor/ceiling constructions are also subject to the provisions for cavity barriers and fire stops. If the surface of the cavity is below Class 1 fire spread, barriers or fire stops could be required at 8 m intervals. Since traditional wood lath or straw does not meet Class 1, expensive and difficult work has been required to satisfy the Regulations. In a double joists floor, with joists running at 90° to each other, it is virtually impossible to fit a functional system of barriers.

2.2.11 External walls

A. Unprotected areas

Besides having to perform their normal structural functions under fire conditions, external walls are required to offer adequate resistance to the spread of fire both over the walls and from one building to another. Some of the 'unprotected area' need have no fire resistance. The permitted amount is calculated on the basis of:

— the distance between the walls and the site boundary;
— the size and shape of the wall;
— the sub-division of the accommodation behind the wall into compartments; and
— occupancy of the building (being a rough guide to the intensity of the fire and therefore of the radiation of heat).

B. Combustible infill

Not only are windows and doors regarded as unprotected areas but so are any areas clad with combustible material more than 1 mm thick, such as weatherboard. Wattle and daub or plaster on straw backing, used to infill a timber building, may not have sufficient fire resistance and would then be regarded as an unprotected area.

C. Upgrading

The Regulations may have necessitated alterations to external walls where, for example, the building was being extended sufficiently to require greater fire resistance. It may have been possible to retain the original appearance by merely reconstructing the infill to a higher standard of resistance. See Case Study No. 6C on St Peter and St Paul, Shellow Bowells, Essex.

See Case Study 6C, pp. 82-3

2.2.12 Internal walls and partitions

A. Fire resistance

Loadbearing walls should provide the same fire resistance as other structural elements. When alterations involve using non-loadbearing walls as part of the structure, or where a change of use converts a partition into a compartment wall, these elements are likewise required to have fire resistance equal to that of loadbearing walls.

B. Timber

Timber partitions are more liable to cause problems, especially where timber panelling forms one or both faces.

Single-leaf timber partitions may be given a fire resisting backing on one side, but this inevitably affects the character of an interior (see Case Study No. 1A, Kingsmead Square, Bath). A new panelled face may be constructed over the fire resisting layer, but this often causes difficulties in matching cornices, dado or skirting mouldings and adjoining panelling and will increase costs. A half-hour standard can sometimes be achieved by applying a clear intumescent coating to single-leaf timber panels (see Case Studies Nos. 5B and 5C on Bedford Row and Great Ormond Street).

See Case Study 1A, pp. 10-11

See Case Studies 5B and 5C, pp. 74-5 and 76-8

Provided that the partition can be dismantled without damage, a twin-leaf timber partition can be inconspicuously upgraded by forming a fire resisting layer or wall between the timber surfaces. However, the problem of achieving non-combustibility may remain and unfortunately old panelling is often impossible to dismantle without damage.

C. Surface flame spread

Almost all changes except those involving a conversion into a house or the sub-division of a house into several houses or flats involves changing or treating any wall surfaces in rooms, circulation spaces, or protected shafts which do not meet the necessary standards under BS 476: Parts 6 and 7. The effect of this is that such fittings as timber panelling, etc, in circulation areas, protected stairs and rooms may need to be treated with a retardant coating. Fortunately there are clear matt treatments available whose affect on appearance is negligible.

D. Wall cavities

There is little doubt that wall cavities exist in most historic buildings with lath and plaster finishes, and the history of fires in such buildings indicates that fire spread often occurs in the interconnecting voids between masonry and laths. *However, we have found no evidence of practical problems involving the application of fire stopping to wall cavities.* It seems that serious attempts to form fire stops in these cavities are not often made or are restricted to points made accessible by other work, such as the creation of compartment walls. But problems do seem to arise with cavities in floors.

2.2.13 Internal doors

A. Fire resistance

Problems associated with the fire protection of doorways form the largest single category of enquiries received by the advisory section of the fire research station, and virtually every one of the case studies involves provision of fire doors. For Building Regulation purposes, existing doorways require fire resisting doors when the wall they are in becomes either a compartment wall or a protecting structure to a protected shaft. In the former case the door has to have the same fire resistance as the wall. In the latter, the resistance needs to be only half that of the wall because, to spread from one level to another via the stair, the fire has to penetrate two such doors.

B. Upgrading

The 1976 Regulations specified that, if tested to BS 476: Part 8, a fire resisting door had to satisfy the requirements for collapse and resistance to passage of flame. Rather than demanding a test certificate for old doors, most building control authorities applied the dimensional criteria of BS 459: Part 3: 1951 and extrapolations from tests of constructions similar to that proposed. This resulted in old doors which were judged to be too thin or cracked having to be upgraded or replaced by new fire doors.

If upgrading is found to be necessary, there are several methods which have varying effects on the existing fabric. Usually the cheapest and ugliest is to infill any panels with a non-combustible insulating board on one side for half-hour standard and apply a sheet of the same material over the whole surface of the door. The door stops usually have to be increased to provide a 25 mm rebate. The door treatment is sometimes disguised by planting mouldings on the flat surface to give a panelled effect. Alternatively the whole door can be split in half and a fire resisting layer slipped into the centre. Both methods, by increasing the overall thickness of the door, may require matching alterations to the door frame so that the door's face does not stand proud of the surround. A third technique, which is possible with raised and fielded doors whose panel thickness is judged to be inadequate only in the tapered fields, is to mortise in a fire resisting sheet around the panel edges only.

These techniques increase the weight of the doors appreciably and, when self-closing devices are fitted, the loads imposed on door and frame can cause serious damage. Because the combined effect of weight and closer make such doors hard to open, they are an inconvenience to the occupants and can present a major obstacle to movement around a building. The fire doors in nearly every building we visited were found to have their self-closing devices disabled in some way, being either wedged open or having the closing devices disconnected.

One other upgrading treatment is sometimes acceptable. This is the application of an intumescent coating to the 'risk' side of the door. The success of such treatment depends on very careful preparation and application, and is liable to result in a coarse, lumpy appearance. Long-term performance and the ability to maintain these finishes properly has still to be established.

Modifications relying on skilled joinery are frequently now so expensive that often the old door is simply scrapped and replaced with a modern fire door.

2.2.14 Roofs (thatch and wood shingles)

Under the 1976 Regulations, roof covering materials not only had to resist ignition by radiation and flying embers, but also limit the rate at which fire could spread over them, once ignited. This particularly affected the use of thatch and wood shingles. Unless a smaller distance was allowed under the relaxation procedures, unrestricted use of thatch or shingles on the roof of a house was only allowed if the house were more than 12 m from the site boundary. *We have found one case – No. 10B, the Old Manor Farm House, Torquay – in which approval to restore thatch to a corrugated-metal roofed house was denied because of the proximity of other buildings.*

2.2.15 Staircases

A new stair that passes from one compartment to another has to be enclosed by a protecting structure with the same fire resistance. For means of escape purposes, the enforcing authority rarely calls for more than half an hour's standard of protection to the stair, but compliance with the Building Regulations may require it to be increased to an hour.

2.2.16 Means of escape

Part B1 of Schedule 1 of the 1985 Regulations, Means of Escape, applies mainly to the erection of shops, offices and both houses and flats of over two storeys.

The problem of protecting stairways has already been referred to, but there are two points that cause problems in particular circumstances. The stairway in a house of two storeys has to be separated from the accommodation by a fire resisting construction if one or more storeys are added, including the conversion of a loft into habitable rooms. Rooflights and dormer windows may need to be designed to allow emergency egress if fire protection of the stairway is not fully obtained. Guidance is provided in BS 5588, 'Fire Precautions in the Design and Construction of Buildings', specifically Part 1: Section 1.1, which deals with single-family dwelling houses. Also means of escape requirements can cause problems when intermediate floors are inserted into an historic building such as a church (see Case Studies Nos. 6B and 6C, St Leonard's, Foscote, and St Peter and St Paul, Shellow Bowells).

See Case Studies 6B and 6C, pp. 81 and 82-3

2.2.17 Part H: Stairways and ramps

Under the 1976 Regulations, there was a tendency for new conforming staircases in small-scale historic buildings to be out of scale. Handrails sometimes had to be higher and the balusters much closer together than those they replaced. Small domestic buildings were often affected because improvement grant conditions specified compliance with Building Regulation standards.

Part K of Schedule 1 of the 1985 Regulations is limited merely to a general concern for the safety of staircases, ramps and other changes of level.

2.2.18 Part G: Sound insulation

See Case Study 10B, p. 132

Part G of the 1976 Regulations only applied to domestic premises. Generally the sound insulation of an historic building is superior to that of modern construction because of its greater weight and flexibility. Domestic conversions of historic buildings should be planned to take advantage of this. *We have found no examples of historic buildings having problems with sound insulation.*

2.2.19 Part K: Ventilation

We found no difficulties over the zones of open space requirements of Part K of the 1976 Regulations but two cases in Inner London concerning daylight to basement rooms and the environmental health requirements for daylight are referred to in Case Studies Nos. 5B and 5C,

See Case Studies 5B and 5C, pp. 74-5 and 76-8

Bedford Row and Great Ormond Street, London, which involve the Housing Acts.

The need in the 1976 Regulations to provide adequate ventilation openings of at least one-twentieth of the floor area of habitable rooms did not appear to raise difficulties in historic buildings (but see Case Study No. 10D on the camping barns at Buckden and Sedbergh, North Yorkshire).

See Case Study 10D, p. 135

1976 Regulations K8, which dealt with the height of habitable rooms, had an important effect on such alterations as the construction of a room in a roof space sometimes involving the construction of bulky dormers which completely changed the character of the roof. The standards of K8 were often made a condition of an improvement grant award. *We have been told of cases in which floors have had to be lowered or roofs raised as a result.* 1985 Regulations merely require that an adequate supply of air be provided in dwellings, toilets and bathrooms.

2.2.20 Part M: Heat-producing appliances and chimneys

The provisions of Part M of the 1976 Regulations only came into effect when a new heating appliance was fitted or the existing arrangements were altered. Changes of this sort must have been made in many historic buildings in the last few years as the economics of heating have changed. *Despite this, we have encountered no difficulties over the 1976 Regulations.*

1976 Regulations L6 made specific requirements for the lining materials to be used in the chimneys of 'Class 1 appliances', which would include normal open solid fuel fires, and there were various other restrictions on having combustible materials in or close to the chimney flue or hearth, etc. Chimney fires in old buildings do sometimes spread into roof or floor timbers through openings in the chimney or because dry and dusty timber is too close to the hot masonry. When a change of use occurred, L6 did not apply, but if alterations involving a chimney were proposed and the authority regarded the original masonry as inadequate, they could require the chimney to be relined. The physical complications of such a job were liable to be expensive and could also cause damage to the fabric of the surrounding areas. A timber lintel over a fireplace could be regarded as contravening the Regulations by being within 150 mm of the flue. An example of this is referred to in Case Study No. 7B, the Wig and Mitre, Lincoln. Severe damage can result from such fires because they are unlikely to be discovered soon enough to be extinguished quickly.

See Case Study 10C, pp. 133-4

See Case Study 10D, p. 135

See Case Study 7B, pp. 101-2

Part J of Schedule 1 of the 1985 Regulations deals with heat-producing appliances in very general terms of ventilation and fire resistance.

2.3 The Public Health Acts

2.3.1 Dangerous structures

The importance of the dangerous structures procedures to historic buildings is obvious. While their aesthetic qualities may be highly regarded, the standard of building construction was sometimes deplorable and the familiar comment 'if they lasted this long they are not going to fall down now' is simply not true. Without proper maintenance and repairs, all historic buildings are bound to deteriorate into a dangerous structural condition, particularly if they were badly constructed in the first place. But the assessment of the structural condition of old buildings is not straightforward: it requires specialist technical knowledge and experience. Situations arise where opinions differ as to the need to apply dangerous structure legislation.

As it is an offence to demolish a listed building or a building in a conservation area without consent, there is a potential conflict between the provisions of swift action on dangerous structures under the Public Health Acts and the protecting powers of the Town and Country Planning Act 1971. Section 55(6) of the Act acknowledges that urgent work for safety or health reasons may be argued in defence, but the courts can only decide when considering the circumstances of a particular case.

The administrative aspects of these conflicts are discussed in Chapter 3.

2.3.2 Section 33 of the 1961 Act

An authority considering a proposal such as that made for the Derbyshire Field Barns (in Case Study No. 10C) for conversion of unserviced agricultural structures into overnight accommodation for hill walkers might feel obliged to reject the plans unless a bath or shower with hot and cold running water was provided. It was a situation for which the county council could find no precedent. To avoid contravening the Act, they decided to treat the barns as 'stone tents' using the legislation under which camp sites are licensed.

In North Yorkshire, at Cam Houses (Case Study No. 10D), a similar scheme for a larger barn was provided with the amenities specified in Section 33 but using the Youth Hostels Association's simplest standard as a guide.

2.3.3. Means of escape

The provisions of S.59 of the 1936 Public Health Act do not appear to be used much by local authorities. They are one of the few means of escape controls that could be applied to public halls used for unlicensable functions such as exhibitions or museums. *No examples have come to our notice.*

Before the enactment of the Fire Precautions Act and for a few years after, Section 60 of the 1936 Public Health Act was the principal control in many kinds of buildings over means of escape from sleeping accommodation on upper floors. Several of the case studies refer to it, including Marshal Wade's House, Bath, and No. 2 Mill, Shardlow (Case Studies Nos. 1C and 2C). Its vague wording unfortunately led to variations in interpretation and application.

Although Section 60 is still in force, its use appears to be diminishing. This is partly because the 1976 Building Regulations included provisions for control of means of escape from 'any part of a building which consists of a flat or maisonette so situated that its floor... is 4.5 m or more above... ground level', and S.30 of the Fire Precautions Act gave the Building Regulations precedence over S.60 of the Public Health Act. Secondly, the provision of S.10 of the Fire Precautions Act give the fire authority scope to tackle seriously deficient premises, including 'sleeping accommodation', thus duplicating Section 60. The building safety officer for the County of Essex reported that the county fire authority is increasingly referring to these sections of the Fire Precautions Act where fire safety in a non-designated building is under discussion and we believe this tendency will grow. Further discussion of these points is included in Chapter 3.

2.4 The Fire Precautions Act 1971

Some of the difficulties raised by the requirements made under this Act are identical to those of the Building Regulations. *In fact we have found that work involving both the Building Regulations and the Fire Precautions Act often seem to confuse all concerned as to which authority is requiring what and by what powers.*

The potential historic buildings problems highlighted by the Fire Precautions Act are:

— devising alternative means of escape;
— protecting escape routes;
— detection, alarms, emergency lighting and fire fighting equipment;
— housekeeping and management; and
— restrictions on the use of the premises.

2.4.1 Alternative means of escape

A. Relevant legislation

Accommodating new doors in an elevation to provide additional exits from a ground floor may present aesthetic problems. This is particularly so in the more formal designs of the Georgian period and in neo-classical elevations. Not only can conflicts arise between Planning and Fire Precautions Act requirements, but a new exit on to a congested highway or narrow pavement may also involve the highways authority. Examples include No. 2 Mill, Shardlow, 57 The Close, Norwich, and Kenwood House (Case Studies Nos. 2C, 3A and 9B).

See Case Studies 2C, 3A and 9B, pp. 20-23, 49-51 and 120-23

See Case Studies 1C and 2C, pp. 14-15 and 20-23

B. Accommodating the escape route

The most difficult and the frequently recurring problem is that of providing an additional means of escape stair from upper floors. The need may arise either because there are too few stairs to ensure that occupants could reach a usable stair from any part of the building, or because existing stairs are not sufficiently protected from fire to be capable of being regarded as means of escape. In addition to the obvious architectural, structural and historical problems of finding a vertical zone in which an opening can be made for a stair, there is the limitation that it must be located both to give direct access to the outside at ground level and to satisfy the travel distance limitations on the floors it serves.

Among the many case studies where the work included provision of a new staircase, those due to the Fire Precautions Act include the Lady in Grey and Broughton House, Derbyshire, and John O'Port's House, Salisbury (Case Studies Nos. 7A and 8A).

See Case Studies 7A and 8A, pp.97-100 and 103-4

Sometimes existing stairs are positioned so that, from some parts of the upper floors, it is necessary to pass through one stairway to reach another. Thus, in such cases, the second stair does not offer a real alternative. If possible, a fire resisting screen can be incorporated across the landing so that, if smoke does get into the first stair, the screen will hold it back and allow passage to the second. The screen inevitably changes the character of the stairway. If this is unacceptable, it may be possible to form a route through rooms flanking the first stair so that it can be by-passed. Obviously the privacy and furniture layout of these rooms is affected.

C. Adjoining premises

Alternatively, it may be possible to form a doorway through a party wall to a property in different ownership so that, by reciprocal agreement, each property has an alternative means of escape (Case Studies Nos. 5B and 8B, Bedford Row and 12 Newgate, York).

See Case Studies 5B and 8B, pp. 74-5 and 105-6

D. External stairs

If access through adjoining premises is not

possible, or the stairs could only be accommodated either at great expense or by destroying important interior features, the other possibility is an external stair. Since Building Regulations have required weather protection for an external stair rising more than 6 m above the ground, and since listed building consent is unlikely to be given for an enclosure whose materials and design are not in keeping with the building, external stairs are usually expensive additions for historic buildings of three or more storeys. It is also very difficult to produce a stair of appropriate design.

E. Openings

The fire authority usually requires all windows, ventilation or other openings that are within 1.8 m horizontally or 6 m vertically below the stair to be made fire resisting and permanently closed. The glazing bars of the typical eighteenth- and nineteenth-century sash window will not accept the 6 mm Georgian wired glass that is normally specified for fire resisting glazing and therefore a second, fire resisting window has to be created either inside or outside the original.

2.4.2 Protecting escape routes

A. Lobbies

Except for small buildings with only one upper storey, a single stair must normally be separated from the accommodation by half-hour fire resisting construction and be approached through a lobby, all the doors onto which must be self-closing and fire resistant. Where doors open directly onto the landing, or where the landings are less than generous in scale, it is often difficult to accommodate a lobby without forming screens or boxy enclosures in either the rooms or the stairway, thereby increasing the cost, inconveniencing the occupants and spoiling the architectural character. If possible, doors onto landings should be sealed and an alternative route devised via an adjoining corridor.

B. Obstructions

The authority may insist on the removal of all combustible or movable fittings from escape stairways, either because they are a fire hazard or because they might obstruct the escape route. The character of large scale interiors, whose circulation spaces are highly suitable for displaying pictures and furniture, tends to suffer when thus denuded. The effect tends to be most noticeable in ground floor entrance halls which form part of the route from a protected stair.

C. Materials

We have found no instances of the materials within an existing stairway being affected by the Fire Precautions Act requirements, only by Building Regulations. Guidance notes have been prepared by the Home Office but they refer only to surface flame spread. The only treatments found in practice have been inconspicuous coatings applied to timber surfaces in stairs, and the underdrawing with plaster or non-combustible insulation board of the soffit of timber staircases.

D. Glazing

Glazing in doors or partitions onto protected stairs or windows must be fire resisting and this generally means that either 6 mm Georgian wired glass or copper light glazing has to be substituted for the original or added in the form of a second skin on the 'risk' side. Thermal radiation passes readily through all normal and wired glass. A window from a 'risk' room onto a corridor could subject people trying to pass it to intolerable heat and thus prevent escape. If there is no alternative means of escape, the authority may require the window to be removed or altered so that its sill is high enough (about 1 m) above floor level to allow people to crawl past.

2.4.3 Detection, alarms, etc

A. Problems

Automatic fire detection is almost always required where the Fire Precautions Act is being applied to historic buildings. In a high proportion of the cases studied, initial fire authority demands for alternative escape stairs have been withdrawn when routes could not be devised and automatic detection requested instead.

The problems seen, or reported, concerning automatic detection involved unsightly surface wiring, the expense of the installation, and inconvenience and loss of confidence due to false alarms.

Generally the wiring is required to be either in screwed metal conduit or MICC cable, both of which are bulky. If surface mounted, they are visually intrusive and, if concealed, relatively expensive to run behind plaster or panelling or through floor joists, etc. Although the equipment – detectors, control panel and power supply – is not cheap, the most significant component of the installation cost in an historic building is the labour of wiring.

B. Smoke detectors

Sometimes comments have been made to us about the

need to conceal the detector heads but this does not seem to be an important problem in the majority of cases. As detectors of the point type (we have found no other type in historic buildings) are ceiling mounted, a low ceiling will make them more noticeable; florid plasterwork, however, can often be used to camouflage the heads. In one case, at Beningbrough Hall, Yorkshire, the smoke detector heads were put within the ceiling depth and holes were formed in the ceiling to let smoke reach them. This seems unnecessarily complicated and in some circumstances would reduce both the sensitivity of the detectors and the fire resistance of the floors in which they were concealed. Where the joists are exposed, the time taken for detectors to respond varies: the spread of hot gases and smoke across the joists will be slow, the space between joists forming a reservoir which has to be filled before the smoke spreads into the next one; on the other hand, smoke spread in the same direction as the joists is likely to be faster even than that which would occur with a flat ceiling. (See Case Study No. 2, Warehouses and Mills.)

C. False alarms

There is considerable debate on the true frequency of false alarms from automatic detection systems. Heat detectors, being relatively less sensitive, have an acceptable record. However, the ratio of false alarms to genuine fire alarms for smoke detectors is put at between 5:1 and 20:1. Historic buildings would not be expected to be any better or worse than others in this respect. It is obviously undesirable to have numerous false alarms: the occupants become blasé, ignoring or reacting slowly to an alarm, and the fire brigade has to make fruitless and expensive visits. For fire stations with 'retained' staff (part-timers who have other jobs they must leave whenever they are called out), the false alarms cause a lot of disruption to the community. A possible future problem for historic buildings may be the unwillingness of the fire service to accept automatic detection as a compensation and instead to insist on more damaging structural fire precautions, additional escapes, etc.

D. Alarm systems

Alarm systems (the bells or sirens which may be activated by automatic detectors if installed, and/or by manual 'break glass call points') have the same wiring problems as detectors, but they constitute only a minor visual intrusion. False alarms with manual break glass systems are negligible and are due mainly to human error or malice. However, malfunctions of automatic telephone dialling machines are reportedly quite common. Fire Precautions Act requirements now hardly ever include direct alarm links to a fire station or control centre, although in the early days of the Act this was quite common.

E. Fire fighting

'First aid' fire fighting equipment is often called for under the Act. It can cause more serious visual and financial problems in historic buildings than elsewhere, because the interiors are more sensitive and the measures needed to accommodate the equipment have to be more elaborate (see Kenwood House, Case Study No. 9B). The cost of the equipment can be greater in some types of historic building than in ordinary buildings. Although the Fire Precautions Act will protect escaping occupants, historic buildings in the country remote from a fire station depend on effective self-help to prevent serious damage.

See Case Study 9B, pp. 120-23

Any historic buildings with fabric or contents of high artistic, architectural or historic value also rely to a great extent on the ability of their occupants to subdue fire in its earliest stages, as critical fire or smoke damage can be caused before the professional fire fighters arrive. The water damage resulting from the full sized 70 mm hose with its 19 mm jet used by the fire brigades can be as grave as that of the fire itself.

See Case Study 2, pp. 16-23

F. Signs

Not only might architectural character be eroded by the removal of furnishings from escape routes, but the Act may also require the addition of signs and emergency lighting fittings. There are two main types of sign: those directing occupants to an exit, and those giving warnings or instruction of some kind. Direction signs must he highly visible but too many signs can create an institutional impression. All too often they are regarded as an addition without any attempt to coordinate their form, finish or mounting with the surroundings.

2.4.4 Housekeeping and management

Because of the high proportion of historic buildings that are required by the Fire Precautions Act to have automatic detection systems, the problem of system maintenance is more serious than in other types of buildings. In some parts of the country, the fire authority stipulates the frequency of maintenance checks which must be carried out by an approved specialist as part of the fire certificate conditions. For all but the smallest installations, the annual maintenance cost is likely to amount to at least £100.

The heavy loading on upgraded fire doors

leads to considerable maintenance problems which get worse as the door frame becomes incapable of receiving new hinges or other fixings such as the self-closing device.

2.4.5 Restricted use

If no way can be found to improve the fire precautions in those parts of a building which are subject to the Act (for example, a top floor served only by an inadequate stair and for which no alternative can be devised), the certificate can prohibit or restrict its use, limiting the number of occupants. At Clarence House, Thaxted, the top floor bedrooms, whose alternative escape is over the roof, are let to young people, and the choice of tenants in the Covent Garden central market building refurbishment; especially for the first floor sites, was most carefully vetted by the fire authority (Case Studies Nos. 5A and 8C). Although these powers can limit the use of a particular building, our research suggests that this happens infrequently, if at all. *We were informed that a large number of small hotels have reduced their number of beds to six or less to avoid having to carry out expensive fire precautions work, but we have only found one example.*

See Case Studies 5A and 8C, pp. 72-3 and 107-10

2.5 The Housing Acts

2.5.1 Houses in multiple occupation – means of escape from fire

The scope of this legislation is limited to providing means of escape where the Fire Precautions Act cannot be used to secure it. In the absence of case law, this is open to interpretation, and the variation in interpretation is discussed in para 3.6.4. The British Standards Institution defines a means of escape as a 'structural means whereby a safe route or routes is/are provided for persons to travel from any point in a building to a place of safety by their own unaided efforts'.

The problems of providing a protected stair in houses in multiple occupation tend to be particularly acute because they often contain more constricted staircases than the hotels, offices, etc, affected by the Fire Precautions Act. Following wide public concern over safety, the Government introduced the Housing (Means of Escape from Fire in Houses in Multiple Occupation) Order 1981 (S1 1981/1576).*

2.5.2 Housing fitness and improvement grants

We believe that the main impact of the Housing Acts on historic buildings has been where local authorities were considering the provision of improvement grants for work affected by the 1976 Building Regulations and the environmental health requirements. The problems arising from the varying interpretations and standards, and the administration of the legislation, are discussed in para 3.5 and Chapter 4.

A. Building Regulations standards

Arguments over the need for structural repairs can arise. At Bunce Street in Chester the building control officer recommended that, before an improvement grant be given, a main elevation should be rebuilt. But the conservation team did not consider that this was essential. The owner's structural engineer advised that the elevation could be tied back without rebuilding and so a grant was provided from the City Conservation Fund instead of the improvement grant.

The replacement of a non-Regulation stair with a new one seems to be a fairly frequent demand of the improvement grant officer. As the original stairs are often defective because they fit into small or awkwardly shaped spaces, these changes can be significant, involving the removal of floor beams and a loss of floor space, and conflicting with small scale domestic interiors.

Part K of the 1976 Regulations particularly affected small domestic buildings subject to improvement grants in setting out the minimum headroom in habitable rooms. Regulation K8 called for a height of 2.3 m minimum with at least 2 m under beams and, for rooms in a roof, a height of 2.3 m over a proportion of the room. Authorities do not all use these dimensions as they are free to set their own standards, and figures of 2.14 m and 2.13 m have been quoted to us. When, as we found in a cottage in Weston, an increased ceiling height was called for on the ground floor, the applicant had either to lower the floor level (which would probably mean that the ground level outside had to be reduced to avoid damp problems) or raise the ceiling level by altering either the roof or first floor. This latter course was liable to change the appearance of the building, and either method was bound to cause considerable expense and disturbance to the original fabric.

B. Environmental health standards

The height of doorways was and is not specified in the Building Regulations but we found that it is nevertheless sometimes included in the improvement grant conditions. Sometimes old doors have to be removed and the doorway modified. In one instance in Norfolk, when a

* This order requires local authorities to use their powers to secure adequate means of escape from houses in multiple occupation of more than three storeys in height (excluding basements) and with a total floor area of over 500 m^2.

row of cottages was being renovated, the architect persuaded the authority that the original low doors could remain where they were in good condition, but, where doors were decayed and in need of replacement, higher doors had to be put in. As a result the door heights now vary from house to house and even within each house.

Under the 1976 Regulations, daylighting requirements are based on the provision of a window area of at least one-tenth of the floor area. Where the existing windows were insufficient the authority usually required a larger window. Architects generally preferred to provide an additional window rather than alter existing ones as this was less disturbing to the scale and character of the building. In one case – 10 and 12 Great Ormond Street, London (Case Study No. 5C) – involving a basement room, the authority insisted that since the window could not be enlarged the usable area of the room had to be reduced by constructing a large 'walk-in' cupboard. In another semi-basement, enlarging the sunken area in the pavement outside the window to provide more daylight caused expensive problems of rainwater disposal. On the other hand, the requirement to provide one-twentieth of the floor area as permanent ventilation was rarely a problem.

2.6 Other Legislation

The problems presented by the other legislation listed in Table 1 are basically the same as those that have been referred to in this chapter – means of escape, fire resistance, structural stability, and fitness for habitation. They differ in the manner of their enforcement and administration, and problems of this kind will be covered in later chapters. The following four groups of legislation which follow this table do, however, display particular physical problems of their own with regard to some historic buildings.

See Case Study 5C, pp. 76-8

Table 1. The legislation

Table 1 sets out the range of historic building types likely to be affected by building legislation, followed by the key number to the legislation listed in the second part of the table.

Against each piece of legislation, an indication is given of the enforcing authority, the department of the authority commonly (but not invariably) responsible. The table gives a brief summary of the content and indicates whether a specific item of legislation can apply:

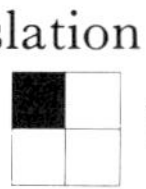 by virtue of a change of use;

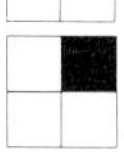 by virtue of physical alteration or extension;

 by virtue of its exising use, whether or not changes of any kind are proposed; and

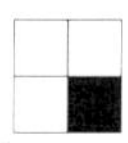 in connection with a house improvement grant.

Abbreviations used are:

H & S Exec: Health and Safety Executive
LA: Local Authority (either County or District)
FA: Fire Authority (County)
DES: Department of Education and Science
DHSS: Department of Health and Social Security

Key number	*Enforcing authority*		*Legislation*
(1)	H & S Exec		Agriculture (Poisonous Substances) Act 1952 and Regulations S.1, 1966 No. 1063: 1967 No. 1860: 1969 No. 843 Concerns provisions for workers' clothing, washing facilities, drinking water, food storage, protective equipment, cleaning and storage
(2)	H & S Exec	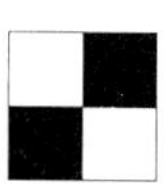	Agricultural (Safety Health & Welfare Provisions) Act 1956 and Regulation S.1, 1959 No. 428: 1959 No. 1216 Sanitation, washing facilities, safety of floors, stairways and stationary machinery
(3)	LA (social services)	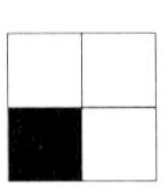	Children & Young Persons Act 1969 Fire precautions, sanitation, environmental health, management, etc, of community houses for children (local authority)

Table 1 (cont.)

Key number	*Enforcing authority*		*Legislation*
(4)	LA (social services)	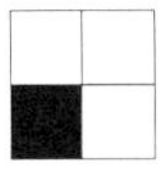	Children Act 1948 Registration requirements for voluntary homes for children
(5)	LA (building control)		Chronically Sick & Disabled Persons Act 1970 and Amendment Act 1976 Access for the handicapped required for new buildings to which the public is admitted including universities, schools and 'maintained' colleges (Sections 4, 6 and 8)
(6)	LA (county or district level – consult FA)		Cinematograph Acts 1909 and 1952, and S.1, 1955 No. 1129: 1958 No. 1530: 1965 No. 282 Licensing requirements include means of escape, seating, lighting, projection room design and equipment
(7)	LA (environmental health)	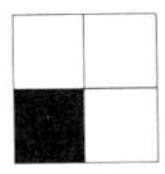	Clean Air Acts 1956 and 1968 and numerous Statutory Instruments (S.1) Chimney heights, appliance design, plant to filter emissions, etc
(8)	LA (social services – consult FA also)	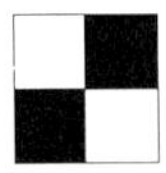	Conduct of Mental Nursing Homes Regulations 1962 Registration requirements including sanitation, lighting, fire precautions, ventilation, etc
(9)	Local education authority for maintained schools. DES for non-maintained		Education Act 1944 and S.1s including: Standards for school premises regulations 1972 (S.1 No. 2051) Building bulletins and constructional standards for educational buildings, issued by the DES
(10)	H & S Exec	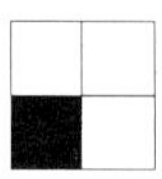	Factories Act 1961 as amended by S.1, 2004, 2009, 2010: 1976 Although fire precautions are no longer controlled under the Act, the safety and environmental health provisions remain
(11)	H & S Exec	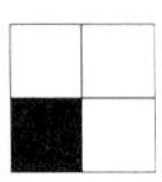	Fire Certificates (Special Premises) Regulations 1970 Premises having large-scale storage or process hazards (e.g. bulk LPG storage exceeding 100 tonnes) are subject to control by Health & Safety Executive
(12)	FA (fire service at county level, fire prevention branch)	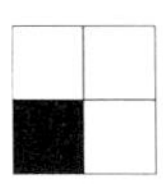	Fire Precautions Act 1971 Designated classes of occupancy require fire certificates (to date they are hotels, boarding houses, factories, offices, shops and railway premises) from fire authority which may make requirements to improve means of escape as preconditions of issuing certificate
(13)	LA (county level inspectors)	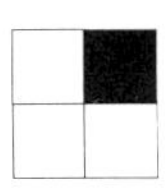	Food & Drugs Act 1955 Provides that regulations can be made for the construction and design of premises where food is produced, handled, stored, prepared or sold by way of business (Sections 13 and 29)
(14)	LA (county level inspectors)	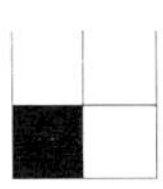	Food Hygiene (General) Regulations 1970 Provisions governing food premises including ventilation, sanitation, washing facilities, segregation of waste, etc
(15)	LA (county level inspectors)		Food Hygiene (Docks, Carriers, etc) Regulations Include provisions for warehouses and cold stores
(16)	Police for Gaming Board and Licensing Magistrates	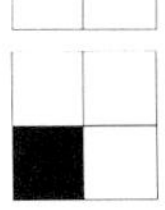	Gaming Act 1968 and S.1, 1969 No. 1110: 1970 No. 242 Licence required for all commercial gaming premises (Schedule 2)

Table 1 (cont.)

Key number	*Enforcing authority*	*Legislation*
(17)	H & S Exec	Health and Safety at Work Act 1974 Wide responsibilities for safety placed on employers, manufacturers and employees. Health and Safety Executive embraced and reorganised factory inspectors and others. Regulations and guidance documents on wide range of topics implemented by executive (e.g. (18) below)
(18)	H & S Exec	Highly Flammable Liquids and LPG Regulation 1972 Provisions concerning both storage and use including construction of enclosures, ventilation, separation from other activities, etc
(19)	LA (building control or environmental health)	Housing Acts 1961, 1964, 1969, 1971 and 1974 Section 16 requires local fire authority to consult the fire authority and to make necessary requirements to provide adequate means of escape from 'houses in multiple occupation' which may include tenanted flats converted from single family dwellings
(20)	Police for licensing justices	Licensing Act 1964 On licence or off licence required for premises where intoxicating liquor is sold; conditions may be attached concerning structure, layout, design and management (Sections 4, 5, 19, 20, 44, 45, 46, 94, 149, 153 and Schedule 2)
(21)	LA (regional variations)	Local Acts: (County Acts, etc) Cover wide range of activities from music to dancing licences to access for fire brigades; although all were due to have expired in 1984 under the Local Government Act, some new County Acts have since been made law and include provisions for tall buildings and high bay warehouses
(22)	DHSS	Medicines Act 1968 Provision for regulations to be made to control design, layout, construction, water supply, etc, of premises where medicines are produced, stored, handled or sold but no regulations made yet
(23)	LA (social services in consultation with others)	Mental Health Act 1959 and S.1 1962 No. 1999 Registration of homes subject to satisfactory sanitation, fire precautions, lighting, heating, etc (Sections 14 and 19)
(24)	LA (social services in consultation with others)	National Assistance Act 1948 and S.1 1962 No. 2000 Registration of old people's homes subject to satisfactory sanitation, fire precautions, lighting, heating, etc (Sections 37–40)
(25)	LA (social services in consultation with others)	Nurseries & Child Minders Regulation Act 1948, and Health Service & Public Health Act (Section 60) Registration of nurseries and child minders subject to satisfactory sanitation, fire precautions, heating, lighting, etc
(26)	LA (social services in consultation with others)	Nursing Homes Act 1975 and S.1 1963 No. 1434 Registration of nursing homes subject to satisfactory fire precautions, sanitation, space, light, heating, etc
(27)	H & S Exec	Offices, Shops & Railway Premises Act 1963, as amended by S.1s Nos. 2003, 2005, 2006, 2007 and 2008

Table 1 (cont.)

		Provisions covering heating, lighting, space, standards, sanitation, etc (fire precautions transferred to Fire Precautions Act) (Section 5–12, 16, 17, 20 and 21)
(28)	County council or harbour authority (fire service)	Petroleum (Consolidation) Act 1928, and S.1 1929 Nos. 952, 992 and 993: 1957 No. 859
(29)	LA (county or district consult FA)	Private Places of Entertainment (Licensing) Act 1967 Licence is required where private entertainment is staged for private gain
(30)	LA (building control or public health to consult FA)	Public Health Act 1936 as amended by the Act of 1961 Section 59 empowers local authority to require that ingress and egress from a place of public assembly is satisfactory Section 60 empowers local authority to require that there is satisfactory means of escape from sleeping accommodation that is above first floor and 20 ft (6 m) above ground level in schools, children's homes, lettable dwellings and the like. Sections 14–25 and 34–42 sewerage; 43–47 sanitation in buildings; 58 dangerous structures; 61–71, as amended, building regulations; 187–199 nursing homes
(31)	LA (building control or engineer or surveyor)	Public Health Acts (Amendment) Act 1890 Only adopted by some local authorities. Requirements may be made concerning the structural security of roofs, balconies, platforms, etc, where large numbers of people may assemble (Section 37). Licences for public music and dancing (Section 51)
(32)	Home Office (certification by county council)	Safety of Sports Grounds Act 1975 Provision governing crowd control barriers, exits, stairs, etc
(33)	LA (district council Environmental Health Department)	Slaughterhouses Act 1958, and Slaughterhouses (Hygiene) Regulations 1958, and S.1s 1958 No. 2166: 1959 No. 1493 and 1958 No. 1971 Licence requirements include construction, layout and equipment
(34)	GLC (entertainment licensing section of Architect's Department)	Technical Regulations for Places of Public Entertainment in Greater London 1965 and 1968 (GLC) Although only applicable to the GLC area, these regulations are often used elsewhere as the basis of local entertainment licensing requirements
(35)	LA (county or district level. Obliged to consult FA)	Theatres Act 1968 Local licensing authority empowered to make any requirements considered necessary in the interests of safety

Legislation affecting historic buildings

Type of occupancy	**Legislation key number**
Residential	
Flat	(29) (19)
Maisonettes	(29) (19)
School (residential part)	(29) (19) (5) (9) (17)
College (residential part)	(29) (5) if 'maintained' (9) (17)
Hotel/boarding house	(12) (13) (17)
Motel	(12) (13) (27) (17)
Hostel	(29) (17)
Old people's home	(24) (17)
Children's home	(4) (17)

Nursing home	(26) (17) (30)
Mental home	(23) (17) (8)
Hospital	(26) if private (5) if public (17)
House in 'multiple occupation'	(19)
Office	(12) (5) if public (17)
Shop	(12) (5)
Depends on goods or service involved	(13) (14) (16) (17) (18)
	(20) (21) (22) (27) (31)
Factory	(10) (12)
Depends upon function, materials handled and processes used	(7) (11) (13) (14) (17)
	(18) (22) (27) (31)
Kitchen	(13) (14) (15) (17)
Audio	(34)
Sound (radio or recording) film or TV	(17) (21) if used for public performances
	(6) (17) (21)
	(34) if used for public performances
Storage	(28)
Vehicle park	
Flammable or explosive material depending on type and quantity	(17) (13) (14) (18) (22)
Cold stores	(15)
Assembly	
Stadium and grandstand	(5) (30) (32) (16) (17) (21)
Passenger transport terminal	(5) (27) (30) (17) (27)
Railway station	(5) (12) (30) (17) (18) (27)
Sports hall and leisure centre	(5) (17) (21) (28) (30) (34)
Public library	(5) (17)
Club	(16) (17) (20) (21) (28) (34)
School – maintained	(5) (9) (13) (14) (17)
	(21) or (28) for non-school entertainment
School – non-maintained	(5) (9) (13) (14) (17)
	(21) or (28) for non-school entertainment
FE college – maintained	(5) (9) (13) (14) (17)
	(21) or (28) for non-school entertainment
FE college – non-maintained	(9) (13) (14) (17) (21)
	or (28) for non-school entertainment
Theatre	(5) (17) (20) (21) (28) (31)
	(30) (34) (35)
Cinema	(5) (6) (17) (20) (21) (31)
	(28) (30) (34)
Concert hall	(5) (17) (20) (21) (28) (30) (34)
Museum, art gallery	(5) (17) (31)
Public house	(5) (13) (14) (17) (20) (21)
Restaurant, café	(5) (13) (14) (17) (20) (21)
Exhibition hall	(5) (17) (21) (30) (31)
Dance hall	(5) (17) (20) (21) (28) (30) (34)
Day nursery	(5) (17) (25)
Church hall	(5) (16) (17) (20) (21) (31)
	(28) (30) (34)
Bingo hall	(5) (16) (17) (21) (28) (30) (31)
Agricultural	(1) (2) (3) (17)
Slaughterhouse	(17) (33)

2.6.1 The Town and Country Planning Acts

There is now sufficient interest in conservation for planning authorities to have recognised that historic buildings can only continue to exist if uses can be found for them. The problem is to find a use which neither involves destructive alterations, nor conflicts with the use of buildings in the adjoining area. Compliance with land use policies and parking standards are the most usual problems, particularly if these are applied with little regard to the merits of the case and difficulties of conforming.

2.6.2 The Health and Safety at Work etc Act 1974

The Act differs from other legislation in that, although there is a health and safety inspectorate acting as enforcing authority, the Act is intended to be 'self-enforcing' to a greater extent than with other legislation. Employers and employees are responsible for ensuring that the Act is complied with. We do not know of any cases of the inspectorate serving notices of requirements concerning historic buildings. Requirements more often seem to arise from discussions with 'in house' safety officers such as a local authority, and therefore tend only to affect buildings owned, run, or funded in some way by an authority.

Industrial (or formerly industrial) historic buildings are affected and, of these, flour mills are by far the most common. The problems are of two kinds: moving machinery and changes in floor level.

A. Machinery

In historic houses which are open to the public it is not always easy to keep the visitors at a safe distance from machinery because of the limited space, and there have been a few fatal accidents. To enclose the moving parts, as would be normal practice in ordinary industrial circumstances, would destroy much of the attraction. Most of these mills rely to some extent on visitors for finance and, by reducing their attraction, the safety measures could undermine their economic use. Another approach is to have more attendants to control visitors, but even when voluntary labour is available there are additional costs.

B. Changes of level

Floor openings, unguarded changes in level and ladder-type stairs are common features in mills which safety officers would disapprove of. Stairs are particularly difficult to upgrade to modern standards without drastically affecting the character of the building. Outside the building, the reservoirs or mill races are potential dangers; the insensitive addition of railings to guard these points can do great harm to the character of the mill in its setting.

2.6.3 The Food and Drugs Act

The only historic buildings adversely affected have been renovated flour mills. Modern hygiene regulations require materials to be used in the construction that will neither harbour vermin nor allow vermin to get into the spaces where the flour or grain is stored or processed. Timber stud and weatherboard, etc, may not fulfil these requirements. Surface finishes and detailing are normally required to be free of places where dirt or bugs can hide, and it should be possible to hose them down for cleaning. Sheet metal or plastic laminates which can satisfy these conditions are hardly in keeping with the predominantly timber interiors of old mills. One old mill, Priston Mill in Bath, has been in continuous use and, although anti-vermin measures and cleaning work is time consuming, no alterations affecting its character have been required under the Food Hygiene Regulations. At Bunbury Mill in Cheshire a compromise was reached with the authority so that flour could be milled in the newly restored mill but could only be sold to the public on the condition that it was not for human consumption.

2.6.4 The Highways Act

The Act enables the highway authorities to set highway design and construction standards, and charges them with improving highways to increase safety and speed the flow of traffic. The negative aspects, so far as historic buildings are concerned, involve the blighting or demolition of historic buildings or parts of them or their surroundings.

A. Demolition

The total demolition of buildings to make way for new roads, as with Travis Mill and the M63 in Stockport, or the new circulatory system around the Eastgate area of Chichester, involves very complex issues. Economic and social considerations may weigh against the retention of historic buildings and, in view of this, we have not regarded their effects as demonstrating the effect of this Act. Demolition on a smaller scale is different, however.

B. Planning conditions

When planning permission or listed building consent is being sought there are often consultations between the planning and highways authorities which can result in highway conditions being attached to the planning permission. For example, at Rake House, Helsby, in Cheshire, permission to convert the stable block and outbuildings into dwellings included the condition that a section of the 1.9 m high stone boundary wall should be reduced to less than 1 m so as to give visibility for 40 m in either direction from the existing gateway onto the road.

C. Sight lines and corner radii

Sight line requirements at bends or junctions can lead to the demolition or realignment of boundary walls, as at Joseph Crossley's Almshouses at Kings Cross in Halifax. The dimensional standards for curves (generally intended to promote more rapid traffic movement) can also increase the area affected by the works. The Eastgate example at Chichester mentioned above involved, among other things, the formation of a very wide gap in a terrace of houses which could have been narrower if a tighter curve had been used, thereby saving one or more of the houses.

The development of the Shardlow Mill and canal basin involved the improvement of the very poor access lane to the A6. Because of restrictions on the minimum distance between junctions on the trunk road, a condition was attached to the planning permission that a new access be provided further from an existing junction. Other difficulties over the acquisition of land for this new access led to the purchase and demolition of a cottage to make way for the road. If it had been of historic interest a conflict of interests would have arisen. See Case Study No. 2C, No. 2 Mill, Shardlow, Derbyshire.

See Case Study 2C, pp. 20-23

D. Blight

Sometimes an impasse is reached between highway requirements and financial or other considerations so that further use or alteration of an historic building for another purpose is blocked. At 1–3 Nuns Road, Chester, the buildings and site have become largely useless. The road is quite narrow and the highway authority allows no access to the site from it. An adjoining site does have access from another road but is in different ownership and, until an agreement can be reached with the owners about access through their ground, numbers 1–3 are unsaleable. At Ravenscroft Hall, Middlewich, the existing drive meets the main road in a dip, so that fast moving traffic could come over the rise to find a vehicle slowly turning into or out of the drive. The highway authority have insisted that a new access is made at a point just outside the existing parcel of land attached to the hall. Two planning applications have failed on this count.

Table 2. Components most affected by the objectives of the legislation

Objective	*Subject of control*	*Components/ aspects affected*
Fire safety	Fire resistance	Walls Floors Doors Glazing
	Escape	Stair protection New stairs New doorways Signs and hardware
	Combustibility	Timber structures Wall/cavity linings Stairs Roof coverings External cladding Fireplaces
	Flame spread	Timber panelling Timber surfaces in stairways Wall/floor cavity linings
Safety/ convenience	Stairs	Staircase Headroom Balustrades
	Headroom	Ceilings Beams Doorways
	Structure	New members Investigation Calculation Demolition
	Highways	Sight lines }* New roads }* Parking provision
Health	Daylight	Window size Usable floorspace
	Ventilation	Fenestration
	Damp	Flooring Levels Wall finish Wall construction
	Sanitation	Wash hand basins and WCs Plumbing Sewage disposal

* demolition

E. Street lighting

All the highway authorities contacted referred either to BS CP 1004: Parts 1–9 or BS 5489: Parts 1–9, saying that these were quite flexible design tools. One authority mentioned that the use of converted gas lighting units, retained in some areas for appearance's sake, presented maintenance problems. Greater Manchester reported that, as a result of public protest against lighting proposals for Mottram in Longdendale Conservation Area in 1975, the planning department arranged to consult with the lighting engineers over all conservation area lighting schemes.

2.7 Summary

To draw together some of the common threads that run through this chapter we have set out in Table 2 the basic objectives of the legislation and the parts of historic buildings that are most often affected.

Case Study 3: Victorian Villas

Such buildings lend themselves to conversion into small hotels, residential homes or flatlets for students or the elderly, or sub-division into two or more smaller houses or flats. Generally, public health matters and dimensional restrictions such as we have reported in older buildings do not present problems in Victorian houses, which were built on a much more generous scale.

Construction

Typical floor construction with good tongued and grooved boards can be upgraded to the half-hour standard of fire resistance by simply laying 5 mm thick hardboard on top. However, residential care establishments (Purpose Group II) require floors of one-hour standard. To achieve this, florid Victorian plasterwork has to be concealed or removed and refixed on the soffit of the new protective plaster layer, or fire protection has to be incorporated within the depth of the floor.

Some other decorative materials are vulnerable to change: engraved or stained glass must either be removed from doors or partitions before they can be made fire resistant, or incorporated in a 'double glazed' sandwich with fire resisting wired glass.

Victorian doors tend to be heavier than older ones and are often of polished hardwood. They are more often accepted as fire resisting than medieval or Georgian doors. If they have to be upgraded, the change from polished wood finish to the painted sheet of insulation board is unfortunate.

Means of escape

Main stairs usually satisfy current Building Regulations, although servants' quarters on the top floors often have much steeper and narrower stairs. The impact of means of escape provisions can be assisted by the existence of a second 'servant' stair; but it was common for the top floor of villas to have only one minor stair, so conversion of those areas may be difficult. Multiple occupancy, institutional or hotel use involves the enclosure of the stairs.

A. No. 57 The Close, Norwich

The example of No. 57 The Close illustrates typical problems of the Victorian villa. The special and aesthetic difficulties are similar to those found in older buildings, but they do not involve the same material and constructional problems, such as light timber partitions.

No. 57 The Close is a detached Victorian villa of three storeys and a basement. It was originally the Archdeacon's residence.

The external walls are of flint with stone quoins, string courses and other embellishments. The interior was virtually unaltered, and retained excellent hardwood doors, decorative plasterwork, ironwork, carving and other details of interest. There were two stairs, the main stair between ground and first floors, and a 'back stair' running the full height.

Architect: Peter Codling

Listed Grade II

Legislation

The house was bought for conversion into an Abbeyfield Home for elderly tenants. Dining facilities were communal but each tenant had his own large bedsitting room. There was a resident warden. The conversion was regarded by building control as a change of use from purpose group I to II. Early on in the project, the architect approached the fire authority for 'goodwill' advice on means of escape and, while this formed the basis of the alterations, the local authority could have served requirements under Section 16 of the Housing Act or Section 60 of the Public Health Act, although the influence of the latter would have been minor.

Doors

Three bedroom doors on the ground floor

The living room showing the heat detector in the original ceiling roundal

opened onto the stairway, which the fire authority advised should be protected. These hardwood doors had a fretted design on the panels and the architects were concerned not to cover them up. It was agreed that it would be adequate simply to increase the rebates to 25 mm.

Means of escape

At the head of the main stair a fire resisting, glazed screen was constructed to enclose the stair so that occupants of the first floor could reach the second stair without passing through the main stair enclosure. It is set back from the top balustrade so as not to hide the decorative metalwork, but, despite the architect's care, it cannot be said to enhance the space.

The 'back stair' was protected. A new route to an external door was formed in what had been a cloakroom at the ground floor level. The basement stair was separated from the upper part by a fire resisting spandrel partition, which incorporates a sliding door. Space restrictions would have made a hinged door impractical and possibly dangerous.

Floors

For approval under the Building Regulations 1976, the upper floors required one hour's fire resistance. Most of the ceilings have plaster cornices and central mouldings. The building control authority accepted that the 10 mm plasterboard, added to the underside, could be butted up beside these decorative features so that their general effect would not be lost, although some cracking has developed at the junction of old and new surfaces.

Fire detection

At a late stage in the project, the architect consulted the fire authority about some changes in door positions. A new fire officer 'strongly recommended' that automatic fire detection should be fitted throughout. As a result, heat detectors were fitted in all bedrooms, usually in the ceiling rose in place of a pendant light fitting, and in the roof spaces. Smoke detectors (ionisation-type) were fitted in corridors and stairheads. The fire prevention officer advised on their position. The architect complied, although there was no statutory obligation.

Cost

The additional capital cost was about £1,100 with an annual maintenance charge of £90. These costs increased the rent paid by each tenant.

References: Paras 1.6.1, 2.2.10D, 3.4.1A and 3.4.3

The exterior

The staircase, showing the fire screen

Case Study 4: Civic Buildings

The Town Hall, Manchester, and The Guildhall, Thaxted, are two examples of the wide range of building types used for public assembly.

A. The Town Hall, Manchester

This fine Victorian building was designed by Alfred Waterhouse (1830–1905) on a triangular plan with four storeys above ground level and a basement. A large hall occupies the centre of the triangle. With the designation of office premises under the Fire Precautions Act, discussions were held between the fire authority and the city's conservation officer, fire officer and chief building surveyor, to find ways of improving fire precautions. An unusual solution has been adopted.

Listed Grade I

An atrium solution

A powerful element of the plan is the arrangement of three circular staircases at the corners of the triangle. They are open to the corridors at each level, which form a continuous route around the building. It was felt that the usual method of separating the stairs from each floor, and sub-dividing the corridors with new fire resisting partitions and doors, would spoil the appearance of the interior and cause inconvenience by impeding circulation. Instead it was agreed that the corridors would be protected from the rooms opening off them by ensuring that the existing partitions and doors had half-hour fire resistance. Thus, for fire protection purposes, these upper levels are akin to an atrium arrangement with each room opening off balconies on to a void which extends upwards through several levels. This

Manchester Town Hall Approximate scale 1:1000

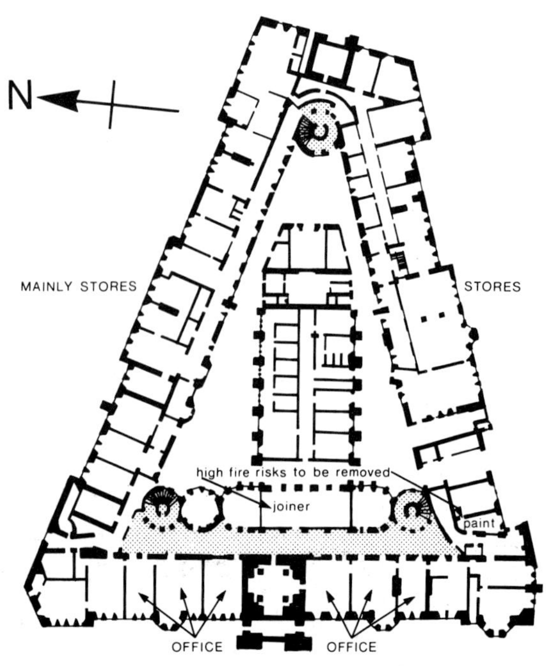

Basement *Protected routes shaded*

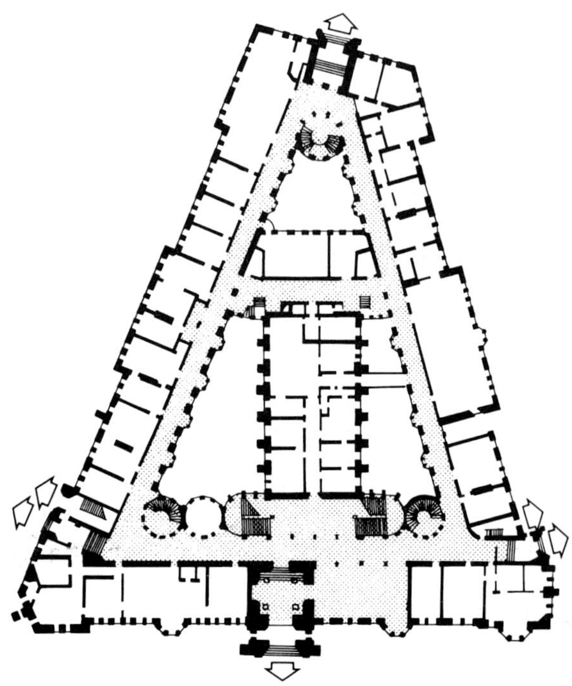

Ground floor *Protected routes shaded*

form has become popular recently for new hotels and offices (e.g. the John Portman hotels in the USA or the new offices of Lloyd's of London) and it is interesting to find the principle being applied to a historic building.

Before the scheme could proceed, a number of detailed problems had to be overcome.

High risk areas

Some joiners' and painters' workshops in the basement – both high fire risk activities – were required to be removed, and the stairs at basement level lobbied in the conventional way, since the smoke spread problems in basements are greater and the harm caused to the interior would be less significant. The basement also had to be compartmented to improve the means of escape.

The kitchens, which are regarded as a high fire risk area, needed to be surrounded by a one-hour fire resisting enclosure. The Lord Mayor's apartments are excluded from the proposals as they are considered to be 'domestic' and outside the scope of the legislation being applied.

Fire separation

To ensure the continuity of the fire resisting walls between the corridors and rooms on the upper floors, some glazing needed to be replaced with fire resisting material such as Georgian wired glass or more expensive clear laminated glass. The doors are of pitch pine and substantially built; their fire resistance was demonstrated in a recent fire and the fire authority asked only that the rebates be increased to 25 mm. Numerous ventilation grilles require sealing and old vents in the offices' external walls resuscitated, with sound attenuation, to replace them.

An automatic fire detection and alarm system extending to every room opening onto the protected corridors had to be included with the wiring concealed for appearances' sake. It was, however, permissible for the doors to

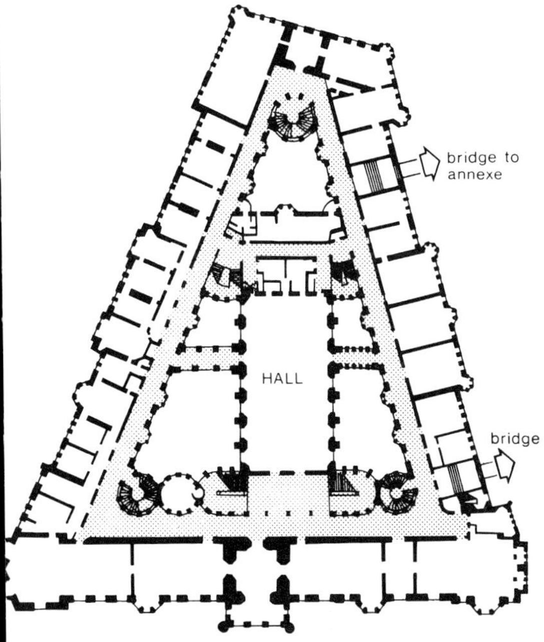

First floor (2nd and 3rd floors similar) *Protected routes shaded*

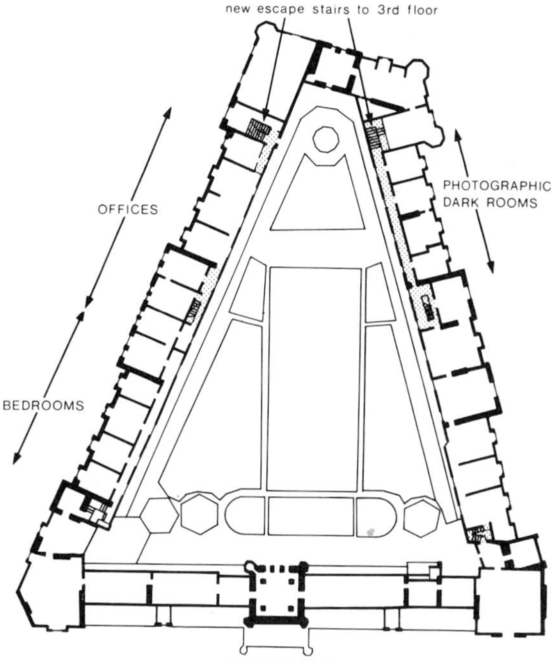

Fourth floor *Protected routes shaded*

Manchester Town Hall

some state rooms to be held open on magnetic catches, connected to the alarm system, for processional purposes. Secondary lighting systems were installed in public areas and in all circulation spaces.

It has been necessary to install some smoke-stop partitions and doors in the second- and third-floor corridors. These levels were regarded as less sensitive to alteration and the fire officer was concerned that smoke spread should be confined to a small part of the corridor, in the event of fire either in the circulation route or from an adjoining room.

Means of escape

To improve the escape from the fourth floor, where there are dead-ends, two new stairs were required. A scheme for escape at this level over a new roof top walkway had been agreed with the Factory Inspector – under the Offices, Shops and Railway Premises Act – shortly before responsibility for means of escape was transferred to the fire authority under the Fire Precautions Act, but the fire authority did not consider that this walkway was suitable as a means of escape and insisted on new internal stairs.

Such a scheme is likely to be more expensive than one which separates the stairs from the corridors. The automatic detection system may be regarded as compensation for the fact that rooms open directly into the volume of the protected stairways. The scheme had a much smaller impact on the appearance of the interior, although many minor alterations (e.g. to fanlights) were required to ensure the continuity of fire resisting partitions.

The proposals demonstrate the benefits of a flexible approach to historic buildings in matters of this sort.

B. The Guildhall, Thaxted, Essex

The Guildhall is a medieval timber-framed building of three storeys and a cellar. It was rescued from its seriously dilapidated condition by the County Council to serve as a local meeting place. The building is of the greatest importance to the townscape, and any alterations would have damaged its character.

Architect: Essex County Architects Department
Project leader: James Boutwood
Consultant structural engineer: J. Mason, M.I.C.E., M.I. Struct.E.

Listed Grade I

Entertainments licensing

Each floor cantilevers beyond the one below so that the top floor has the largest area. Even this is only 87 m^2, 20 per cent of which is taken up by the stairway. Discussions were held with the fire service and the county building safety section with a view to achieving a standard adequate for a music and singing licence and bearing in mind that the space precluded more than about sixty people attending at any time.

The limited area made a second internal stair impractical and the prominence of the building, exposed on three sides, ruled out an external escape on aesthetic and planning grounds. It was decided that the stair would be adequately protected by making the first floor access doors half-hour fire resisting. The plastered stud partitions to the stair were considered to have sufficient fire resistance. The stairs were provided with an electric fire alarm with a manual break glass call point and a second handrail. The door from the main room at first floor level was rehung to open inwards so as not to obstruct the stair.

The district council, which is the licensing authority for entertainments, normally accept the advice of the county building safety section, who vet all applications. However, they chose not to do so in this case and the application was refused. It is therefore illegal for a group of people to sing in the Guildhall. The use of the building apparently has not been prejudiced by this restriction and it continues to be a social asset. The terms of hire of the main room stipulate that no more than sixty people should be admitted at a time.

Thaxted Guildhall

Thaxted Guildhall, Essex
Approximate scale 1:200

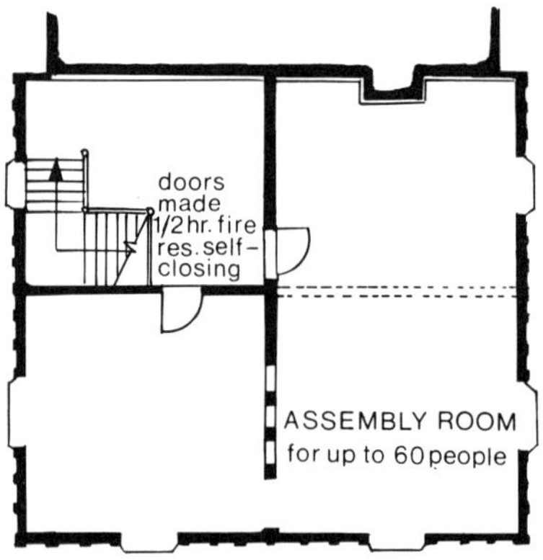

Second floor

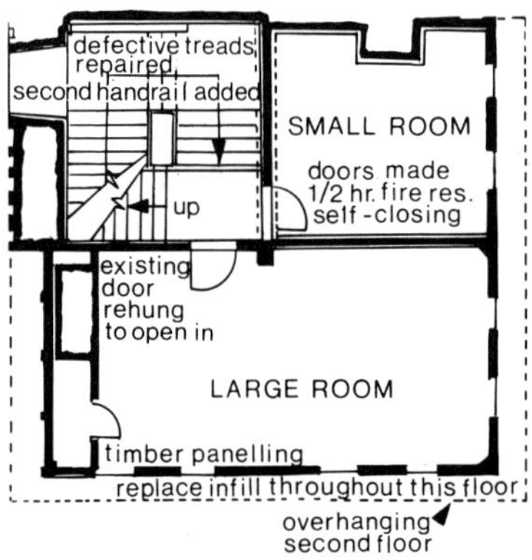

First floor

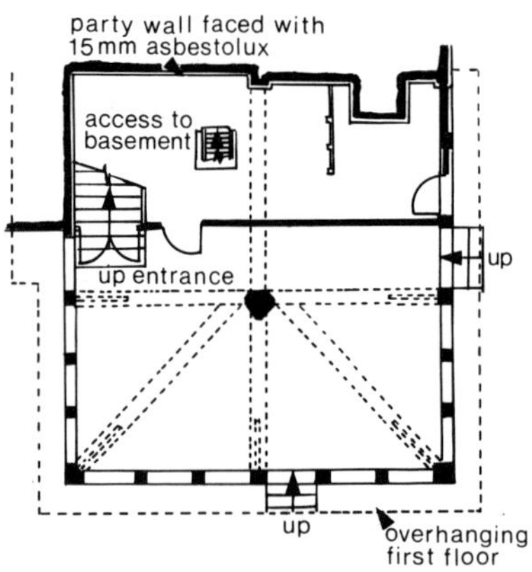

Ground floor

Structure

Before 1970 the Guildhall was owned by a local society. Its upkeep was becoming increasingly burdensome and, when a survey showed serious structural defects, they closed the building altogether. By the time the county bought the building it was in a dangerous state, although not actually subject to a Dangerous Structures Notice. As the work to restore it was essentially maintenance and no change of use was involved, Building Regulations did not apply. A consulting structural engineer experienced in the restoration of this type of building advised on the work, which included a major reconstruction of the foundations, repairing the timber structure, replacing most of the floors and incorporating lateral bracing into the infill panels of a new external wall. No structural fire resistance was involved other than replastering the ceilings, after renewal of flooring. The plain-edged elm boards are exposed at first floor level.

References: Paras 1.7.4, 2.2.7 and 5.4

3

Administration and enforcement

3.1 Introduction

The purpose of this chapter is to examine the various procedures involved with a view to their application to historic buildings.

Legislation, being principally concerned with ends rather than means, generally makes few stipulations about how it is to be administered. Responsible authorities are nominated, sometimes consultations with other bodies are specified, powers are defined, and appeals procedures are usually described. Sometimes, time limits are set for carrying out particular functions. It is too early to forecast the results from the rationalisation of the changes in the legislation introduced since 1984, or to anticipate the procedures which are likely to arise from them, but the intentions behind the consolidation of the numerous Acts and controls, together with the simplified statements of intent, bode well for the future. However, a common endeavour will be needed to make such a scheme succeed.

Table 3 shows which level of authority dealt with the pre-1984 legislation referred to in this study. Each council determined its own organisational structure, so there were many different structures reflecting varying local requirements and attitudes.

With some legislation, the choice of enforcing officer was quite obvious; for example fire authorities made use of the fire service; but some legislation was open to a wider range of possibilities. In Table 4 we have listed the more important building legislation relating to historic buildings and indicated some of the different groups we found enforcing it in different authorities.

Some of these were differences of name only, but where they reflected different hierarchical groupings they could have a strong effect on approaches to historic building problems and on the liaison that may or may not have been possible between specialists.

Figure 1 gives examples of two different district authority organisations. They obviously do not show all of the functions that such authorities actually carried out.

Such intricacies and differences made it difficult for architects and the owners of historic buildings to find the right person to deal

Table 3. Levels of authority

Regional level	Water Authority (usually delegated to district level) Gas Electricity Health and Safety Inspectorate
County level	Planning (county matters) Education (but at district level in the Outer London and Metropolitan area) Police and Fire – organised into divisions on a geographical basis Highways – may delegate some power to districts
District level	Housing Public Health Highways (if delegated) Planning Building Regulations 'Registration' – of old people's homes, nurseries, nursing homes, etc Entertainments licensing Improvement grants Liquor licensing – a judicial function outside the local authority as normally defined, but performed at a local level

Table 4. Enforcing officers

Legislation	Title of responsible group
Building regulations	Building control/surveyors/ building inspectors
Public Health Acts Ss 59 and 60 dangerous structures	Building control/health engineers/surveyors/ building inspectors
Highways	Highways/engineers/ surveyors
Housing Acts	Housing/health/building control – or a combination of these

with, and our experience has shown that personal contact is important to success. Bodies such as the National Trust or the Landmark Trust, who deal with many authorities, find these differences particularly troublesome.

The conservation officer has to deal with, or make representation to, most of the other specialists in Figure 1 and some of the most important contacts – on dangerous structures and Building Regulations – could be particularly difficult to maintain.

It would be unrealistic to suggest that local authority organisation should be regimented for the sake of improving the handling of historic building matters. However it is recommended that, in recognition of these problems, every authority should nominate an individual or group known as the historic buildings officer/section within the planning department.

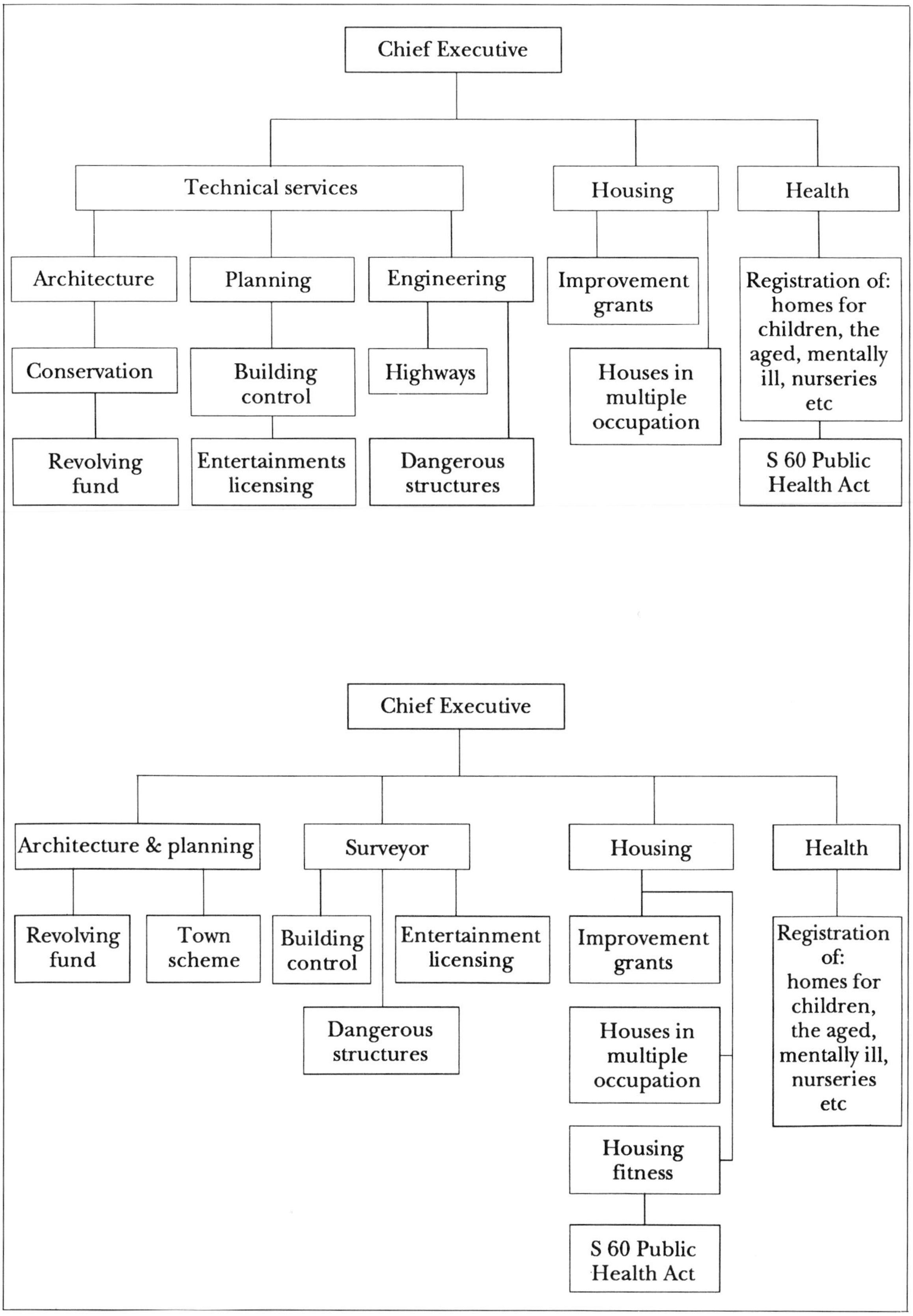

Figure 1

The liaison role of these officers should be strongly supported. Through their knowledge of their own authority's organisation they would be able to act as first reference on all historic building enquiries and refer these to the correct specialists throughout the organisation.

Many local authorities have already appointed conservation or historic building officers.

3.2 Problems Common to most Legislation

3.2.1 Knowing the legislation

The first problem is that of deciding what legislation, if any, applies to a scheme or building. While the enforcing officer will be aware of which places or projects might come under his jurisdiction, the building owner or his agent needs to find out which legislation might apply, who would enforce it and what scope it may have. With some legislation, such as S.16 of the Housing Act 1961, or S.60 of the Public Health Act 1936, it is not always clear whether a particular establishment should be subject to the legislation or not. Even with the Fire Precautions Act, whose scope is defined in detail, there are still uncertain areas – such as university premises – where education and office functions are combined. Sometimes the problem is to know which provisions apply to a particular aspect. As an example, Table 5 lists the many guidance documents on means of escape legislation. Chapter 4 explains the consolidation and rationalisation that has developed in the legislation since 1984.

Because of the wide range and complexity of statutes, the average historic building owner very often needs professional advice about the full extent of his obligations and rights. However, for financial reasons, owners quite often do not seek professional advice. Most authorities will, however, give advice; the building control officer sometimes has not only to lead the do-it-yourself applicant through the legislation but give a run-down on the rudiments of building construction as well. But the complicated problems that many historic buildings jobs can pose, with a variety of different possible solutions, are beyond the scope of an enforcing officer to handle on the owner's behalf. The architect's role here can be most important.

Unfortunately, architects find the legislation equally confusing and they do not all have the sort of detailed understanding of it that is often needed if its effect on an historic building is to be minimised. Yet they should be ready to advise an owner against those uses of an historic building which are unsuitable owing to the effect the legislative requirements would have. To gain a full grasp of most of the legislation one needs to work with it fairly constantly. Enforcing officers receive formal training on the legislation with which they work. Most architects, by contrast, are self-taught and this can put them at a disadvantage when dealing with the authorities.

We have met officers of the local authority in several historic towns who have told us of their disquiet about the competence of some of the submissions made to them by architects. They naturally base this assessment, in part at least, on the understanding of 'their' legislation shown in the submission. The officer's view of the architect is important where historic buildings are concerned because it is likely that the architect will take the lead in conservation matters. Very often authorities have told us that historic building cases are considered 'on their merits'. In the absence of their own historic building experts, these authorities would rely on the architect to make the building's merits clear to them. If the officers doubt the architect's competence they are less likely to be persuaded by his conservationist arguments to make a special effort to avoid harming the building.

3.2.2. Statutory 'requirements' and 'recommendations'

There is a need to make a clear distinction between the requirements that an enforcing authority issues and the advice or guidance it may offer. The former has to be complied with, the latter does not.

Fire authorities' correspondence seems to be more prone to misinterpretation in this respect than that of other bodies. In one case encountered, the fire authority was actually giving advice, but by mistake issued a schedule using a standard form that gave the impression that it had the force of law. We have been shown a large number of fire authority letters and schedules from which it is apparent that there is a form of language sometimes used in them that gives the impression of compulsion, even when recommendations are being made. The word 'shall' is used where 'should', 'could' or 'ought' is the correct form.

Most building owners are, we believe, predisposed to take the fire officer's observations very seriously. It is therefore most important that they should not be confused about the exact extent of their legal responsibility. The owner can of course do more than the legal minimum amount of work if he or she chooses; but clear distinctions between requirements and recommendations can ensure that the extra cost and the possible damage to historic fabric are not incurred in the mistaken belief that they are essential.

Table 5. Guidance on escape route design in existing buildings

Building type	Guidance
Private house	None
Institutional homes	1. Home Office Draft Guide to Fire Precautions in Existing Residential Care Premises, January 1983 2. DHSS Local Authority Circulars (e.g. (77)3) (not generally available to the public)
Hotels and boarding houses	Guide No. 1 to the Fire Precautions Act
Non-maintained schools	None (residential or otherwise)
Maintained schools	DES Building Bulletin No. 7 (5th edition). Only available to non-residential areas
Flats and maisonettes	None
Offices	Guide No. 3 to the Fire Precautions Act. (Guide to Offices, Shops and Railway Premises Act – fire precautions – now superseded)
Shops	Guide No. 3 to the Fire Precautions Act. Home Office FP Guide No. 1, 'Fire Precautions in Town Centre Redevelopment' (Guide to the OSR Act now superseded)
Factories	Guide No. 2 to the Fire Precautions Act
Places of public entertainment	None. (Local documents often based on GLC Code and Technical Regulations)
Places of public assembly	None
Licensed premises (liquor)	None
Licensed premises (petroleum)	None
Storage	Home Office FP Guide No. 3, 'Fire Fighting and Fire Precautions in Automated Warehouses'
Residential homes for the elderly	1. Home Office Draft Guide to Fire Precautions in Existing Residential Care Premises, January 1983 2. Circulars to Chief Fire Officers and/ or Local Authorities 6/ 77 and FIR/74 422/ 8/1 (not available to the public)
Residential homes for children	Home Office Draft Guide to Fire Precautions in Existing Residential Care Premises, January 1983

3.2.3 Delays

The word 'delay' is a pejorative term: the dictionary definition of it includes 'hinder the progress' and 'put off acting'. In the world of building legislation one party's 'delay' is another's 'due process'. For example, the delay in obtaining consent for the demolition of Brough Hall in Yorkshire enabled the planning officer to find a developer who was prepared to convert it. However, this is unusual. Normally delays tend to be to the detriment of historic buildings. They suffer decay or vandalism, promised grants may lapse, or people may simply lose interest and turn their attention to something less troublesome.

The different kinds and causes of delay are discussed below under the different pieces of legislation.

One other very important general effect of delay should be mentioned at this stage. Because they know or fear the consequences of delay, architects are sometimes prepared to accept legislation requirements without 'fighting' them, even though the quality of the project may suffer. It takes time to resolve appeals or to go through court proceedings, the outcome is not certain and ill-will may be engendered between architect and authority which might hamper future negotiations on both the project in hand and on others. Although most legislation incorporates appeal or relaxation procedures, we have found many instances where we think considerations such as these have stopped them being used. A senior officer of the GLC Historic Buildings section (now the London Division of the Historic Buildings and Monuments Commission for England) emphasised to us most strongly that he considered most historic building problems could be solved if there was enough time, but so often time is at a premium and in those cases one may have to be satisfied with a solution that falls some way short of the optimum.

3.3 Building Control Authorities

Building control sections within local authorities carry out a wide range of activities besides the enforcement of Building Regulations. The comments in this section refer to these activities as far as they affect historic buildings. Table 6 indicates how many other building control activities are carried out by the enforcement officers.

3.3.1 Attitudes

The most noticeable feature of our contacts with building control offices around the country has been the variation in attitude to historic buildings. With occasional exceptions, the offices in areas with a high concentration of historic buildings showed the greatest sympathy to the special nature of the relationship between these buildings and modern regulations. Case Studies Nos. 1A, 1B, 8B and 11B include buildings in Bath and York which illustrate this point very well. Comparisons between buildings must be qualified by remembering that there are always differences in the circumstances surrounding each case but, allowing for this, if one compares Kenwood House with Brocket Hall, or the King Street warehouse conversion with those of Coalbrookdale's Great Warehouse or the Shardlow No. 2 Mill, a different attitude is apparent, in our opinion (Case Study Nos. 2B, 2C and 9A).

See Case Studies 1A, 1B, 8B and 11B, pp. 10-11, 12-13, 105-6 and 144

See Case Studies 2B, 2C and 9A, pp. 18-19, 20-23 and 117-19

A. The effect of experience

We believe there are simple reasons for these differences. These historic towns have recognised the value of retaining architectural character, and have policies directed to that end. The building control officers are therefore individually and collectively aware that there is something special about many of the buildings with which they deal. They also acquire experience in dealing with the structural and constructional peculiarities of these buildings, so that they come to know their strengths and weaknesses and can agree workable solutions with confidence even though they may depart from modern practice. We have previously mentioned the difficulty of calculating the structural action of an old timber frame. An inexperienced officer is likely to ask for calculations to prove the adequacy of a proposal whereas the experienced one may be content to make his assessment by eye. This is not simply a matter of saving historic building owners the expense and trouble of obtaining the services of a structural engineer, although the time factor can be very important. With old buildings, the interpretation of calculations (which are a hypothetical and usually highly simplified model of reality) must be based on a sound understanding of the principles. The assessment of calculations is often done by an engineer outside the building control office who may be even further removed from historic buildings consideration than the building control officer. If historic buildings are treated like modern structures they may end up looking like modern structures.

The same principle applies to those aspects of fire safety administered by building control officers. Those in the City of Bath are in the happy position of having the results of a full-scale fire test in a typical Georgian house to draw upon when assessing the likely performance of traditional construction (the Chatham Row tests of 1967). Unfortunately,

Table 6. Activities of building control offices in addition to building regulations

Activity	% of offices
Control of dangerous structures	82.4
Control of demolition	67.4
Cinema and theatre inspections	56 (Theatres Act, Cinematograph Act, etc)
Enforcement of planning conditions	28.3
House renovation grants	23.5 (Improvement grants)
Means of escape in case of fire	13 (Public Health Act Ss 59 and 60, etc)
(from Local Training Board Working Party on 'Training for Building Control' Report – Stage One, April 1978)	

there have been no other local tests of this calibre to our knowledge, and so general reliance is placed on either the published work of the Fire Research Station or the tests of proprietary fire resisting materials promulgated by the material's manufacturer or importer. The solutions proposed by these sources may not always be appropriate in an historic building, and may be unnecessarily onerous.

B. Legal liability

The local authority's policy on liability is probably not related to the number of historic buildings in its area but it can certainly affect those buildings. The *Annes vs London Borough of Merton* case in particular has made councils aware of their vulnerability to claims in matters of construction defects. Some councils, stimulated by their insurers, have since sought to protect themselves by instructing their building control staff to be punctilious in their enforcement of the Regulations; this has increased the time needed to obtain approval while every minor point is resolved and documented. It has also discouraged the granting of relaxations because they are seen as a departure from the norm and therefore as potential liabilities. The relaxation may still be available if an appeal is made to the Secretary of State, but again this takes time.

*C. Personal attitudes**

In addition to the authority's attitudes and policies and the effects which the nature of its building stock can have on the experience of its building control officers, the personal attitudes of the individual officer should not be overlooked. The typical building control officer regards himself as a practical person and has worked in the building industry as a tradesman. He is in a position not only to apply the Regulations but to relax them (within limits) where applicable. Where there is a clear-cut practical problem he is happy to negotiate a practical solution to it, and he may or may not consider that a formal relaxation is needed. He may be less happy with points that are theoretical or outside his experience and be anxious to avoid basing decisions on topics he considers to be subjective, such as aesthetics. In such cases he may wish to refer to a higher authority, either informally within his own organisation, or formally by denying a relaxation and hence passing the matter to the Secretary of State on appeal; or he may demand the written attestation of a recognised authority before giving the relaxation. The Fire Research Station is often asked to act as a recognised authority in cases of this sort.

D. Training

There is no uniform training for building control officers. Age on entry, experience prior to building control and academic and professional qualifications vary enormously. There has been a switch in recent years away from staff with extensive trade experience to younger people with little practical experience but higher qualifications, but the professional bodies are exerting considerable influence to raise the standards.

3.3.2 Interpretation and comprehension

A. Interpretation

The 1976 Regulations were written to satisfy the legal draughtsmen and, largely as a result of this, were quite hard to understand. Some passages had to be read several times to be comprehended and two people were quite likely to read different meanings into the same passage. As an example, we reproduce in Figure 2 a passage which states in legal jargon, that any alteration or extension of a building must not result in a building which contravenes the Regulations more than it did previously.

It is unfortunate from an historic buildings point of view that one of the most difficult Regulations to interpret, A7, was designed to determine how the Regulations should be applied where new work in existing buildings took place.

We see from Figure 2 that, according to paragraph A7(1), Regulation A7 applied to everything except the exemptions listed in Regulation A5, to Means of Escape (Section II of Part E), and Works and Fittings (Parts M, N and P). Regulation A7 therefore appears to have allowed old buildings quite a large measure of exemption. But when we proceed to paragraph A9(3) we find that not only was there a series of specific regulations to be applied as though the building, or the parts affected, was a new one, but that A7 was to be applied to involve any *additional* requirements not stipulated in the series of specified ones. It was therefore advisable to discuss any proposed alteration or extensions with the local authority in case Building Regulation approval was required.

B. Comprehension

Sometimes the purpose of the 1976 Regulations was not clear, so that the importance of

* Based on interviews with senior building control officers by Peter Bedford, BA, RIBA, as a member of the Local Government Training Board Working Party on 'Training for Building Control' Report Stage One, April 1978 (see Table 6).

Figure 2

A7 Application to alterations and extensions

(1) Subject to the provisions of Regulation A5, Parts A to L except Section II of Part E shall apply to:
 (a) a structural alteration or extension of an existing building (irrespective of when that building was erected); and
 (b) the existing building as affected by that alteration or extension to the extent (subject to the provisions of regulations A9 and K3) of prohibiting any alteration or extension which would cause a new or greater contravention of any regulation.

(2) In applying the regulations under paragraph (1) (a), the alteration or extension shall be treated as if it were part of a building being newly erected identical to and to be used for the same purposes as the altered or extended building.

(3) In determining for the purposes of paragraph (1) (b) whether the alteration or extension would cause a new or greater contravention of any regulation, the following provisions shall have effect:
 (a) the regulations shall be applied to the altered or extended building, such building being treated as if it were being newly erected in its proposed form but for the purposes for which it will be used;
 (b) the regulations shall be applied to the existing building, such building being treated as if were being newly erected in its existing form but for the purposes for which it will be used when altered or extended; and
 (c) the alteration or extension shall be regarded as being such as would cause a new or greater contravention if (when the regulations are applied as directed in sub-paragraphs (a) and (b)) the altered or extended building:
  (i) contravenes any regulation which does not apply to the existing building; or
  (ii) contravenes any regulation which is satisfied by the existing building; or
  (iii) contravenes to a greater extent any regulation which is contravened by the existing building.

applying a requirement to some marginal case was unknown. The London Building By-laws have shown themselves to be superior in this respect in that before each one there is a general statement of the intention of the clauses that follow. However, a statement of purpose without any supporting standard also causes problems of interpretation because there can be disagreement as to whether a proposal does in fact fulfil the required purpose. For example, Regulation C10 stated:

The roof of any building shall be weatherproof and so constructed as not to transmit moisture due to rain or snow to any part of the structure of the building which would be adversely affected by such moisture.

On the basis of this Regulation, some authorities did not accept proprietary roof windows.

It had long been the aim of many architects to have the Regulations re-written in plain language with drawings and diagrams to explain the requirements in a clear way. Again, the GLC's Codes of Practice on Means of Escape and on Section 20 (special requirements for large buildings), and the London Building By-laws were held up as models.

The Inner London method of building control was generally thought to work much better than the national system. The widely accepted reason for this is that more emphasis was put on control of the building process on site, using very highly qualified district surveyors who were given considerable freedom to use their discretion. The flexible attitude of the well-trained central staff in the GLC's Building Regulation Division was also helpful. The Department of the Environment's Manual to the 1985 Building Regulations, together with the Approved Documents, etc, goes some way towards providing the type of assistance available from the GLC District Surveyors. The Approved Inspectors, whom the applicant under the new Regulations can employ to supervise the work instead of going directly to the local authority, may be able to provide similar expertise.

C. Purpose groups

A particular problem occurred in many of the case studies in this report as to which purpose group or groups should be applied to a building. For example, should a mill really be considered a place of public assembly when the public is admitted on no more than twenty-eight days a year? Again, there seemed to be a common view on the subject of residential accommodation within a building that serves some other principal purpose (e.g. the caretaker's flat in a museum) to the effect that it should always be fully compartmented. With other purpose groups, however, it was hard to find a consensus. A large warehouse with a small office was likely to be all in one group but, as the office area increased, so did the chance that the authority would insist on the two purpose groups being compartmented. The purpose group problem at Brocket Hall was so severe that the matter went to determination (Case Study No. 9A).

D. Public Health Act

The application of Section 60 of the 1936 Public Health Act is a local authority matter often handled by building control. The section simply gives the local authority power to make requirements to improve the means of escape where they are not held to be satisfactory. It does not qualify or define these terms and there is no standard of guidance to which officers can refer. It is probably fortunate, therefore, that the Fire Precautions Act is, to a large extent, superseding this legislation.

E. Charges for building control services

The applicant is obliged to include a payment for those parts of the project which are subject to Building Regulations. A second payment is due when the local authority makes its first inspection of work on site. The charge is made on an incremental scale unless the cost of relevant work is less than £1,000, when no charge is made. It can be difficult to decide whether a particular regulation applies to an old building or not. The method of charging makes these decisions doubly important, as the more the work is regarded as within the Regulations' scope, so the greater do the charges become.

3.3.3 Building control officers

A. Continuity and consistency

It is usual for one building control officer to deal with a project from start to finish, so it is unusual for the building control requirements to change in the course of the work. Also the approval concerns the proposal to build rather than the building itself, so that having approved the plans it is administratively inconvenient for the building control officer to enforce some overlooked requirement. Nor are amendments to the Regulations retrospective. However, several architects have described how, on re-submitting plans altered to comply with some request of building control, further objections have been raised by the authority to points which had attracted no comment before. We think that this may have been due partly to human fallibility – plan checking is complicated and it is easy to miss something – but chiefly it is because the authority does not have to cite every failing when it rejects a plan. An officer with a heavy workload may not be inclined to search for every defect in an architect's plans when he has found one serious enough to warrant rejection. In his opinion the architect is being paid to 'get it right' and he sees no reason to do the architect's work for him. This problem may be largely resolved by the use of Approved Documents and Approved Inspectors.

See Case Study 9A, pp. 117-19

B. Delays

Building control authorities have five weeks to give a decision on a building notice or plans. This may be extended to eight weeks with the applicant's approval. If the authority pass the plans or fail to reject them within that period, they will not be able to serve a notice requiring the alteration of work which is in accordance with the plans.

Unfortunately, not every case is settled in five or even eight weeks. Where the authority considers there is not enough information on the plans for a decision to be made, the applicant/architect will be asked for more information. For example, calculations may be requested to show that an existing floor is capable of sustaining the loads imposed by some new use. If the information will take longer to provide than the five or eight week limit, either the plans may be rejected for lack of information or they may be withdrawn for resubmission when the information is available. According to the architects and building owners we have spoken to, considerations of liability have led authorities to ask for more information on drawings and particularly for more structural calculations.

There is a time limit of two months on relaxation decisions unless extended by agreement. It seems that some authorities, instead of rejecting an application for relaxation, indicate to the applicant those measures they wish to see taken, and then they wait until the applicant gives an undertaking to implement them. This appears to have happened at the Coalbrookdale Great Warehouse, for example (Case Study No. 2B).

See Case Study 2B, pp. 18-19

C. Dangerous structures

The control of dangerous structures is the most common non-Building Regulation activity of building control officers (over 82 per cent of officers, according to the Local Government Training Board survey set out in Table 7).

Whether or not the dangerous structures legislation is the cause of widespread demolition depends on the attitude of the local authority and its officers. If the staff keep an eye on the buildings in their area, and liaise with the conservation or historic buildings officers when they see an historic building deteriorating, it is possible to take steps to

Table 7. Standards affecting historic buildings

Health	Safety	Convenience	Consumer protection	Energy conservation
Daylight	Fire and smoke	Stairs and ramps	Durability	Thermal insulation
Ventilation	Structure	Access for handicapped	Nuisance*	
Damp	Falls	Headroom		
Smoke	Highways	Space		
Sanitation	Industrial risks	Noise		
Water supply	Explosion			
Heating	Electricity supply			
Vermin	Gas supply			
Refuse				
Food hygiene				

* 'Nuisance' refers to development control over non-conforming users and similar considerations of the licensing courts over liquor licence applications.

repair it. There are cases where the owner does not want to repair it because he would rather demolish and redevelop, and the local authority may be reluctant to serve a repairs notice because this could lead to their having to purchase and maintain the building and they may not have the funds. The City of Chester is unusual in having an historic buildings fund supported by a rate levy which can help in such cases, but elsewhere public opinion and the activities of amenity societies and building preservation trusts may be the only hope for saving such buildings from demolition. These measures all take time, and so it is important that the local authority should not see its dangerous structures duties as a 'fire brigade' activity but should anticipate trouble and warn the people who may be able to do something positive about it.

See Case Study 10A, pp. 130-31

D. Cinema and theatre inspections

The Cinematograph (Safety) Regulations 1955 and 'Recommendations on safety in Cinemas' contain detailed requirements and guidance, which apply nationally. Fifty-six per cent of building control offices carry out cinema and theatre licensing inspections. Their role varies according to local administration from a comprehensive investigation of technical matters, such as electrical services and ventilation, seating layout and fire prevention, to a much more restricted function concerned mainly with the state of the structure and fabric. In the latter instance specialists, such as the fire service and electrical engineers, are brought in to check other points. The sophistication of the standards enforced and the expertise of the officers doing the work varies widely. Where the legislation is less frequently applied, the officers involved have fewer opportunities to gain the experience needed for a flexible approach.

E. House renovation grants

Problems over the impact of housing grants are discussed in para 2.5.2. About a quarter of all building control departments deal with house renovation grants. The grants officer may ask for compliance with Building Regulations even where the work does not otherwise have to comply. For example, in Case Study No. 10A (Nos. 5 and 8 St John's Square, Wilton) a 'non-conforming' stair, which could have been retained under normal Regulation enforcement, had to be replaced. In the 1985 Regulations, the Approved Document dealing with staircases states that 'there is no obligation to adopt any particular solution in the document if you prefer to meet the requirements some other way'. Rigid and unnecessary compliance with specific solutions will therefore not be so easy to enforce in future.

F. Liaison with planning officers

Owners of listed buildings are not always aware that they have to apply for listed building consent and/or planning permission as well as submitting plans under the Building Regulations. The building control officer can therefore act as a long-stop to prevent unapproved alterations by drawing such cases to the attention of planning officers. This is most likely to happen where the planners are in the same department as the building control officer. Some authorities have formal arrangements whereby a planning officer checks each Building Regulation submission to see whether planning/listed building consent submissions have been made.

3.3.4 Central government

Government interest in conservation matters is centred in the Department of the Environment, which is also the Department responsible for Building Regulations. The DOE sends Circulars to local authorities on matters of policy and procedure. A particularly important Circular from the point of view of this report is No. 8/87, which deals with historic buildings and conservation areas and recommends, among many other things, that Building Regulations could be relaxed in the interest of historic buildings (para. 19). Since half of the building control officers do not work in planning departments this advice may not have reached some of them.

Except for the case given in para 3.4.8 below, there is no attempt by the Department of the Environment to supervise building control officers other than by the limited means incorporated in the enforcement procedures of the Regulations themselves (e.g. determinations, the classes of relaxation that have to be referred to the Minister, appeals, etc).

3.4 Fire Authorities

3.4.1 Introduction

Fire service personnel are recruited by a single-level entry system and all fire prevention officers have come up through the ranks of the operational branch of the service, so that they have extensive experience of fire fighting before they join the fire prevention side. Many officers' careers take them from the operational to the fire prevention branch and back again several times, all officers attend courses at the Fire Services College at Moreton-in-Marsh, Gloucestershire, and promotion is often gained by moving about the country from one fire authority to another. Compared to the building control officer, the fire prevention officer's training and experience should therefore result in a high degree of uniformity.

The fire authorities exist at county level, and the fire service in each county can be regarded as the executive arm of the fire authority. Although all county fire services are entirely independent of one another, they are all subject to regular appraisal by Her Majesty's Inspectorate of Fire Services in the Home Office. As well as working to ensure that consistent and adequate standards are maintained, the Home Office provides specialist technical resources that would be uneconomical for individual authorities to maintain.

3.4.2 Attitudes

Fire prevention officers become fire-orientated by their fire fighting experience in the sense that to them fire is not an abnormal or infrequent occurrence. By contrast, the rest of us are unlikely to experience more than one or two very minor fires in a lifetime. Also, the officer's legislative responsibilities concern human safety and not building conservation. It is therefore difficult for him to accept any suggestion of a departure from his normal standards in the interests of conservation.

In requiring or recommending fire precautions, an officer has written guidance (the Home Office Fire Precautions Act Guidance Notes, or his own authority's code on means of escape from houses in multiple occupation, for example) which he has to apply on the basis of his training and experience, to what he perceives to be the significant risks. As an example, we would refer to our discussions with fire officers in Lancashire, and contrast their attitude to textile mills with that of the Shropshire Authority's attitude to the Coalbrookdale Great Warehouse in Case Study No. 2B. In Lancashire, cotton fires were apparently common and the officer's attitude to them was 'philosophical'. The means of escape and compartmentation in the old mills were rudimentary by modern standards, but the risks are known and it seems that all concerned have learned to cope with the problems.

See Case Study 2B, pp. 18-19

3.4.3 Inconsistency and additional requirements

The main source of complaint from building owners and architects against fire authorities is that they change or add new requirements or recommendations as projects progress. This may occur when there are changes of personnel. At 57 The Close, Norwich (Case Study No. 3A), for example, the provision of automatic fire detection later in the project resulted from a meeting with a different fire officer. The same effect can be seen at the policy-making level. For example, in Derbyshire the fire authority accepted an intumescent paint for the fire protection of existing doors, but, following the appointment of a new senior fire prevention officer, the authority decided no longer to accept that material. A third reason for changes in the requirements is that characteristics are revealed in the finished scheme which were not apparent to the officer from the drawings, resulting in further requirements or recommendations.

See Case Study 3A, pp. 49-51

The Fire Precautions Act sanctions the issue of additional requirements at late stages in a project. Fire authorities issue schedules of work against, for instance, proposed alterations, as the starting point in the certification process, and the recipient assumes (not unreasonably) that the certificate will be available on completion of this work. In fact, the authority is not bound by these requirements and the certificate will only be issued when the authority is satisfied with the building when it is in operation. There is thus scope for second thoughts on the part of the fire officer and for new thoughts if a different person makes the 'final' inspection.

The fire service inspectorate has stressed to us that architects and owners should explain the particular problems that the historic building presents so that the fire authority may suggest alternative solutions.

3.4.4 Documentation

The distinction between recommendations and requirements can be blurred by the inappropriate use of the imperative form in some fire officers' reports.

We have noted the poor performance of some fire authorities as correspondents; some authorities do not acknowledge minutes of meetings or other notes of agreement on important points. If there is a change of fire officer the new man may have no record of his predecessor's negotiations and no evidence that he agreed to something the applicant claims was agreed. The explanation for this probably lies in the relatively small amount of clerical support available to the fire prevention officer. The use of a standard letter to acknowledge the receipt of such minutes, or notes of agreement, would ease this problem in those authorities where it occurs.

3.4.5 The time factor

Under the Fire Precautions Act the authorities impose a time limit for the execution of their requirements, but they appear to be very reasonable in extending this limit where they can see that serious efforts are being made to comply.

3.4.6 Approach to historic buildings

Fire Service Circular 14/1972 states that, under Section 43 of the Fire Precautions Act, the fire authority may not make requirements which would conflict with any legislation directed towards the preservation of historic buildings. The senior fire officers we have contacted expressed sympathy with conservation aims, but over one-third of them also said that there is a lack of guidance on how their staff should balance historic or architectural interests against those of fire safety. At the moment this is done in the form of adversarial debate: the fire officer responds to the building or proposed works from the fire safety point of view; then the architect or owner makes a case for not doing it as he suggests, either because of some point of conservation interest, or because of the great cost involved; the fire officer then assesses that case and so the debate continues until agreement is reached. If the conservation case is not made strongly the building may suffer; if it is made too strongly the level of fire safety may be lowered.

A Code of Practice for historic buildings that discussed the issues, set out basic principles and gave examples could support all the parties to negotiations of this sort.

3.4.7 Changed role of fire officers

The legislation has had the effect of changing the role of the fire prevention officer over the years. Under the Fire Services Act, his job traditionally includes inspecting premises and advising on the possible risks of fire outbreak and spread. But this is less the case than it used to be: nowadays he is more an 'enforcement' officer ensuring conformity to Regulations, so that his inspection visits become those of a 'policeman' ensuring compliance. There is thus a feeling that the goodwill element of positive and helpful advice is in danger of being lost.

3.4.8 Restricting and prohibiting use

Special reference should be made to Section 10 of the Fire Precautions Act. If, in any building within a wide range of occupancies, the fire authority are satisfied that the risk to persons in case of fire is so serious that the use of the premises ought to be prohibited or restricted, the authority may seek a court order to do so until the necessary steps have been taken to reduce the risk.

The section, as framed, does allow for wide interpretation. The assessment of risks is imprecise and subjective, and the courts attach considerable importance to the view of the fire services. The fire authorities submit an annual return to the Home Office on the use of Section 10 and usually provide fairly full reports on the progress of each action.

3.5 Improvement Grant Administration

These grants are provided under the Housing Acts by district level authorities. Their administration varies. Some authorities have sections which deal with all aspects from site inspection to checking estimates and dealing with the paperwork. Others have an administrative team which calls on the resources of other departments in the authority to advise on the work needed, the acceptability of proposals and of the completed job, etc.

Strong criticism has been expressed about the inflexible way in which some grant authorities set and enforce their particular standards and this is exacerbated by the lack of an appeals procedure. The Housing Act gives the local authorities considerable latitude in adjusting their requirements to take account of circumstances, but it seems that they do not often do so.

Owners are not well placed to argue. As improvement grants are not given retrospectively, an owner cannot start work until the scheme and estimates, etc, have been vetted. If there is any negotiation over points of difference, the whole process can take months. Meanwhile, inflation increases costs so that the value of the grant is reduced and tradesmen become committed to other work. Thatchers, for example, have to be 'booked' about a year in advance.

The NBA report on improvement grant administration of July 1979 indicated that improvement grant officers needed more advice from the DOE. DOE Circular 21/80 now provides some help and suggests what type of repairs and improvement works may be eligible for grant aid.

3.6 Environmental Health and Housing Authorities

3.6.1 Introduction

In dealing with historic buildings, the health officer is mainly concerned with fitness for habitation. In some local authorities this is dealt with by the housing department, in others by the environmental health department. In either case there may be little contact between these officers and the conservation or planning officers dealing with historic buildings, or with the building control department. Notice may thus be served on the owner of a listed building under Section 16 of the Housing Act without reference to these departments.

In some local authorities, responsibility for Section 60 of the Public Health Act (means of escape from sleeping quarters on upper floors) is split between building control and housing, with the former applying requirements to new buildings and the latter being responsible for existing buildings.

3.6.2 Attitudes

The application of these pieces of legislation is subject to some of the problems that occur with the fire authority. The health or housing officer's sphere of interest is entirely separate from conservation and the individual officer has no authority to depart from the rules he is charged with applying. Some of his responsibilities, such as means of escape from fire, are technically complex. The fire officer can have problems with historic buildings, even though he has considerable experience of his subject: a health or housing officer confronted with similar situations, but with nothing like the same experience or training, is much less likely to be able to find a satisfactory compromise.

3.6.3 Appeals

We know of no formal appeals made against health or housing fitness requirements for historic buildings. The officer dealing with the Great Ormond Street case (Case Study No. 5C), which related to the level of natural light in basements, told the architect there was no appeal against his ruling.

See Case Study 5C, pp. 76-8

3.6.4 Housing in multiple occupation

Difficulties arose in the interpretation and application of Section 16 of the Housing Act 1961, concerning houses in multiple occupation, and it is now replaced by Schedule 24 of the Housing Act 1980. The local authority is obliged to consult the fire authority in each case before serving notices of requirements under this section. In Greater London and Greater Manchester, the fire authorities have prepared Codes of Practice for the local authorities and compliance with these is deemed to constitute consultation. The Act defined a house in multiple occupation as being 'a house which is let in lodgings or is occupied by members of more than one family'.

We asked twelve local authorities how they interpreted the term. Nine authorities replied, one of them at length, as described below:

Multiple occupation is defined as a house occupied by persons who do not form a single household.
There are many varied occupancies which could be classed as such:
— *a housing cooperative (several persons purchasing a house);*
— *student accommodation sharing communal kitchen and lounge facilities and separate bedrooms;*
— *a house occupied by one main householder with varying numbers of individuals who do not form part of that household, although in certain circumstances an individual lodger might form part of a household;*
— *lodging houses (not registered under Part IV of the Public Health Act 1936);*
— *mother and baby homes;*
— *battered wives homes;*
— *flats if not under the Public Health Act 1936, Section 60; (see para 1.2.3 for details of this section);*
— *hostels; and*
— *some types of homes for the elderly, etc.*
There is conflicting case law on what has been accepted as being multiple occupation particularly in respect of occupation by students. The Ministry of Housing and

Local Government give advice in Circular 67/69, but it is up to the local authority to decide after consideration of each individual case.

Two other authorities stated that they judged every case according to its individual circumstances and one admitted that its interpretation '...one which has some common shared facilities, i.e. shared kitchen or bathroom' was legally open to doubt. Most of the remainder more or less reiterated the definition given in the Act or enlarged upon it by stating what did not constitute multiple occupation, such as a self-contained flat, a boarding house or an hotel. Confusingly, one authority stated that 'multiple occupation means where a number of persons do not live in a separate household', and another interpreted it as 'people who do not share a common meal'!

Given this sort of variation in interpretation it seems likely that historic buildings around the country are not receiving uniform treatment.

Some of the uncertainties in the application of Section 16 were illustrated in the court case that arose over requirements that the local authority served on the University of Hull. More details are given in para 5.3. The matter went to the Court of Appeal over what could and could not be required under the Act, and an important ruling was given on how the 'reasonableness' of requirements should be judged.

A joint DOE/Home Office/Welsh Office Circular (DOE No. 25/1982) on Fire Safety in Houses in Multiple Occupation was published on 25 October 1982, with the aim of giving guidance to local housing and fire authorities on the changes in the law governing fire safety in houses in multiple occupation, and clarifying the scope and nature of the wide variety of statutory powers and responsibilities that they have for improving fire safety. Details of a recent code of guidance are given in Chapter 4, together with a discussion of the current legislation on housing in multiple occupation.

3.7 The Health and Safety at Work Act

Unlike any other legislation, all employers and employees have a duty to take action themselves. Employers have a duty and employees have a right to investigate the place of work to ensure that it and the methods for work, etc, adopted in it are safe. As we have said, the only historic buildings we found frequently affected were working mills.

The danger to historic buildings is that *ad hoc* alterations are made on the initiative of either a relatively unskilled employee safety representative or a manager who has been given health and safety responsibilities on top of his other work. Reference to a fully trained safety officer employed by the health and safety executive may not be made. However, from our research we would conclude that this danger has not amounted to a significant problem.

3.8 Residential Care Establishments

Local authorities have to register non-National Health Service residential care establishments, such as old people's homes, children's homes, day nurseries and the like. It is quite common for old buildings to be converted for these purposes, and so listed buildings may often be affected.

The registration is subject to the premises having satisfactory sanitation, fire precautions and means of escape, heating, freedom from damp, etc. It is usual for the registration officer to call on the fire authority and other departments for reports on all these specialised matters. If defects are reported, the officer may decide to serve requirements on the applicant.

A case has been reported in which a fire officer's requirements were passed on in this way. They included putting an external metal stair down the centre of an important elevation of a neo-classical country house. Appeals to the registration officer to reconsider were to no avail because he did not feel competent to overturn the fire officer's advice. The fire officer would not agree that any of the alternatives the architects proposed were satisfactory. The listed building consent application was rejected and actually went to appeal, which was refused.

3.9 The Licensing Act

The position of listed buildings under the Licensing Act is administratively similar to that described for residential care establishments. The police and the fire authority are consulted and considerable importance is attached to their observations.

The applicant is given notice by the fire authority of their observations and can usually discuss them and suggest alternatives with the fire officer before submissions are made to the licensing court. This also gives the applicant an opportunity to enlist the aid of the local conservation officer, or any other help to support this case, if he feels the quality of the building will be harmed by the fire safety measures, etc. But, as with residential care establishments, this is no guarantee of success.

3.10 Conservation Officers

Full-time conservation or historic buildings officers are now to be found in many, if not most, local authority planning departments. In the architect's department additional specialist staff may be more actively involved in the design and supervision of contracts involving the council's own historic buildings. Some authorities operate revolving fund schemes to rescue historic buildings.

The officer's liaison duties can strongly influence the effect of the legislation on historic buildings. By cultivating contacts within the council's departments and with officers of other authorities, the officer is in a position to bring the interested parties together when an old building is threatened. The importance of such contacts has been stressed to us by several conservation officers and by architects, and is borne out by our personal experience.

The success of the conservation officer depends both on the abilities of the individual and the way his local authority is organised. Some officers appear to take a far more active role than others, seeking out cases and putting forward points of view in the interests of conservation that may be at odds with the particular interests of other officers of their council. Many of them have expertise in the field of historic buildings grants and loans which may help to overcome financial obstacles to meeting legislative requirements. However, our impression was that their knowledge of legislation outside the planning field was often rather limited, and this reduced the effectiveness of even the most active.

The effectiveness of the conservation officer is influenced by the structure of his council's organisation. Formal contact between departments is usually in the name of the chief officer and may be ponderous and even subject to internal political considerations that distort the views or aims of the officers at lower levels. It might therefore be an advantage if the conservation officer were in the same department as the building control officers and, where there is a technical services department, it would be an advantage for the group to include highways engineers and environmental health officers.

Conservation officers are encouraged to discuss topics of common interest at the local level through local authority regional forums and nationally through the Conservation Area Committee of the Society for the Protection of Historic Buildings and the meetings of the Association of Conservation Officers. In this way problems can be discussed, and the success of different practical or administrative approaches reported. Stimulation of such contacts is strongly recommended.

3.11 Highway Authorities

Apart from legislation affecting trunk roads, which is administered by the Department of Transport, the enforcement of the Highways Act is undertaken by the county authority. It may devolve some of its functions to district level, although the county retains a right to vet the district's scheme.

Under the general development order, highway authorities have a right to be notified of, or to be consulted on, planning applications that involve forming a new access or generating more traffic. In most of the highways related cases, improvement or access road realignment have been imposed as conditions of the planning consent. Under such arrangements it ought to be the case that no requirement injurious to a listed building would be passed on by the planners. The effect of highways requirements is not always immediately apparent, however, and innocuous conditions can ultimately have a detrimental effect. For example, a new use cannot be found for Ravenscroft Hall, Cheshire, because it requires a new access, something for which no developer has been prepared to pay.

3.12 Statutory Undertakings

Statutory undertakings are exempted from most building legislation and from the need to obtain planning permission for much of their normal 'works' development. In Chester – and particularly in the city centre where the raised arcaded pavements make it difficult to use the normal arrangements for running concealed services such as electricity from beneath the street into the buildings – the conservation officer has been concerned at the lack of power to control the undertakings. Although consultation meetings are held between undertakings and the conservation staff to plan acceptable routes for new services, work on site does not necessarily comply with the agreement. The conservation officer considered that an action could be brought against the undertaking under Section 57 of the Town and Country Planning Act 1971 (Part IV) for an 'act which causes or is likely to result in damage to a listed building...' To date, this action has not been taken and we do not know whether it would be successful in restraining a statutory undertaking.

Case Study 5: Town Houses

The survey set out at the beginning of Chapter 2 (pp. 24-29) shows that a quarter of the cases we came across in this category involved Building Regulations. The Fire Precautions Act and Offices, Shops and Railway Premises Act taken together affected one case in five. The Public Health Act, Housing Act and Highways Act account for most of the remainder. Two cases involved the London Building Acts.

A. Clarence House, Thaxted, Essex

This elegant Georgian three-storey brick house is in a prominent position on the main road through Thaxted. The top floor is a semi-attic with coombed ceilings. The building is used by the County as a short-stay residential centre for young people, and the existing pair of vertical external ladders were considered inadequate as emergency escapes.

Architect: Essex County Architects Department

Project leader: James Boutwood

Listed Grade I

The work was done of the county's own volition to forestall the service of statutory requirements to do other, more damaging, work under Section 60 of the Public Health Act or Section 10 of the Fire Precautions Act, to bring the means of escape from the top floor up to current standards.

There were two stairs to the first floor and earlier fire precautions work had involved separating these from each other, creating a series of doors and hatches between the small dormitories (each sleeping four or five people) which enabled the occupants to by-pass one stair to reach the other. However, only one stair served the top floor. An alternative route had been devised via dormer windows onto the parapeted roof and thence to two vertical ladders down the east gable. The authority considered that this drop of well over 7 m and the rooftop route were not adequately safe by modern standards.

The only location for a new stair would have been outside the east gable which is prominent as one approaches Clarence House from the centre of Thaxted. The Building Regulations 1976 and architectural considerations would have required this to be enclosed, presenting a very difficult design problem.

The solution was to provide a floor hatch and internal ladder whereby the top floor occupants could reach a first floor bedroom from where they had access to both stairs.

Reference: Para 2.4.5

Clarence House, Thaxted, Essex Approximate scale 1:200

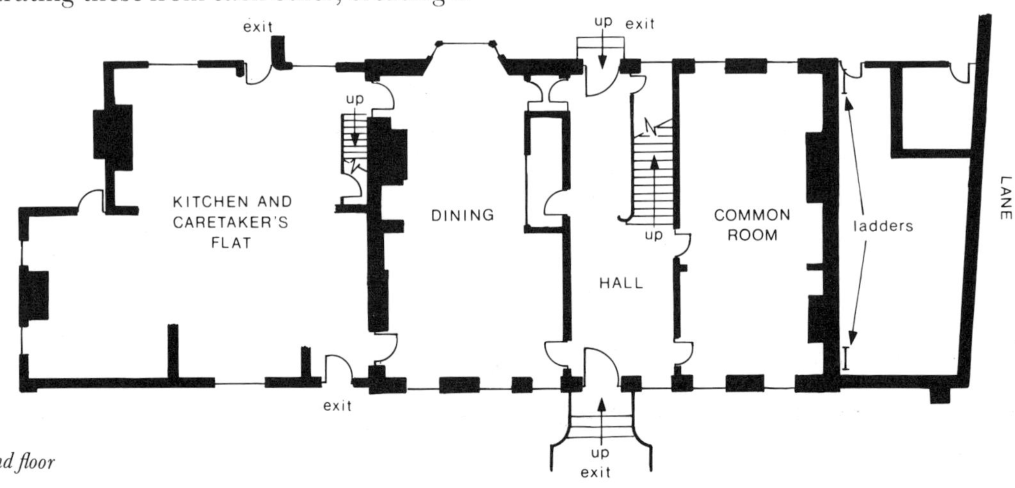

Ground floor

Clarence House, Thaxted

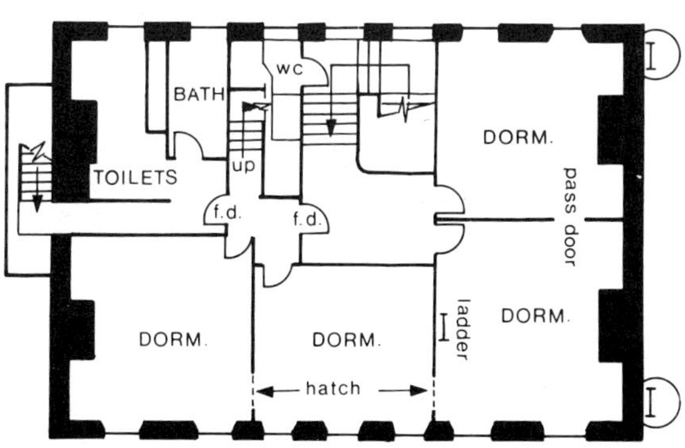

First floor

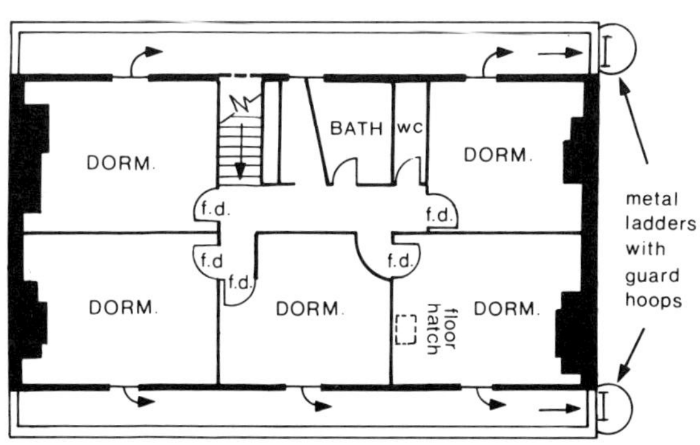

Second floor

B. Nos. 12/13 and 42/43 Bedford Row, London WC1

These two pairs of town houses in the Bloomsbury conservation area are now used as offices. Nos. 42/43 date from about 1692 and have a rebuilt street façade, while Nos. 12/13 were built in about 1718. All have four storeys and a basement.

Listed Grade II

Legislation

Listed building consent applications were submitted to the Historic Buildings Section of the GLC for alterations to each pair of houses. The applications were entirely separate but presented similar problems.

Construction

Of particular interest and attraction were the panelling and other details in the rooms and stairways of the lower floors, which were original and in quite good condition. But the timber partitions between stairways and rooms were not considered to offer a half-hour's fire resistance.

Problems and solutions

Initially, the Building Regulations Division advised the applicant for Nos. 42/43 that two-door protection would be required, which would necessitate lobbies in the rooms, and that the combustible panelling to each stair would have to be either replaced or covered by fire resisting construction. The Historic Buildings Division were opposed to this and an alternative solution was agreed with the Building Regulations Division.

Party wall openings 1.2 × 0.610 m were to be formed at each level, coinciding with the existing panelling, providing crawl-way routes between the rooms giving access to either stair. Nos. 42/43 were then treated as a single building with two staircases. Automatic fire detectors were installed and a surface treatment was applied to the timber in the stairways to reduce surface flame spread.

Nos. 12/13 presented a similar problem. Lobbies were again avoided by providing party wall openings giving access to an alternative stair. Automatic smoke detection was installed as a further safeguard.

In their correspondence with the Surveyor of Historic Buildings, the Building Regulations Division expressed reservations about 'reliance upon mechanical devices to give automatic early warning... in the event of fire', which they felt was a 'pale substitute for structural fire protection'. They also maintained that 'ensuring the maintenance and renewal of such equipment in the future could create an unacceptable workload on the council's officers'. They did, however, accept that the circumstances justified amendment to their original requirements.

References: Paras 2.2.12B, 2.2.19 and 2.4.1C

Bedford Row

Nos. 42/43 Bedford Row, London WC1 Approximate scale 1:200

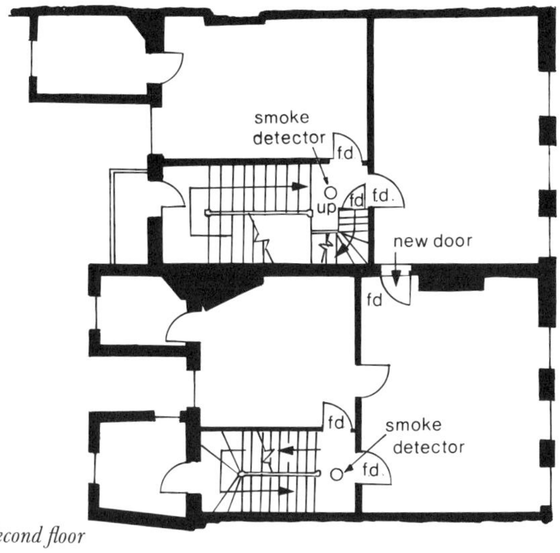

Second floor

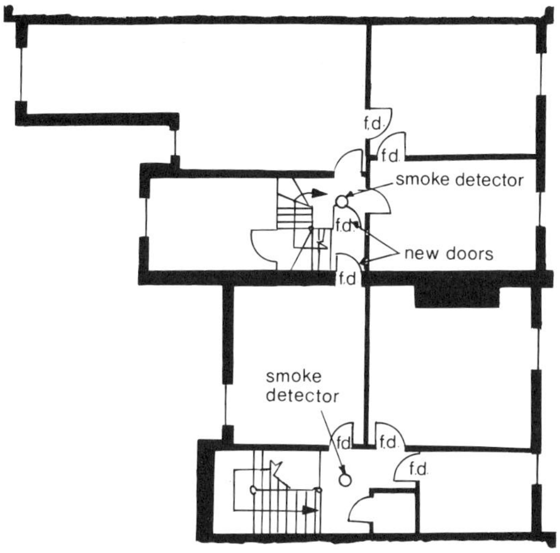

Third floor

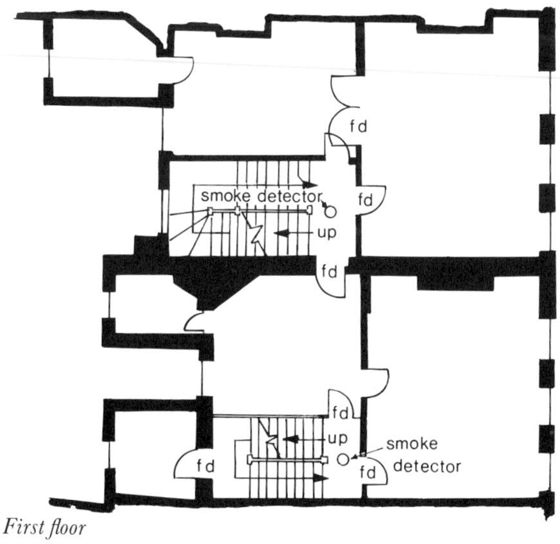

First floor

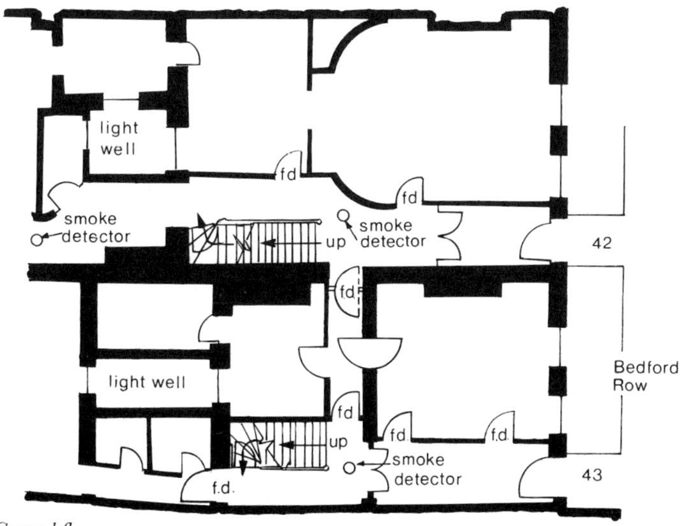

Ground floor

C. Nos. 5, 7, 10 and 12 Great Ormond Street, London WC1

Great Ormond Street

This row of five-storey terraced houses (including basement) dating from the early eighteenth century was acquired by the Borough of Camden from the Rugby Estate, refurbished and converted into flats and maisonettes.

Architects: Donald W. Insall & Associates

Listed Grade II

Legislation

Section 35 of the London Building (Amendment) Act 1939 applied and, as the premises were wholly residential, the structural fire precautions and means of escape were dealt with by Camden Borough Council under delegated authority from the GLC. Under the Housing Acts, the responsibility for daylight levels within dwellings is that of Camden Borough Council.

Structural fire precautions

The compartment floors of Nos. 10 and 12 were 25 mm plain-edged boards on joists with nominal 19.8 mm plaster-lath ceiling. Two layers of 12.7 mm plasterboard were applied to the underside of this to satisfy fire resistance requirements. There were difficulties with ceiling cornices. The timber cornices were removed and replaced after the plasterboard had been added but, where they were of plaster, the operation proved more difficult and expensive.

Means of escape

To sub-divide the principal rooms of Nos. 10 and 12 as little as possible, maisonettes were formed on the basement/ground and first/second floors with a flat on the top floor.

For means of escape purposes, the building control authority required a half-hour standard fire resistance for the partitions and doors enclosing the common stairways. There was considerable timber panelling internally, including partitions of only a single thickness of timber. At many points there were extensive cavities between the lath and plaster and the brickwork. While the partitions on the lower floors were quite substantial, the single-thickness timber panels at the upper levels were regarded as totally inadequate. Yet the age and form of assembly of the timber partitions made it virtually impossible to dismantle them to add a fire resisting interlayer.

After consultation with the GLC, it was decided to use an intumescent coating reinforced with glass tissue to upgrade the timberwork without hiding it. The GLC advocated the use of fire-resistant sheeting over the thin timber panelling of the upper and less historically important areas; the coating to panels in the lower, more important areas was favourably considered only because of the substantial construction of the panels. Other timberwork in the stairways and escape route was painted to reduce the surface spread of flame.

Daylighting

In the lower maisonettes, the larger ground floor rooms were converted to living or dining rooms and the smaller basement rooms to bedrooms. With all four houses, the level of the pavement outside reduced the effective area of the basement windows for daylighting purposes below one tenth of the floor area, the minimum required by the environmental health officer. No account could be taken of indirect reflected light and the Department insisted that any area of a room which was in excess of that permitted by the effective win-

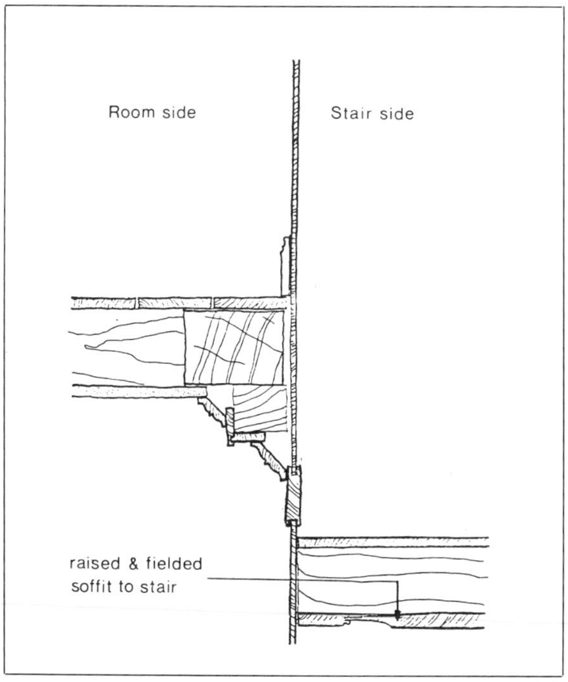

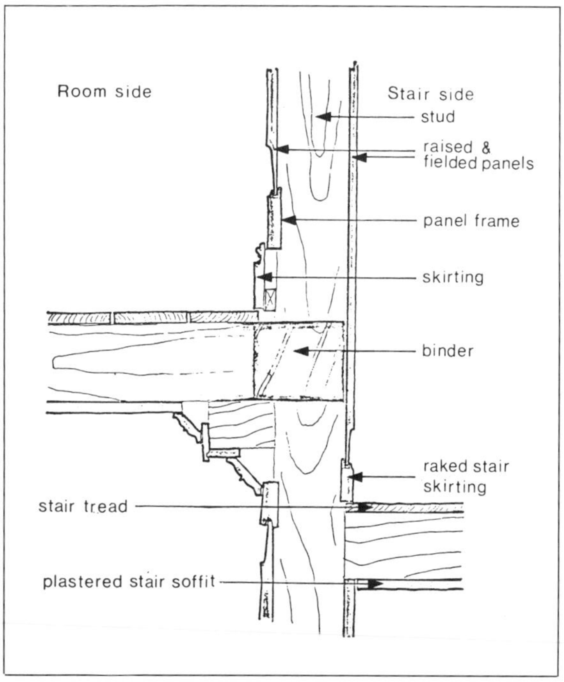

Nos. 10 and 12 Great Ormond Street, London WC1
Sections through single and double thickness timber stair partitions
Approximate scale 1:10

dow area should be partitioned permanently in a way that would prevent it from being used as a habitable room. Large parts of the rooms in Nos. 5 and 7 had to be made into cupboards. The drawings show how the basement windows were obstructed and the effect on the plan. *We seriously question the benefit of these measures.*

In Nos. 10 and 12 the architects overcame the problem by very careful planning and changes to the windows. The Georgian windows were removed – unfortunate, because they were the only original ones – and replaced by Victorian-styled ones with only four panes instead of twelve and set back in the window reveals using spring sash balances

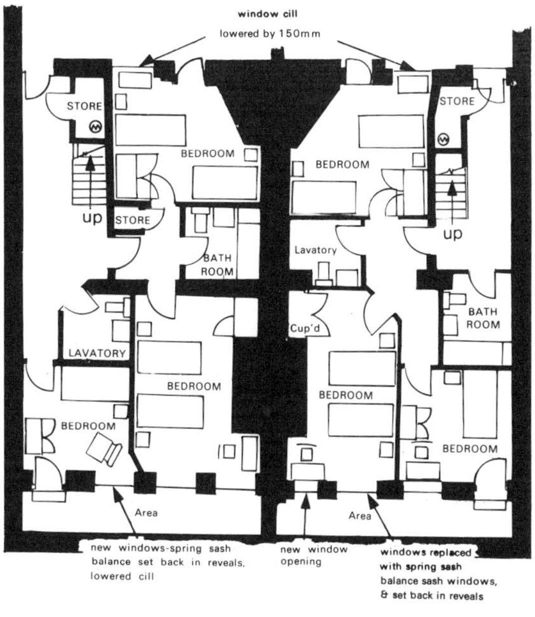

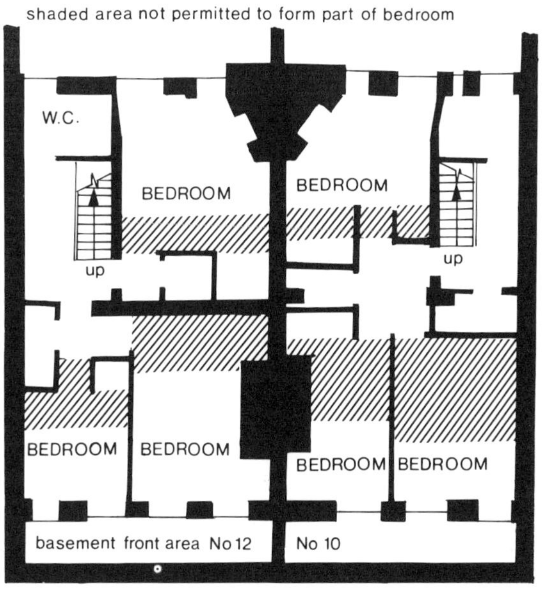

Basement showing area blighted by daylight requirements and layout permitted by increased window areas and reduced kerb
Approximate scale 1:200

Section through basement before and after increasing window area and reducing kerb height Approximate scale 1:50

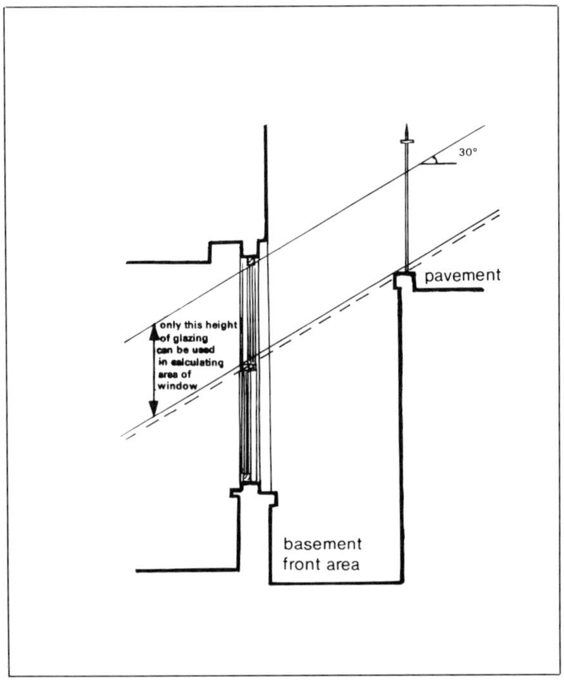

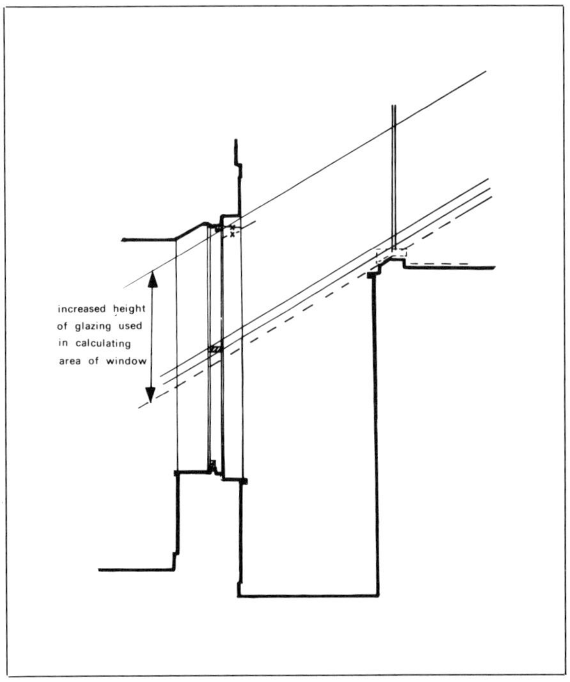

Front elevation showing increased window size and reduced kerb height (below)

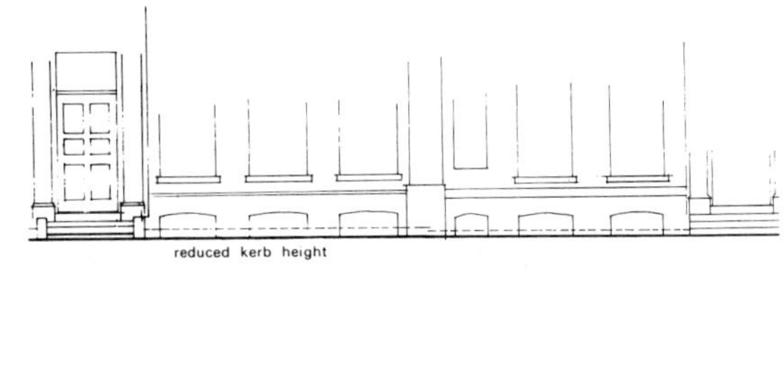

that were narrower than the original sash boxes. The pavement kerb was lowered and chamfered to increase the light angle (see section) and in some cases the window sills were lowered to bring the window mid-rails below the light path and increase the useful glazed area. One new window was also added in the front of No. 10. With the useful glazed area increased as much as possible, the maximum bedroom sizes were determined on the basis of the 1:10 ratio, and the interiors were replanned accordingly. Parker Morris space standards were achieved.

Some of the other properties in the Great Ormond Street scheme were too dilapidated to conserve and were rebuilt in facsimile. The basement daylight problem was overcome by raising the level of the basement and ground floors 160 mm and raising the basement window heads as much as possible.

References: Paras 2.2.12B, 2.2.19, 2.5.2B and 3.6.3

Case Study 6: Churches

Building Regulations apply to all churches, but we have no evidence of any adverse effects or special problems. Few of the Regulations would affect the typical masonry church anyway.

Entertainments licensing for secular musical performances may be required. Only one entertainments licence case was called to our attention. At a cathedral in the Midlands the main west doors were required to open outwards for means of escape, in connection with a music licence application. As churches were originally built as places of assembly, and as their interiors are generally of a very low fire risk, it would be most surprising if they were not found acceptable for ordinary licensed functions without alteration. It is only when a change to secular use occurs that churches are subjected to the full effects of building legislation.

A. St James', Pockthorpe, Norwich

St James', Pockthorpe, has been converted into premises for a professional puppet theatre company, housing a workshop and base for their touring operations, as well as an auditorium with bar and refreshment area. New exits, fire separation of the backstage area, protected escape from the auditorium and attention to the road access were all called for, and relaxation of Building Regulations 1976 was obtained for a new stairway.

Architect: Peter Codling

Means of escape

Two new doorways had to be made in the external wall which, being constructed of flint with loose fill, presented practical structural problems, the more so because there was a buttress on the doorway centre-line. The auditorium seating is entirely new, on a raked pattern, with the main public access at the back about 3.2 m above ground entrance level. A relaxation had to be obtained to fit in a stair whose width and tread dimensions were a little outside the limits in the Regulations. It had to be protected from any fire originating in the bar area on the ground floor by putting a glazed screen on the line of the arch and columns that formerly marked the west lobby.

Structural precautions

The main auditorium was to be separated from the bar and storage accommodation beneath, for acoustic purposes as well as for fire safety.

The height of typical church windows often makes the detailing of the junction of any new intermediate floor with the middle of the window very difficult. The problem here, where the new floor cuts obliquely across the window, was resolved by bricking up the window on the inside. This also reduced noise transmission from the road and provided blackout conditions for the theatre lighting. The windows still appear as before from the outside.

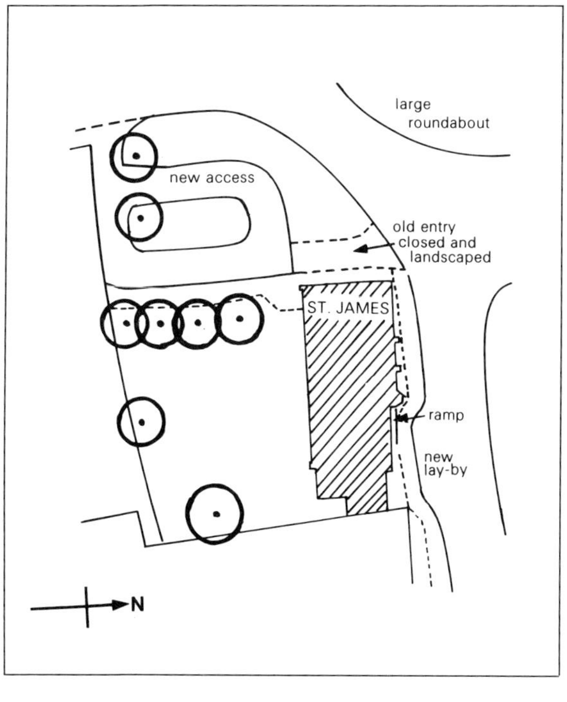

St James', Pockthorpe, Norwich

Site plan Approximate scale 1:1000

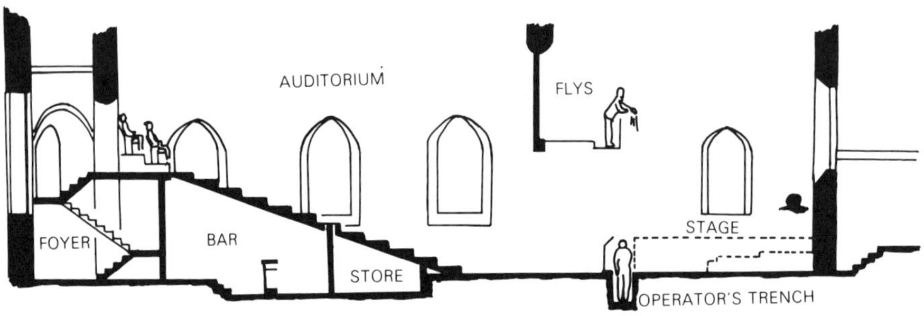

Section A-A
Approximate scale 1:200

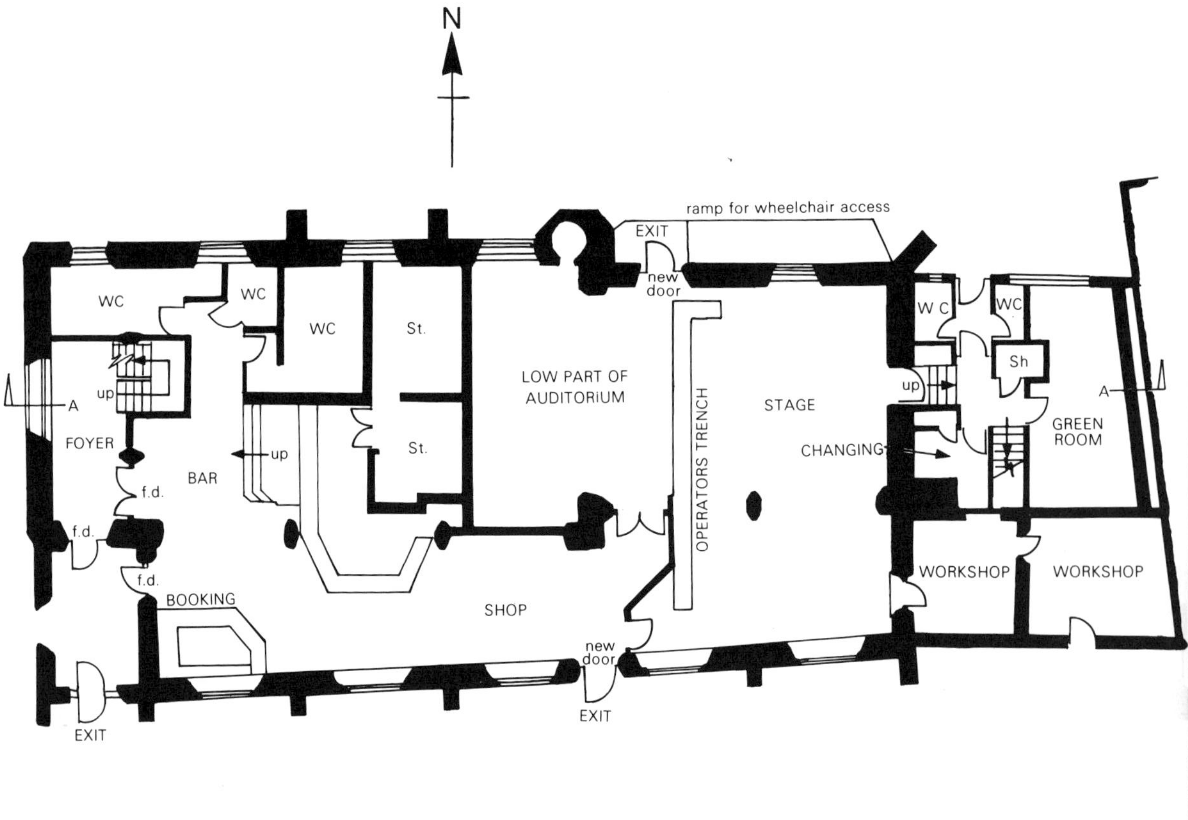

Ground floor plan

B. St Leonard's, Foscote, Buckinghamshire

Because the typical church is a high-ceilinged space, church conversions, especially domestic ones, usually involve the construction of some new structure internally to create one or two upper levels within this space. At St Leonard's the Building Regulations 1976 required that the stairs should be protected from fire, and an interesting problem of interpretation arose which could be of significance to conversions of this sort in the future.

As the drawings show, the first 'floor' in the conversion consists of a bathroom with open galleries overlooking the studio and dining room. If this had been interpreted as a floor, so that the house then had three storeys, the whole stair would need to be protected from the accommodation by an enclosure of half-an-hour's fire resistance. This would completely change the nature of the interior space. When the Regulations approval plans were lodged, showing the three level arrangement, they were passed. Work proceeded slowly and about three years later (in 1980) the Building Inspector advised the architect that the stair ought to be enclosed. An application for relaxation of the enclosure requirement was made by the architect. The local authority refused this, but an appeal to the DOE was successful. Subsequently, the architects submitted an invoice to the district council for the costs incurred in gaining approval, which the council paid.

Reference: Para 2.2.16

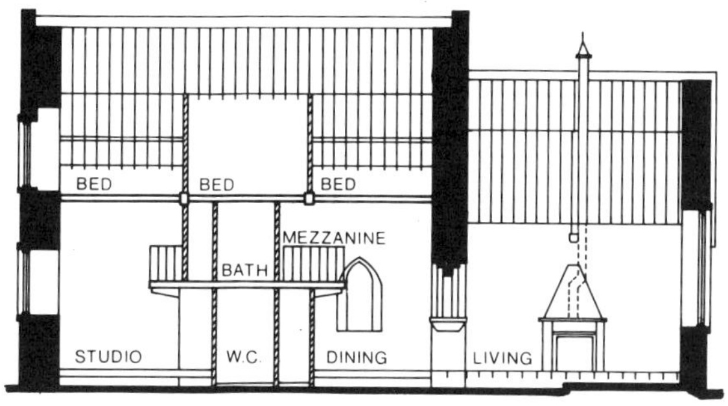

Section A-A

St Leonard's, Foscote, Buckinghamshire Approximate scale 1:200

Walls added during conversion

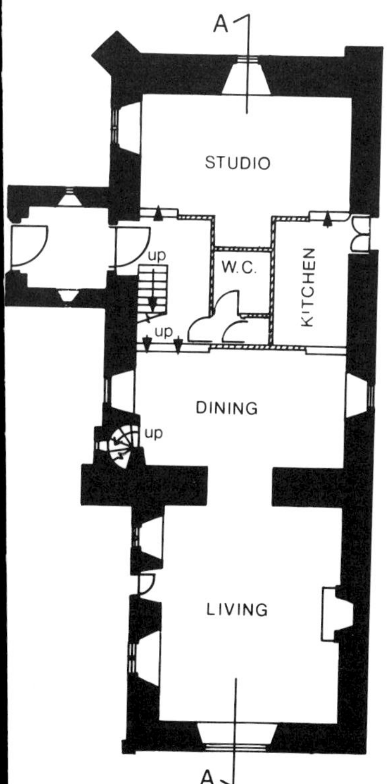

Ground floor

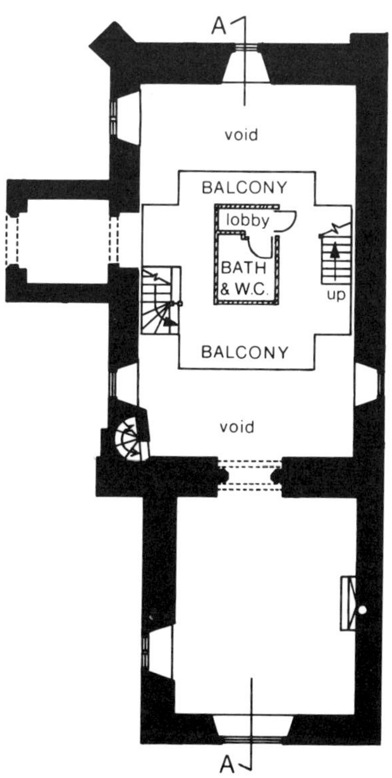

Mezzanine

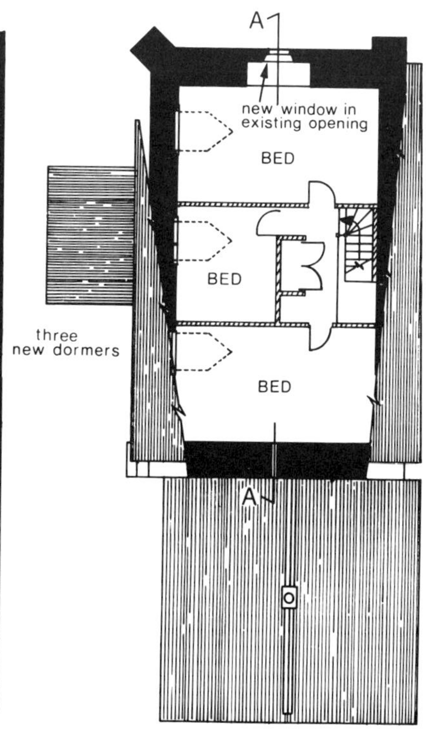

First floor

C. St Peter and St Paul, Shellow Bowells, Essex

This case set a precedent, involving both planning permission and approval under the Building Regulations 1976. This small stone church in rural Essex was redundant and an application was made for its conversion into a house. The Church Commissioners wanted to retain control of the surrounding graveyard and only sold a 0.914 m wide strip of land around the church.

The problems of the site boundary

Planning application was refused because the house would not have enough garden, although a 'satisfactory' garden size was not defined. Building Regulations approval was also refused because the area of unprotected openings (windows and doors) was too great considering that the boundary of the property was only 0.914 m away.

The new owner put these problems to the Church Commissioners, who agreed to sell additional land around the church, the exact amount being determined according to the requirements of Part E7 of the 1976 Regulations. The Planning Authority was also satisfied by this measure. It became standard practice for the Church Commissioners to base the minimum area of land sold with a church on that permissible under Regulation E7.

The three-storey house

There were two phases to the conversion. The first involved constructing a gallery and a bedroom on the first floor, in the second phase, the stair was extended up to a second floor to accommodate another bedroom. When the Building Regulations application was lodged for the second phase the local authority wanted the stair to be enclosed, as the dwelling now had three storeys. They would not accept that the first floor gallery had too little habitable accommodation to make this necessary. However, a relaxation of the requirement to enclose the stair was given when the applicant agreed to fit an automatic fire detection and alarm system.

References: Paras 2.2.11C and 2.2.16

St Peter and St Paul, Shellow Bowells, Essex Approximate scale 1:200

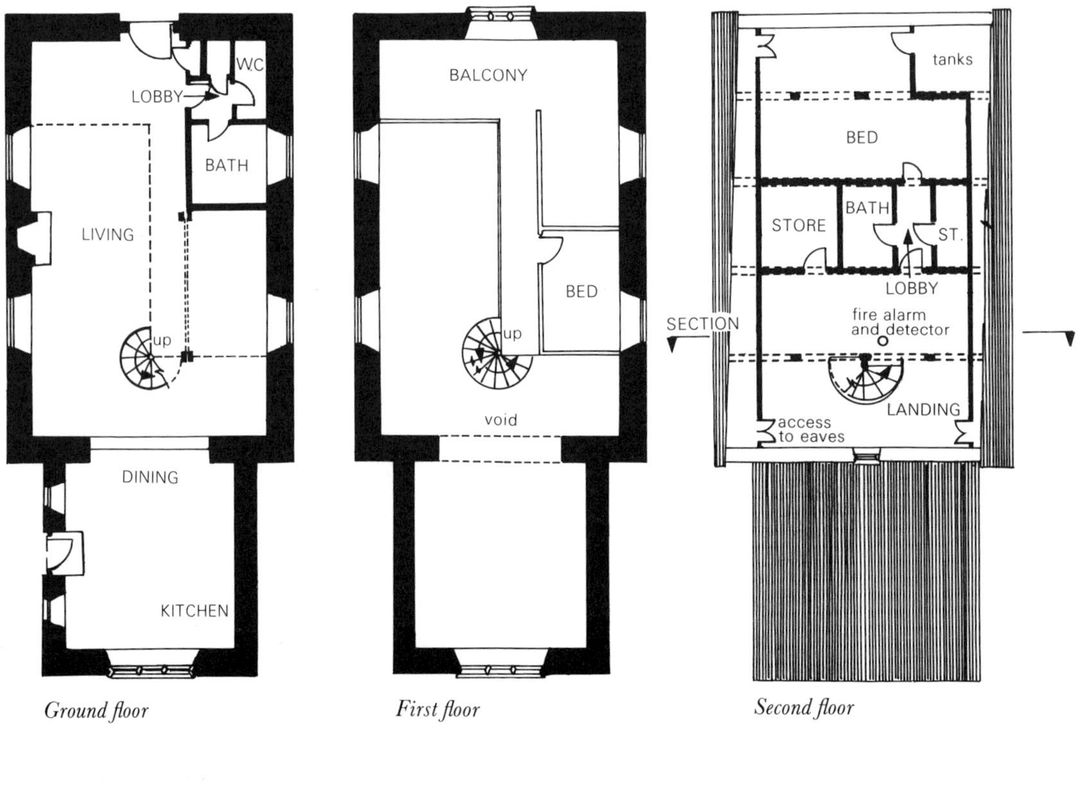

Ground floor *First floor* *Second floor*

Exterior

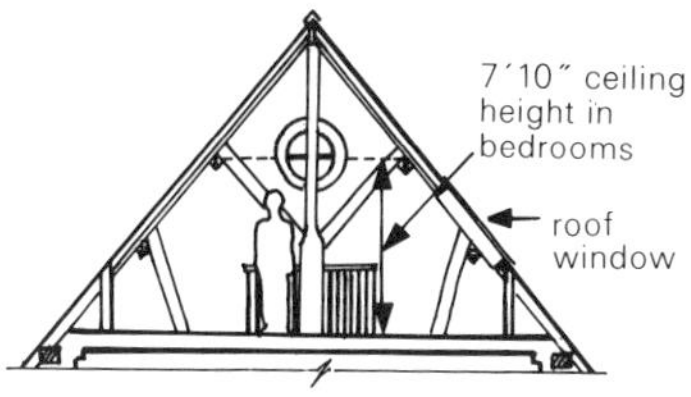

Section through second floor looking eastwards

Interior ground level

4

Recent changes in legislation

4.1 The Building Regulations 1985

4.1.1 Introduction

This chapter gives an overall assessment of the significance of the Building Regulations 1985 for work on historic buildings, particularly their potential for resolving some of the problems raised in Chapters 2 and 3. The Building Regulations for England and Wales (apart from London) were made under the Public Health Act and were defined 'to protect the health and safety of building users and to promote energy conservation'. From the date of their inception they became increasingly complex as various governments added technical amendments to the original contents so that they became progressively more difficult to assimilate.

In 1980 the Secretary of State for the Environment published a consultative paper provoking discussion in an attempt to streamline the Regulations by means of:

— maximum self-regulation;
— minimum Government interference;
— total self-financing; and
— simplicity in operation.

As a consequence of these discussions, Command Paper 8179, 'The Future of Building Control in England and Wales', was published in 1981. It reviewed the current problems of the existing Regulations and set out some policy commitments. It concluded that the present cumbersome nature of the Regulations had been caused by their having been originally derived from the Model By-laws, which were mainly concerned with domestic buildings and public health, and then expanded in an attempt to cover other building types. The 1976 Regulations were thought to have become over-complicated and legalistic, and local authorities, designers and builders had difficulty in interpreting them. They also inhibited innovation. This resulted in widespread dissatisfaction with both their scope and form.

The Command Paper recommended that a radical re-examination was needed to simplify the Regulations. It redefined the purpose of Regulations as applying only to public health safety and energy conservation and therefore requiring an urgent review to weed out ruthlessly any unnecessary requirements. It proposed that the new Regulations should be expressed as 'functional requirements', clearly indicating the purpose and the standards to be achieved, and that these should be supported with 'Approved Documents' which would give guidance to designers.

In considering the administrative system the paper recommended that;

— the Regulations need only be concerned with public health, safety and energy conservation;
— they should be recast as broadly expressed functional regulations supported by approved documents;
— many public organisations should be able to lay down their own requirements;
— the procedures should allow the authority automatically to exempt from Regulations a range of minor works where the health and safety risks were slight;
— a system of private certifications, by appointed inspectors, should be set up to run in parallel with the local authority building control system, as an alternative available to developers, but without enforcement powers; and
— there should be two stages of approval, one certificate being for the proposed design and another to confirm that the building complies with the Regulations on completion.

4.1.2 Comprehension

Many of the Command Paper's proposals have been incorporated in the new Building Regulations, which came into operation on 11 November 1985. The Regulations, which were made under the Building Act 1984, comprise a brief description of the way in which they are to be applied, and four Schedules: 'Requirements', 'Facilities for Disabled People', 'Exempt Buildings and Work' and 'Revocations'. Schedule 1 replaces Parts A–R of the 1976 Regulations with a far briefer statement of the requirements affecting specific aspects of the building and the limits on their application. It was hoped that the omission of detailed technical provisions from the principal Regulations would enable a more flexible approach to be taken on work to buildings, and this would of course include historic buildings. The Schedule is supported by a series of Approved Documents indicating some possible ways in which the requirements might be met; since they are not statutory instruments. they do not need to be expressed in legal language. A manual has also been prepared which contains explanations of the Regulations and their requirements. Table 8 compares the arrangement of the 1985 Regulations with that of its predecessor by placing, against the items in Schedule 1, the equivalent Part of the 1976 Building Regulations (as amended) or sections of the Building Act 1984.

Table 8.

Schedule 1	*1976 Regulations (as amended) or section of the Building Act 1984*
A: Structure	D: Structural stability
B: Fire	E: Safety in Fire
C: Site preparation and resistance to moisture	C: Preparation of site and resistance to moisture, and Section 29: site containing offensive material
D: Toxic substances	S: Toxic substances
E: Resistance to the passage of sound	G: Sound insulation
F: Ventilation	K (Part): Open space, ventilation and height of rooms F (Part): Thermal insulation of dwellings
G: Hygiene	Sections 26, 27 and 28: provision of WCs, bathrooms and food stores P: Sanitary conveniences
H: Drainage	N: Drainage, private sewers and cesspools, and Section 23: Provision of facilities for refuse
J: Heat-producing appliances	L: Chimneys, flue pipes, hearths and fireplace recesses M: Heat-producing appliances and incinerators
K: Stairways, ramps and guards	H: Stairways, ramps, balustrades and vehicle barriers
L: Conservation of fuel and power	F: Thermal insulation of dwellings FF: Conservation of fuel and power in buildings other than dwellings Q: Control of space and water heating systems R: Thermal insulation of pipes, ducts and storage vessels

4.1.3 Flexibility

The main purpose of the Regulations is stated as being to ensure merely that buildings meet 'reasonable standards of health and safety' for people who use or are affected by the standards used in the construction of buildings. The new system will give a greater degree of flexibility to designers and builders than was available under the previous Regulations. It will not be obligatory to follow the guidance in an Approved Document provided the functional requirement contained in the Regulations is met.

4.1.4 Exemptions

The new Regulations make significant reductions in the amount of control exercised under the 1976 Regulations. Figure 3, taken from the manual to the Regulations, shows where they do not apply. Categories of relevance to historic buildings in Schedule 3 include:

— Ancient Monuments;
— detached buildings of less than 30 m^2 floor area, with no sleeping accommodation;
— buildings into which people do not normally go, or only enter intermittently to inspect or maintain fixed plant or machinery;
— greenhouses and agricultural buildings; and
— small extensions such as conservatories, carports and porches.

4.1.5 Work to existing buildings

We have explained in para 3.3.2A and in Figure 2 (p. 64) how complex the 1976 Regulations were when dealing with work to existing buildings. In the 1985 Regulations, existing buildings are catered for in para 2(4), which states:

For the purposes of Regulations 3(2)(a) and 4(2) work shall be regarded as adversely affecting an existing building ... if the building ... as extended or altered:
(a) would not comply with any applicable requirement of Schedule 1 ... which the existing building ... complies with, or
(b) would not comply with a requirement ... which does not apply to the existing building ... or
(c) would not comply with any such requirement which related to the existing building ... and would, in

Do the Building Regulations apply?

YES		NO
As a general rule the Regulations will apply if what you propose is listed in this column. But there are exceptions listed in the NO column.		
The erection of a building	except →	buildings for certain specialised uses, temporary buildings and small detached buildings (with total area not more than 30 m^2) with no sleeping accommodation. For details see Schedule 3
The extension of a building	except →	the addition at ground level of a greenhouse, conservatory, carport open on at least two sides, porch, covered way or covered yard (with total floor area not more than 30 m^2)
The 'material alteration' of a building, as defined in Regulation 3(2)		Any other alteration and repairs, i.e. making good, replacing like with like but see para 3
The provision, extension, or material alteration of:		electrical installations
• Sanitary equipment drainage for a building unvented hot water systems fixed heating appliances in which fuel is burnt	except →	in small buildings (see above)
• Insulation and energy – saving controls for space heating and hot water systems, hot water pipes and warm air ducts	except →	in dwellings or for industrial purposes
A change of use of an existing building, as described in Regulation 5		Any other change of use

relation to compliance with such a requirement, be more unsatisfactory than the existing building.

The requirement would therefore appear to be easier to understand than that in the 1976 Regulations. However, Regulations 3 and 4 deal with 'building work', which is defined in 3(2) broadly as the erection, extension or *material* alteration of a building, and 'building work' is deemed to be material if, carried out by itself, it would at any stage adversely affect the structure, means of escape or fire spread (Parts A, B1, B3 and B4 of Schedule 1) of the building, or if it involves underpinning or cavity insulation.

4.1.6 Alterations

Alterations which do not adversely affect the building as regards these items are not material and therefore not 'building work', and do not require a building notice, etc. This would also apply to alterations which affect Parts A, B1, B3 and B4, but not adversely. If other work is done to prevent the alteration from adversely affecting 'building work', the alteration would therefore not be 'material' and not controlled by the Regulations. Page 21 of the manual to the Regulations gives examples of this type of work to guide the builder. It follows that alterations which would have formerly conflicted with other requirements of the Regulations are now permitted. However, if a material alteration is carried out, the Regulations apply to it regardless of when the building was constructed. Despite this, the 1985 Regulations offer greater freedom from control over alterations to historic buildings than did the 1976 version.

4.1.7 Material changes of use

Regulation 5 explains the meaning of a material change of use. Broadly, a change of use is not considered to be 'building work' unless the change involves:

— the provision of sleeping accommodation, including hotels or institutions;

— the use was previously exempt and the new use is not; or

— the building is used as a public building.

Different parts of the Regulations apply, depending on the type of new use, and whether the change applies to the whole building or only part of it.

4.1.8 Repair work

Repairs are not subject to the Regulations if they do not involve a material change of use, or either entail merely making good the existing fabric or replacing like with like. However, no guidance is given as to at what point repair work becomes alteration or new work, except that the guidance manual to the Regulations explains that if repair work is so extensive – for example, where a whole building has suffered serious damage – that the local authority considers it should be treated as a new building, the Regulations would apply.

4.1.9 Materials and workmanship

The Regulations stipulate that the 'work shall be carried out with proper materials and in a workmanlike manner'. 'Proper' is not defined but an Approved Document supporting Regulation 7 provides guidance as to its interpretation. For example, local authorities are empowered to take samples of materials to ensure that they are satisfactory and the Approved Document gives restrictions in the use of short lived materials, the standards required for the resistance of moisture and the areas affected by the house longhorn beetle. It also acknowledges that past experience, together with British Standards, Agrement, quality assurance, tests, etc, is an important factor, by stating that a building material or a method of workmanship will be considered adequate if it can be shown to be adequately performing the function for which it was intended in a building in use. Such a means of fulfilling the required standards of materials and workmanship is of course particularly significant for historic buildings.

4.1.10 Structure

The structural requirements are far more simply expressed than in the 1976 Regulations. Part A of Schedule 1 requires that loads be safely sustained and transmitted to the ground without causing instability, both dead and wind loads affecting the building at all times and loads imposed while the building is in use; also that ground movements be allowed for, and that larger buildings be protected against disproportionate collapse.

The Approved Document A concerned with structural matters also gives the opportunity to consider alternative solutions to structural problems beyond those covered by British Standards, etc, where they may be more suitable for historic buildings. It advises that, where other solutions are adopted, enough safety factors should be incorporated into the design to allow for the loading, the properties of the materials involved, the details of construction, the quality of workmanship and the overall design analysis, since change in any one of these aspects could disturb the safety of the structure.

4.1.11 Fire safety

A. The requirements

The requirements relating to means of escape and fire spread are covered in Sections B1 to B4 of Schedule 1.

Section B1, which requires that means of escape be provided, is mandatory and can only be met by complying with the HMSO publication 'The Building Regulations 1985 – Mandatory rules for means of escape in case of fire'. However, it only applies to residential buildings (of three or more storeys), offices and shops.

These and other building types are also dealt with in other legislation. The Housing Act 1980 requires a means of escape from houses of three or more storeys (excluding basements) which are over 500 m^2 in area. Certain factories, offices, shops, railway premises, hotels and boarding houses require a fire certificate under the Fire Precautions Act 1971; this may entail the provision of fire alarms or fire fighting equipment. And buildings of more than two storeys to which B1 does not apply may require means to escape to conform to S.72 of the Building Act.

Section B2 requires that walls and ceilings offer adequate resistance to the spread of flame and do not give off an unreasonable amount of heat 'in the circumstances'.

Section B3 requires that a building which is on fire shall retain its stability 'for a reasonable period' and inhibit the spread of fire by being sub-divided into compartments.

Section B4 requires that external walls and roofs be adequately fire resisting and prevent fire spreading to other buildings.

The generally accepted standards to satisfy B2, B3 and B4 are based on British Standard tests and are set out in the Approved Document. They depend on the use and size of the building and the distance to the site boundary.

B. Varying the provisions

The provisions of the Approved Document can be varied where they might prove unduly restrictive, taking into consideration:

— the fire properties of the materials;
— the degree of fire hazard and fire load;
— the distance of the building from property boundaries and other buildings;
— the means of escape in case of fire;
— the ease of access for fire fighting;
— the provision of any compensatory features such as sprinklers or automatic fire detection systems; and
— whether the building is new or existing.

The opportunities provided by such variations are obviously significant for historic buildings, since they can be based on careful assessments of the condition of the fabric compared with structures or materials whose resistance to fire has been tested or is known by experience. Hazardous materials or processes can then be identified, and precautions which are sympathetic to the character of the building can be taken to reduce fire risk.

For example, thermal energy and smoke production can now be accurately calculated for specific situations to determine the fire load and its effect on means of escape, limitations on fire brigade access, evacuation times and obscurity from smoke.

The designer can thereby build up a package of fire safety while fulfilling the Regulation requirements for means of escape to suit the particular historic building. It might be possible, for example, to vary the orthodox forms of means of escape by increasing the standards of the automatic fire detection system or ease of access for fire fighting. Such features may already be incorporated to meet other requirements, such as insurance conditions or the provisions of the Fire Precautions Act.

The Approved Document merits thorough study at the design stage to check if other statements can help to ease the problems of historic buildings, such as those relating to stairways, linings, and variations relating to special purpose groups.

C. British Standards

The original Codes of Practice covering fire precautions in buildings specifically apply to new buildings, but the recent revised editions published under the general BS 5588 series have amended the introduction so that it is now to be used to provide guidance in protecting the lives of people using the buildings and the buildings themselves against the effects of fire, not only in new buildings but also in alterations to existing ones. While only the sections on means of escape are mandatory, the Codes are comprehensive and cover the whole range of fire safety matters, and must therefore be carefully considered when any alterations or extensions to historic buildings are under discussion.

4.1.12 Stairways and ramps

The Regulations merely state that stairways and ramps shall enable people to circulate about the building safely, and have guardrails, etc, where necessary. Despite this, there could still be some conflict with the similar provisions for stairways forming part of a means of escape. These can only be resolved in discussions with the appropriate authorities. Although there is no longer a specific limitation for 'one step' situations, or for any steps or stairways which do not form part of the building, such arrangements must still provide safe passage.

Considerations for relaxations, etc, may still be necessary where steps or stairways and their handrails are to be altered or extended from or adjacent to existing stairways which do not have the same limiting dimensions.

4.1.13 Sound insulation

Part E of Schedule 1 requires that some walls and floors of habitable rooms of new buildings be reasonably resistant to airborne and impact noise. This Part therefore only applies to dwellings and other buildings containing residential accommodation.

Approved Document E, 'Airborne and impact sound', allows the standards of sound resistance of new construction to be based on the performance of existing buildings, and it describes the test procedure required to ensure that the existing fabric is adequately sound-resistant. This test is therefore extremely useful in checking the degree of sound-resistance of existing buildings, particularly when it is being brought into residential use.

4.1.14 Means of ventilation

Under the 1976 Regulations it was necessary to divide habitable rooms from toilets by means of separating lobbies and to construct habitable rooms to a minimum ceiling height. Both these requirements caused considerable difficulties in historic buildings. It is significant therefore that these conditions have not been transferred to the new Regulations and that the Approved Document on ventilation illustrates alternative methods of meeting the requirements with both natural and mechanical means, so that the opportunities are now far greater to meet the requirements without necessarily affecting any historic features.

4.1.15 Facilities for the disabled

Schedule 2 of the Regulations sets out facilities required for disabled people. It applies to all floors of new shops and offices and to new single-storey factories, educational buildings and other new single-storey buildings open to the public. There is at present no Approved Document. Compliance with the recommendations given in BS 5310: 1979, or DES Design note I8, published in 1984, are deemed to be satisfactory, but are not mandatory.

One could argue that this section therefore does not apply to historic buildings, but it could apply to any extension or substantial addition and could therefore affect the existing building. Even then, it is possible for a local authority to set aside the requirements of Schedule 2 in suitable cases. While no Approved Document is available there is a draft BS 'For fire precautions in the design and construction of buildings – Part 8, Code of Practice for means of escape for disabled people' (to be published as BS 5588: Part 8).

The basic premise for means of escape for the disabled is to enable them initially to reach a place of relative safety on the floor at risk, either by entering an adjacent compartment or a 'place of refuge' such as an extended lobby to a protected stairway. In the event of further evacuation being necessary, it is assumed that rescue will be organised, either from the adjacent compartment or from the 'refuge' lobby.

The Code places reliance on an integrated management emergency plan which should be preplanned and rehearsed to ensure that the correct procedures are adopted and evacuation of the disabled starts immediately a fire is detected. This implies installing automatic detection systems and alarms, and the Code provides detailed information on the formation of fire warden groups, etc, to control such evacuations.

The Code describes the use of stairways and ramps, and special lifts. Such a lift would have an isolated control switch so that it can be independently operated in an emergency, overriding the automatic controls.

Appendix B, 'Application of the Code to existing buildings', strongly recommends the adoption of the principles of safety for the disabled in existing buildings in the same way as for new ones, including the provision of refuges and lifts. It is therefore essential to consider this aspect in development of any future projects requiring Building Regulations approval, or indeed on moral and social grounds where approval is not required.

The draft Code is under review and is being applied by fire prevention officers and building control officers on Building Regulations applications and has been the subject of at least one Determination by the Minister of State. However, it is not yet a British Standard and must not be used as one, since the final version may be in a totally different form.

4.1.16 Future developments

At the end of 1986, the DOE introduced a second stage review of the Regulations in an effort to further simplify and clarify them. This included suggestions for improving the Parts relating to structure (A), fire spread (B), the conservation of fuel and power (L), durability of materials, and alterations.

A. Structure

Part A may be recast to provide a general requirement for all buildings to possess structural robustness.

B. Fire spread

The general intention is to restructure the fire safety requirements to relate them more directly to the protection of life and, as far as is appropriate, to the protection of adjacent property. This could result in the reduction of minimum periods of fire resistance and a simplified way of determining space separation between different types of buildings.

Guidance on the use of automatic fire detection and alarm systems in combination with – or perhaps as a trade-off against – the traditional passive measures of structural fire resistance and compartmentation are to be introduced in the Approved Document. Ways are also to be sought of making the requirements for means of escape more flexible.

C. Conservation of fuel and power

Part L prescribes insulation values for different elements of a building. It is proposed that it be recast in a functional form giving guidance in an Approved Document on different ways of reaching reasonable standards of energy conservation, and thereby providing designers and builders with the opportunity to use a variety of combinations of energy conservation measures.

D. Durability of materials

The Approved Document supporting Regulation 7 (materials and workmanship) does not specifically mention durability, but the section on short-lived materials contains guidance which is relevant, including the following paragraph (1.3):

Some materials, in the absence of special care, may be considered unsuitable because of their rapid deterioration in relation to the life of the building. It is not possible to set down any specific criteria from which the length of life of a material can be considered against the requirements of the Regulations. Often the selection of materials will be influenced by economic judgements which will not be proper considerations as matters affecting health and safety of persons in and around the building.

Ease of inspection, maintenance and replacement and the consequences of failure are also mentioned as factors affecting the suitability of a short-lived material in a particular situation.

Although the DOE doubts the need for any specific requirement for durability in relation to health or safety, and considers it would be very difficult to define, it has invited comments on this aspect of the Regulations.

Durability is a crucial element in the quality of materials appropriate to historic buildings, and a guidance document on their use could help considerably in maintaining appropriate standards.

E. Alterations

Since the recommendations in the Approved Documents are primarily directed at new construction, they tend to bear unduly onerously on alteration work, and it has been suggested that these could have a separate Code of recommendations for alteration work.

Although the DOE considers that there is now sufficient flexibility in the 1985 Regulations and their Approved Documents to cater for alteration work, the Department is interested to hear of problems that have arisen and for ways of improving the guidance.

4.2 Supervision of the Regulations

4.2.1 Introduction

Compliance with the Regulations is to be ensured through building work being supervised by means of either local authorities or approved inspectors.

The system of supervision by approved inspectors is set out in the Building (Approved Inspectors, etc) Regulations 1985 and could well be advantageous to historic building owners in that it may be possible to find sympathetic inspectors who have a profound depth of knowledge pertaining to works in historic buildings and who will be able to identify work which meets the standards of the Regulations without harming the historic character, structure and finishes of the building.

Parts of these Regulations were introduced on 1 September 1985, but to date only one body, the National House Builders' Council, has been recognised by the Minister as an approved inspectorate body. They have published well illustrated guidance documents of their approach to the new Regulations as they apply to housing provided by their members and which demonstrate the standards that they expect when they are appointed to act in this capacity.

The other professional bodies identified by the Minister, such as the RIBA, RICS and the Institute of Structural Engineers, have yet to establish the standards of requirements for any of their members wishing to serve in this capacity, and for which they will set examinations, etc. The main stumbling block involves resolving the problems of professional liability and therefore the necessary insurance cover indemnity and premiums, etc.

4.2.2 Local authority control

There are two forms of local authority control, known as 'deposit of full plans' and 'building notice' procedure.

A. Deposit of full plans

The local authority must pass or reject plans within five weeks, or up to two months if the applicant agrees to an extension of time. They can reject them if they contravene the Regulations, and are incomplete or unsatisfactory as regards one of the local authorities' 'linked powers', or any local Act. Instead of rejecting the application they can, with the written agreement of the applicant, approve it subject to the specified modification or the submission of further plans.

The applicant may also deposit a certificate stating that the plans show compliance regarding structural stability (Part A) and/or energy conservation (Parts L2 and 3), provided he is an approved person under Section 16 (9) of the Building Act and is covered by an approved insurance scheme. If so, the local authority cannot reject the plans on the grounds that they contravene the Regulations in respect of matters covered by the certificate.

B. Building notice procedure

Alternatively, the applicant can simply submit his application together with a site plan and any information prescribed in Regulation 12. However, this procedure is not possible if the work relates to means of escape (B1) and the building is intended to be put to a use designated under the Fire Precautions Act 1971, which concerns offices and shops.

C. Starting work

Work may start at any time after full plans or a building notice have been deposited, provided the local authority is given forty-eight hours notice of commencement. Further notices must be given at certain stages.

D. Contraventions

If a local authority considers that work contravenes the Regulations they may serve a notice under Section 36 of the Building Act requiring it to be altered or taken down within twenty-eight days. Failure to comply with a notice within this period allows the local authority to carry out the work themselves and to recover the costs from the owner. If the developer does not agree with the local authority he can submit a report of an independent expert and, should the local authority not withdraw the notice, he can appeal to the magistrate's court. A person contravening the provisions of the Building Regulations is also liable to a fine.

The local authority cannot serve a Section 36 notice for work which is shown on and conforms with 'full plans' passed by the local authority. They may, however, seek an injunction in the courts requiring alteration of the work. The court, in granting an injunction, may require the local authority to pay compensation to the owner.

4.2.3 Supervision by an approved inspector

A. Initial notice

If an approved inspector is to supervise the work, an 'initial notice' and a declaration that an approved scheme of insurance applies to the work must be given to the local authority. The authority has ten working days to consider the notice and may only reject it on grounds prescribed in Regulation 8 and Schedule 3 of the Regulations. If they do not reject it within the ten working days, they are presumed to have accepted it. It is a contravention to start work before the initial notice is accepted by the local authority.

B. Work in progress

The approved inspector is responsible for supervising the work and may require to be notified at certain stages. Except for minor work, such as the alteration or extension of a one- or two-storey house or work on services or fittings, the approved inspector must have no financial interest in the work.

The approved inspector must consult the fire authority if the regulations controlling means of escape under Schedule 1 (B1) apply. This would also be desirable in any case where the building is a type designated for control under the Fire Precautions Act 1971.

C. Certification

The approved inspector may certify by means of a 'plans certificate', issued to the local authority and the developer, that plans of the work (or part of it) comply with the Building Regulations.

When the work is complete, the approved inspector should give the local authority and the developer a final certificate. This must state that the work, or a specified part of it, is complete and that the approved inspector has discharged his building control functions.

The final certificate cannot be issued after a

new building or extension has been occupied for six weeks or, in the case of a building where means of escape is controlled by Section 1 of the Fire Precautions Act or Section 24 of the Building Act, after one day. If premature occupation occurs it can lead to the initial notice ceasing to have effect and the revival of the local authority's powers to enforce the regulations.

D. Withdrawal

The initial notice must be cancelled if the approved inspector cannot continue to supervise the work. If this happens another approved inspector can be appointed and a second initial notice be given to the local authority to cover any work which has not already been the subject of a final notice. Alternatively, the local authority will become responsible for supervising the work. In this event the local authority may require plans of parts of the work not covered by a final certificate. They will also require the full fee for the uncertified work as prescribed in the fees regulations.

If work continues following the withdrawal of an approved inspector and the cancellation of initial notice, the local authority may require that the work be opened up or pulled down so that they can check that uncertified work complies with the regulations.

E. Contraventions

Unlike a local authority, an approved inspector has no direct power to enforce the Building Regulations. He is, however, required to inform the developer if he believes that any work being carried out under his supervision contravenes the Building Regulations. If the work is not made to comply within three months he is obliged to cancel the initial notice. He must inform the local authority of the contravention unless a second approved inspector is taking over responsibility.

4.2.4 Relaxations and dispensation

If, because of special circumstances, it would be unreasonable to meet all the terms of a requirement of the Building Regulations in full, or at all, a local authority may grant an application for relaxation or dispensation of that requirement. Application for relaxation or dispensation should be made to the local authority even if an approved inspector is involved, as he has no power to dispense with or relax the requirements of the regulations. Should the local authority refuse to relax or dispense with a regulation, the applicant has the right to appeal within one month to the Secretary of State. Until that appeal is resolved, enforcement action for compliance is affectively suspended.

Regulations which are drafted as 'functional requirements' will not need to be 'relaxed' as it is implicit that the interpretation should be flexible and have regard to particular circumstances. The only regulations which are not drafted as 'functional requirements' are:

— Schedule 1 B1, means of escape;
— Schedule 1 L2 and L3, conservation of fuel and power; and
— Schedule 2, facilities for disabled people.

It may be necessary to apply for relaxation of these in cases where special circumstances apply as they contain 'specific requirements'.

Dispensation is the complete setting aside of a regulation and this will be possible for functional regulations as well as for specific ones when particular circumstances make them unreasonable.

4.2.5 Determinations

If the local authority rejects the application or the 'full plans' deposited for Building Regulations approval, or an approved inspector refuses to issue a plans certificate, on the grounds that they show a contravention of the Regulations, the aggrieved party may ask the Secretary of State for a determination.

4.3 Building Regulations in Inner London

4.3.1 Introduction

The Building (Inner London) Regulations were laid before Parliament on 16 December 1985 and came into force on 6 January 1986. They apply the national system of control to Inner London, except for the requirements for drainage, sanitary conveniences and solid waste storage. These will be applied at a later stage. The Regulations repeal and amend many of the London Acts, national Acts and even some parts of the Building Regulations. They bring into force in Inner London:

— the Building Act 1984 Sections 8, 9, 10, 16, 32, 36, 37, 39 and 40;
— the Building Regulations 1985;
— the Building (Approved Inspectors, etc) Regulations 1985; and
— the Building (Prescribed Fees, etc) Regulations 1985.

The Inner London Regulations repeal all the London building By-laws, many sections of the London Building Acts, and amend many other Regulations.

4.3.2 Remaining legislation

The Acts and sections which remain are as follows:

— London County Council (General Powers) Acts, 1954, 1955, 1956, 1958 and 1959;

— Greater London Council (General Powers) Acts, 1965, 1966, 1968, 1975, 1976 and 1978.

— The London Building Act 1930; Part XI: Dangerous and noxious businesses; and Part XII: Houses on low-lying land.

— The London Building Act (Amendment) Act 1935; Sections 1–3, 8, 11 and 14.

— All sections of the London Building Act (Amendment) Act 1939; except Sections 16–18, 22–8, 32, 71–2, 83–5, 92–3, 98–100, 127–31 and 140.

Section 20 (as modified by Schedule 3(2) of the Inner London Regulations) applies where a building has a storey at a greater height than 30 m (25 m for buildings of more than 930 m^2) or where a trade building has a volume of more than 7,100 m^3. Trade buildings can be divided up by division walls but, as they are not dealt with in regulations B2–B4, the requirements for their construction are given in detail. The Council can also require a wide range of fire protection, such as alarms, sprinklers, detectors, smoke extractors and access for fire fighting. Although Section 149 of the Act exempts a number of historic and other buildings from the operation of Section 20, the requirements of this Section are likely to have a significant effect on large period buildings in London.

Plans must be deposited with the Borough Council before any alterations are made. The Council has five weeks in which to give its decision (or longer by agreement) and must consult with the London Fire Authority before issuing a consent.

Sections 33–43 deal with means of escape in case of fire and, although buildings which are subject to the national Building Regulations B1 are exempt from 5.34, these Sections cover a wider range of buildings and more stringent conditions can be applied.

Sections 44–59 cover the rights of buildings and adjoining owners and are particularly relevant to historic buildings in congested areas.

Sections 60–70, dealing with dangerous and neglected structures, provide stiffer and more effective procedures than under the Building Act 1984.

Section 132 is concerned with the re-erection of buildings of architectural interest.

4.3.3. Organisation

Now that the responsibility of administering the Regulations has been transferred from the defunct GLC to the Boroughs, they are having to apply a combination of old and new legislation, making building control in Inner London more complex than in other parts of the country. Architects and builders are having to cope with modified national Building Regulations, with many modified sections of the London Building Acts and many general powers Acts. There are different definitions and fire requirements, different applications to be made, and different exemptions and enforcement measures.

However, this complexity can be justified as being necessary to retain the required standards of fire protection and fire safety, and the more effective means of dealing with party walls, contraventions and dangerous structures.

Although the number of district surveyors' districts has been reduced from twenty-eight to thirteen – one for each of the Inner London boroughs and the City – each is headed by a similarly titled 'principal building control officer/district surveyor'. *We have already commented on the high standards of achievement and the good working relationships resulting from the district surveyor system and we believe that these will still remain.*

4.4 The Fire Precautions Act 1971

In 1980 a Green Paper published by the Home Office entitled 'A Review of Fire Policy' pointed out that a great deal of fire service time and manpower has been taken up in the enforcement and administration of the Fire Precautions Act, but without being effective in reducing fire damage or loss of life. It is suggested that, in future, it would be more cost-effective to concentrate on the larger risk buildings only, employing some kind of two-tier system which would, at the lower level, not involve the amount of detailed inspections, surveys, documentation and record keeping that the fire service is required to do under the Act.

It also pointed out anomalies which had been revealed in applying the Act, where many premises which were more at risk than those defined in the Act were not being controlled.

A further consultative document was published in 1985, 'A Review of the Fire Precautions Act, 1971', which spelt out in far greater detail the basic proposals for reducing the costs of administering this Act, including extending the technique of 'self-regulation' so that it applied to building owners and occupiers in the same way that the Health and Safety at Work, etc, Act controls all places of work.

This document was published after the Bradford football ground disaster but before the Popplewell enquiry had completed its work. As a consequence a further consultative document was published in 1986, 'Fire Safety and Safety at Sport Venues', and included recommendations by the Home Office relating to 'A Review of the Fire Precautions Act, 1971' as follows:

— certification should be retained for normal and high risk premises;
— the fire authorities should have the powers to exempt premises in specific categories from the need to have a fire certificate;
— guidance should be drawn up to determine which premises may be considered a low risk and could be exempted;
— fire authorities should be notified of changes of use to determine if a previously exempted building should now be controlled;
— owner/occupiers of exempted buildings should be required to maintain reasonable means of escape and fire fighting equipment;
— a Code of Practice should be drawn up to set out how the statutory duty could be met and how a 'deemed to satisfy' procedure could be implemented. It should include a provision whereby owner/occupiers could fulfil their duties in other ways provided an equivalent standard was achieved;
— churches would no longer be exempt;
— no change would be made in the control of multi-use buildings;
— open spaces around buildings should be included in provisions for means of escape; and
— fire authorities should charge for the issue and amendment of fire certificates.

There are many items in this list which could be favourable to historic buildings but it will all depend on the definitions of low risk premises. We can only wait and see how the provisions will be met when the Bill is published, possibly in the 1986/7 Parliamentary session, in order to assess the changes in operation and application.

4.5 The Housing Acts

The various Housing Acts have been consolidated under the Housing Act 1985, and the relevant controls described in Chapter 1 are incorporated. Also, local housing authorities are authorised to make requirements for the improvement on the provision of means of escape in multi-occupation premises, and the Home Office has recently published a 'Guide to means of escape and related safety measures in certain houses of multiple occupation'. This generally applies to houses of at least three storeys (excluding basements) and with a total floor area of $500\,m^2$.

It is now possible to calculate the calorific load of the contents and wall and ceiling linings of rooms in historic buildings. From these figures, accurate assessments can be made of fire growth and heat and smoke generation in volume, temperature rise and cooking, and thereby the resultant layers of smoke. A clearer picture can be therefore be given of the risks to life in terms of escape time, fire brigade access, etc. Such a process could prove far more beneficial in preserving the character of historic buildings than the strict interpretation of legislative requirements. See, for example, Case Studies Nos 9C and 9D, Hardwick Hall, Derbyshire, and Cliveden Manor, Buckinghamshire.

A more flexible approach may well arise from the additional rationalisation of the 1985 Building Regulations Act discussed in para 4.1.16.

Case Study 7: Hotels and Public Houses

The Fire Precautions Act is by far the most significant piece of legislation for hotels, and the Licensing Act has the same significance for public houses.

One effect of the Fire Precautions Act on hotels which has been brought to our attention is the closure of establishments where the cost of meeting the requirement was too great. At Kenny's Manor in Chepstow, plans to develop a public house into a hotel were abandoned in the face of these costs. An attempt to find a use for a greater part of the building has been frustrated. However, damaging alterations have not been made and a suitable alternative may be found instead. These points are further discussed in Chapter 4.

The problems raised by legislation in hotels and to a lesser extent in pubs are:

— the provision of alternative means of escape;
— the provision of fire resistance in walls and floors to safeguard the means of escape; and
— the expense of installing and maintaining detection, alarm and emergency lighting installations.

A. The Lady in Grey and Broughton House, Shardlow, Derbyshire

These are two different buildings about one hundred yards apart, in common ownership. The Lady in Grey is a two- and three-storey group of buildings, parts of which are probably eighteenth and others nineteenth century. Broughton House is a small, eighteenth-century Georgian mansion with two storeys.

The Lady in Grey is *Listed Grade II* and Broughton House is *II**

Legislation

The Lady in Grey has been run as a licensed restaurant with residential accommodation above. Broughton House was in use as offices for some time, but fell into a poor state of repair. It had no grounds and when new users were being sought this shortcoming proved to be a major limitation. The owner of the Lady in Grey, whose grounds adjoined Broughton House, eventually bought it with a view to converting it into a bedroom annexe. He was also extending the guest accommodation at the Lady in Grey and so both buildings were involved in the fire precautions certification process at the same time.

Means of escape

The fire authority officer who inspected Broughton House told the owner that an alternative stair would be required from the upper floor and that the existing main stair would have to be enclosed. This posed several problems. The county historic buildings officer, who was involved in the discussions, considered that an external stair was not likely to be acceptable. Not only would a new internal stair take up usable floor space, but there was no obvious place for a new stair that did not affect the architectural character of the interior. Listed building consent might therefore have been unobtainable. The enclosure of the head of the main stair would also have posed listed building consent problems as it would have destroyed the spatial effect. The solution to this impasse came when the owner agreed to use the first floor of Broughton House as his own flat, and convert his former flat on the first floor of the Lady in Grey into guest rooms. The ground floor doors onto the stair in Broughton House were required to have fire resistance of half an hour, but no enclosure or second stair was required.

The Lady in Grey, Shardlow, Derbyshire Approximate scale 1:200

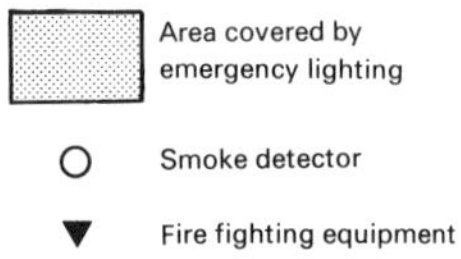

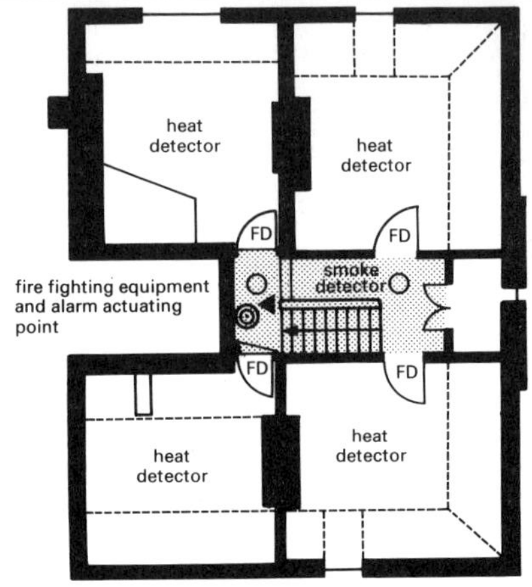

Second floor plan

First floor plan

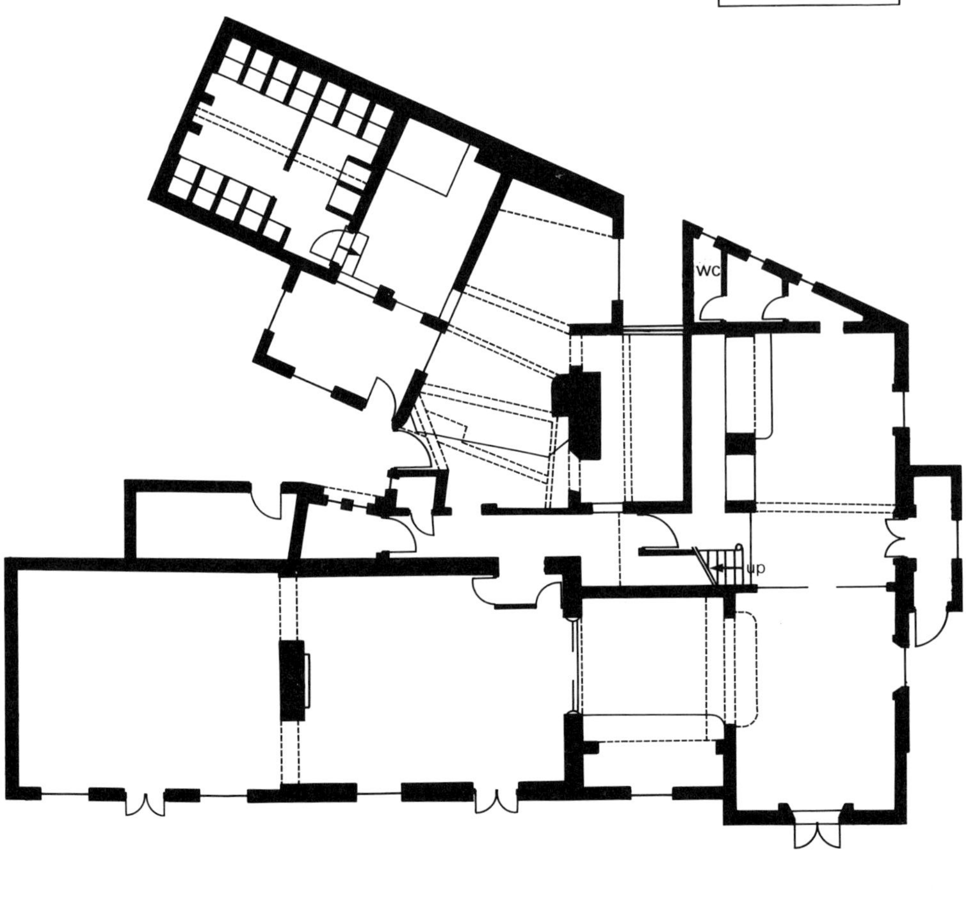

Ground floor plan

Broughton House
Approximate scale
1:200

Area covered by emergency lighting

○ smoke detector

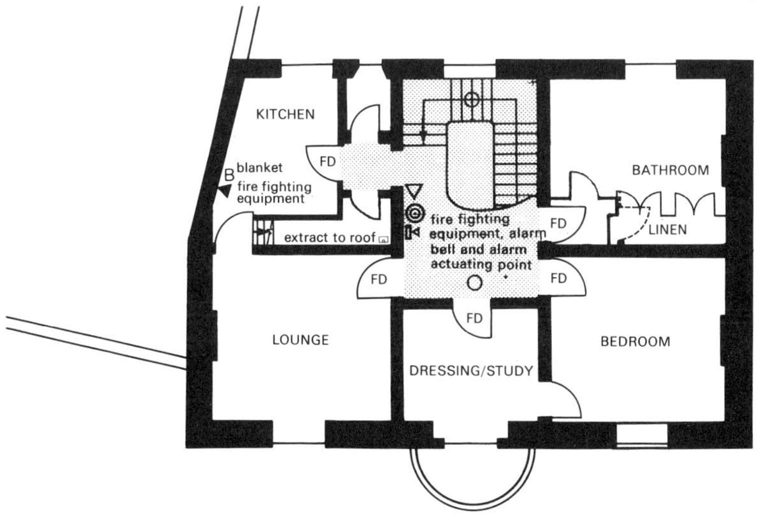

Second floor plan

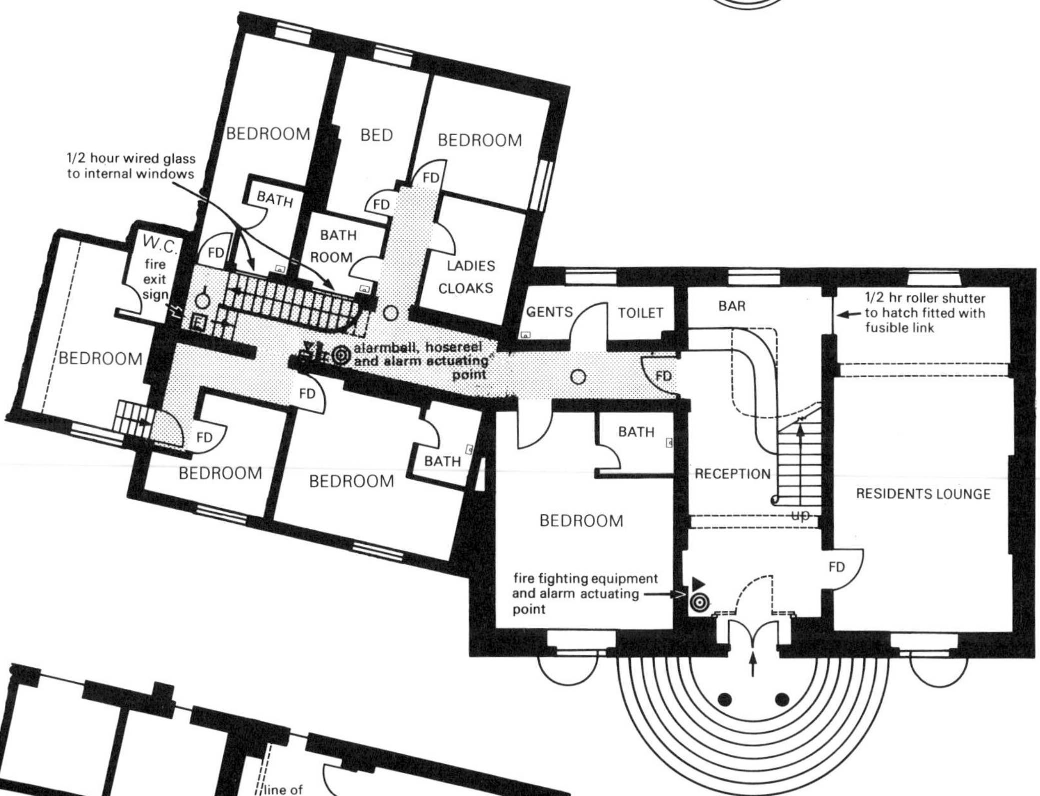

First floor plan

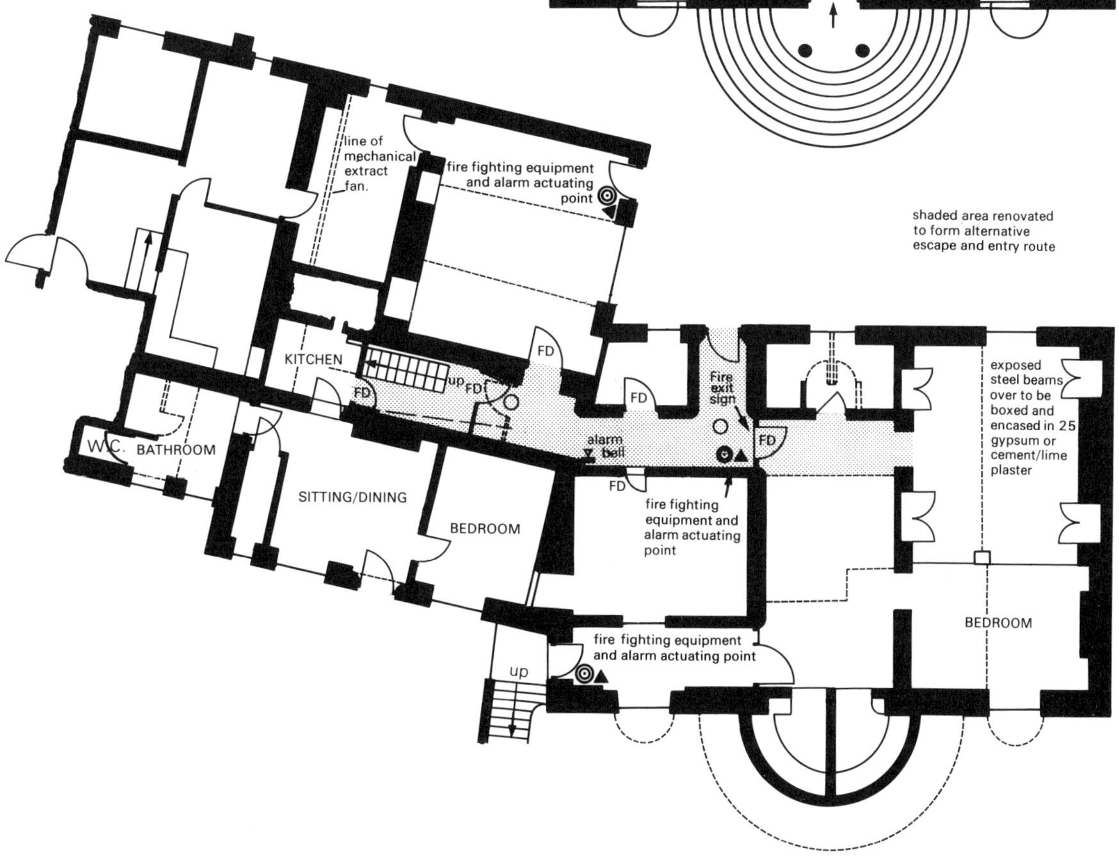

Ground floor plan

In the Lady in Grey there were two stairs from the first floor. Neither stair was important in a historic building sense and their protection did not damage the character of the buildings. The main stair is not enclosed at ground level and the exit from it is through the reception and lounge area.

Fire detection

The fire authority required automatic fire detection covering the stairs and corridors. The owner decided to extend the coverage with heat detectors in all first floor bedrooms.

Doors

The character of the rooms has been harmed by the measures to upgrade their panelled doors to a half-hour fire resisting standard by infilling the panels on the room side and sheeting over the whole face of the door with fire resisting material.

Reference: Para 2.4.1B

B. The Wig and Mitre, Lincoln

This important building, close to the Cathedral precincts, was originally one of three fourteenth-century tenements of timber construction with a range fronting the narrow medieval street and, in the case of this particular building, a large two-storey hall to the rear. Much of the original timber had been replaced with brick. Before the application was made to turn it into a public house, it had been partly used as a shop with storage and display in the hall. There was a conflict between the conservationist desire to preserve the remaining details of timber construction and the fire resistance principles embodied in Building Regulations 1976 and the Fire Precautions Act.

Architect: Brian Wright of Simons Design Services Ltd

Listed Grade II

Building Regulations

There was a party wall of timber studs with plaster infill panels. In order to expose this as a feature and yet provide adequate fire resistance, the whole wall was treated with an intumescent paste.

The roof structure was to be made visible and new oak was used in the repair. No fire resistance was required by the Regulations for roof structures. To satisfy the building control officer, new purlins had to be put in to stiffen the structure against lateral forces.

Elsewhere the timber construction was covered up except that a 'representative sample' of the lime-ash on reed walling was made visible behind a fire resisting glass panel. A section of the attic floor, also of lime-ash on reed, was retained, having been given a surface flame spread treatment (this section is not walked on, only looked at).

There were timber lintels over the fireplaces in the seventeenth-century chimney stack. To comply with Building Regulations controlling the proximity of combustible material to hearths, fireplaces and flues, stone lintels were required, despite the precedent of three centuries and the possible use of A7 of the 1976

The bar of the Wig and Mitre

The Wig and Mitre, Lincoln Approximate scale 1:200

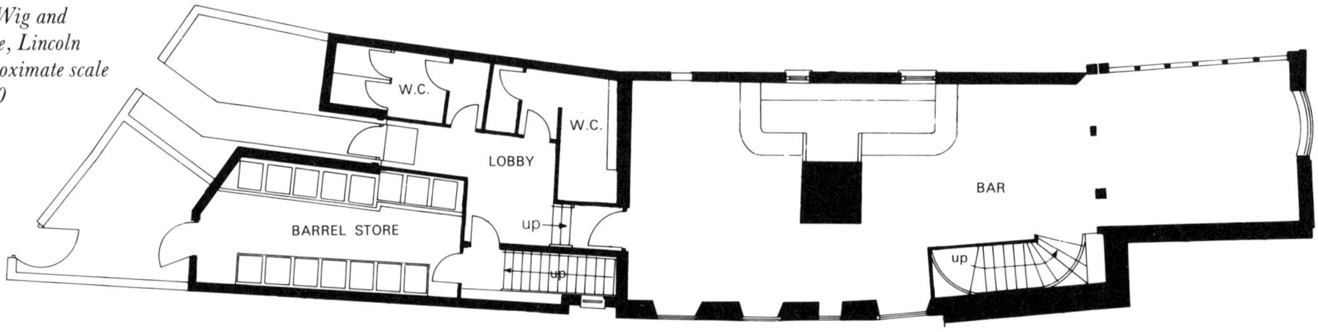

First floor plan

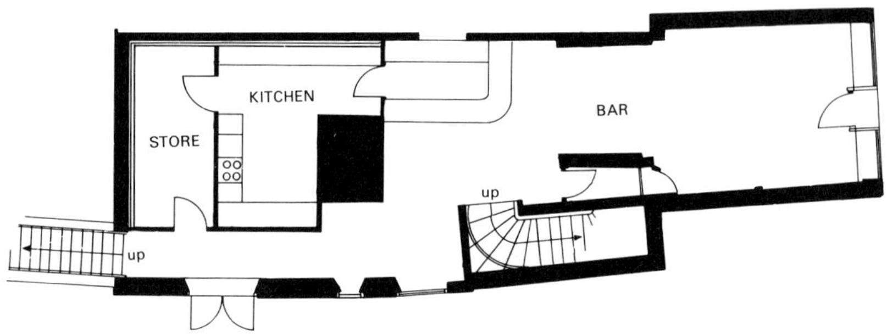

Ground floor plan

Regulations, under which the existing fabric should not have contravened the Regulations any more than it did before the alterations were carried out.

Means of escape

To have protected the stair with a lobby enclosure at the main stairhead would have intruded very badly into the first floor bar. This was avoided by separating the stair from the rest of the accommodation at ground level by using a large new self-closing door. It is held open magnetically and closed automatically if the smoke detectors are triggered. The building control authority did not object to the absence of a landing resulting from this arrangement.

Reference: Para 2.2.20

Front entrance to the Wig and Mitre

Case Study 8: Shops

We have found that problems tend to occur where an attempt is made to combine the shop with some other use or uses on the upper floors, as shown in Case Study 1. Fire precautions and Building Regulations 1976 are the two areas of legislation we found most likely to affect the use of historic buildings as shops.

A. John O'Port's House, Salisbury

This building forms part of a china shop and became involved in Building Regulations 1976 and Fire Precautions Act requirements as a result of a phased programme of internal alterations. Considerable efforts were made to expose the medieval timber structure and to avoid having to enclose the old stairs and gallery.

Architect: Brandt Potter and Partners

Listed Grade I

Means of escape

The shop is a little over 33 m deep and escape is possible at ground level at the front. Because a large new development was being carried out at the rear of the site it was also possible to arrange new exits (to car park and service areas of the new development) from ground, first and second floor levels. The main problem for escape was at the second floor office area over the front of the shop, and from the gallery immediately below it in the shop. The stairs serving these areas were old and the architects and owner neither wanted to move them nor to enclose them below the level of the gallery. The gallery overlooks a double height space which is spanned by a hammer beam structure and it was desirable that this space should not be altered by enclosing the gallery or stairs. The solution was to provide an alternative route leading from the gallery upwards through the second floor office and thence via a hatch and ladder into the store room, from which a new exit to the car park could be provided at the back. The stair up to the second floor was enclosed at its head, where a heat detector was also fitted. There were some very low (1.7 m) roof beams in the office which coincided with tie beams 200 mm high at floor level, but it was accepted by the fire authority that nothing could reasonably be done to change this. The arrangement of an exit from the office to the rear part of the building involved reconciling the fire officer's requirements for an easily traversed route with the practical limitations on cutting through parts of the timber structure and the formation of openings.

The owners required an accommodation stair near the back of the shop for customer circulation; the fire authority asked for this to be enclosed either at head or foot so that smoke could not spread up it, since this would prevent first floor occupants reaching the exit at the rear.

Structure

Only the ground floor of the shop had been used for the previous forty years. The old roof structure, wall framing and its trefoil windows, etc, had been concealed behind a succession of alterations in previous centuries; the present owners were unaware of their existence and had been thinking of demolition and rebuilding rather than restoration. When the historic importance of the structure became apparent – the roof structure is one of the earliest known examples of its type – the building control and fire officers were advised and both agreed that the timber frame and trusses could be exposed without causing a fire hazard. The building control officer was satisfied with the architects' repair proposals without calling for detailed structural calculations to back them up. *The end result is most satisfactory.*

Reference: Para 2.4.1B

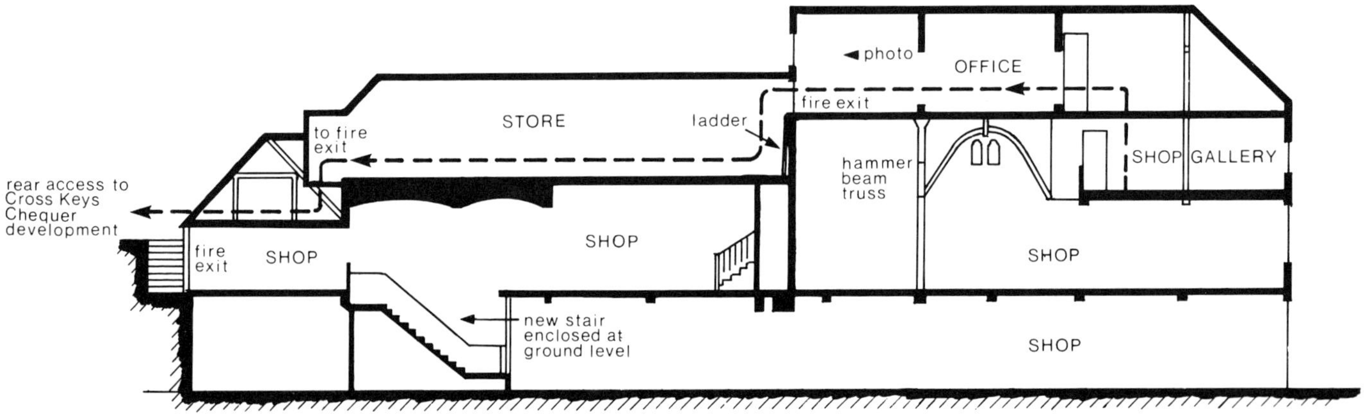

Section

- - - - - escape route

Second floor plan

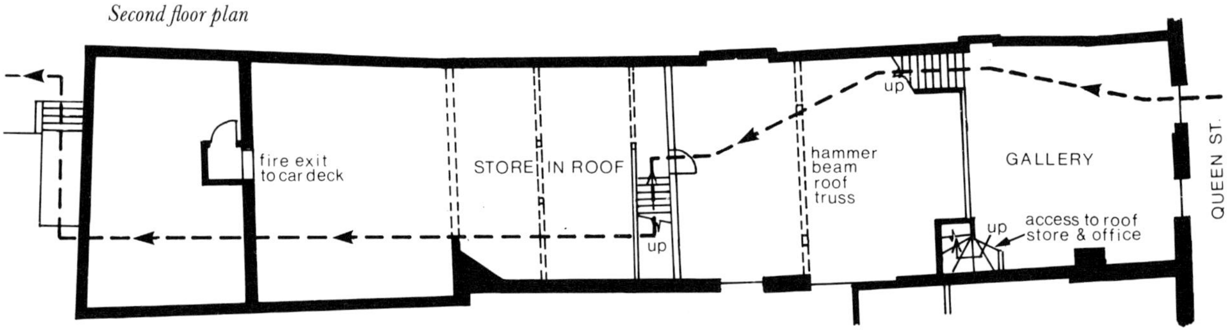

John O'Port's House, Salisbury Approximate scale 1:200

B. No. 12 Newgate, York

This three-storey, timber-framed, medieval building was regarded by the City of York conservation officer as a classic example of the problems that are presented by this building type. The small size of the premises is the root cause of many of the difficulties. In this case Building Regulations 1976, environmental health and means of escape considerations were involved.

Architects: Brierly Leckenby Keighley and Groom

Listed Grade II

No. 12 Newgate, York

Second floor

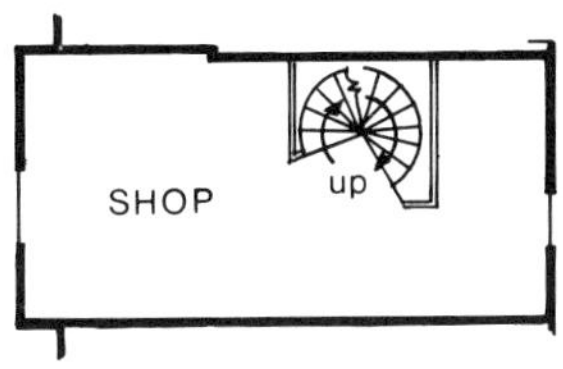

First floor

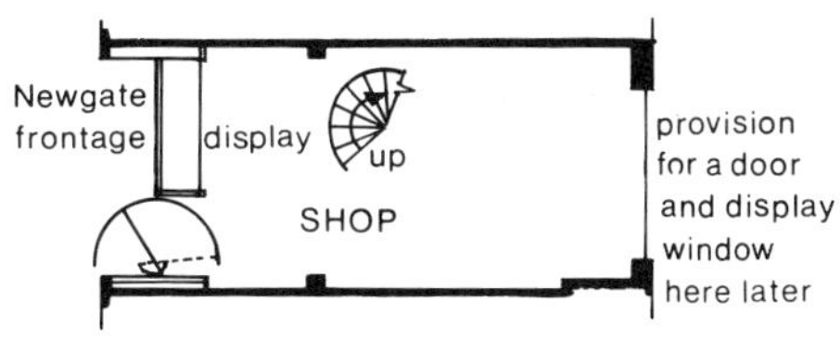

Ground floor

The project

The client wanted to convert the building, which had previously been a house, into a showroom and shop on the ground and first floors and associated office space on the top floor. The gross floor area was less than 20 m^2 at each level. Dual access for customers was required at ground floor level. Floor to ceiling heights varied between 2.4 m at ground level and 2.16 m at first floor to 2.26 m at the highest part of the coombed top floor.

Means of escape

The existing stairs were steep, narrow and winding. They were to be replaced and, between 1969 and 1973, several different arrangements were investigated, none of which could be protected for escape purposes without taking up a substantial proportion of the floor area. The fire authority considered that an alternative route was essential from the top floor and this became a requirement under the Offices, Shops and Railway Premises Act. An agreement was negotiated with the owner of the adjoining property for a party wall opening into his attic. Steps were built up to the floor level of this attic and a door 1.78 m high was formed, fitted with glass bolts so that it could be opened from either side in an emergency.

Building Regulations

There is no requirement to compartment a shop of this size and, in the 1972 Regulations, shops of less than 150 m^2 such as this could have zero structural fire resistance above ground floor level. Because of the small floor area, the ceiling required only a class 3 surface spread of flame classification, enabling a simple treatment to be used. The floorboards were lifted for repairs and, before relaying, a cellulosic insulation board was laid fair face down on the joists. The fair face then provided the ceiling finish for the room below and the joists were left exposed. This would not have been permitted under the 1976 Regulations.

Despite the low floor to floor height, it was not possible to fit in a stair which complied with the Regulations. A spiral stair was used for its compactness but, to meet the 38° pitch line requirement, it should have had a larger diameter than the 725 mm available. This dimension was fixed by the clearance needed on the top floor from the steps to the emergency exit and for a passage to the WC cubicle.

Environmental health

Before the conversion there was a WC at the back of the ground floor. This area was to become one of the two entrances. After considerable discussion with the authorities it was accepted that a single WC in a compartment under a new dormer on the top floor would be adequate.

Reference: Para 3.3.1

C. The Central Market Building, Covent Garden, London WC2

This three-storey building (including the extensive basements) was erected in 1830 for the Covent Garden fruit and vegetable market. In its original form it consisted of four parallel rows with aisles between them. At the east end the buildings were linked by a stone terrace. In 1875 and 1890 the south and north aisles were covered by cast-iron and glass roofs whose structures are independent of the original buildings.

The traders' accommodation consisted of basement storage, reached through floor hatches and steep ladder stairs, ground floor 'shop' spaces with access from both sides, and first floor offices above the shops which were also reached by steep timber stairs. The basement was something of a warren. Two firemen have been killed in fires there since the Second World War.

Architects: GLC Department of Architecture and Civic Design

Listed Grade II

Legislation

Until local government reorganisation and the formation of the GLC, the market was, by an Act of Parliament, outside the scope of any Building Regulations. When the market moved out of central London in 1974, the need for fire safety improvements was one of the many factors involved in the selection of a new use for the building. After some debate the GLC decided to develop it themselves into a shopping arcade with allied facilities such as restaurants and a pub. The physical form of the development was also discussed at length. Here the choice was whether or not to remove the Victorian glazed roofs. In addition to the historical or philosophical arguments, this was of great significance from a building control point of view since, with the roofs retained, the building would come within the scope of Section 20 of the London Building Acts (Amendment Act) 1939 because of the volume of the space they covered.

Compartmentation

The Building Regulations division accepted the use of the basement for shopping but favoured restricting the size of individual units as much as possible. Some basements interconnected and most shops and basements had exits at front and rear.

Means of escape

Access to the basement had been improved by forming two major stair wells in the ground floor and providing other stairs to basement level direct from the outside. No unprotected connection between ground and first floor accommodation was allowed by the Building Regulations division and new timber stairs were formed serving the first floor directly. The ground and first floors were required to have one hour's fire resistance.

For historical reasons the shop fronts were rebuilt in timber and small panes of glass were used as this was in the interests of both restoration and fire safety. Since the original doors were very narrow and unacceptable for

The Central Market Building, Covent Garden, London WC2 Approximate scale 1:500

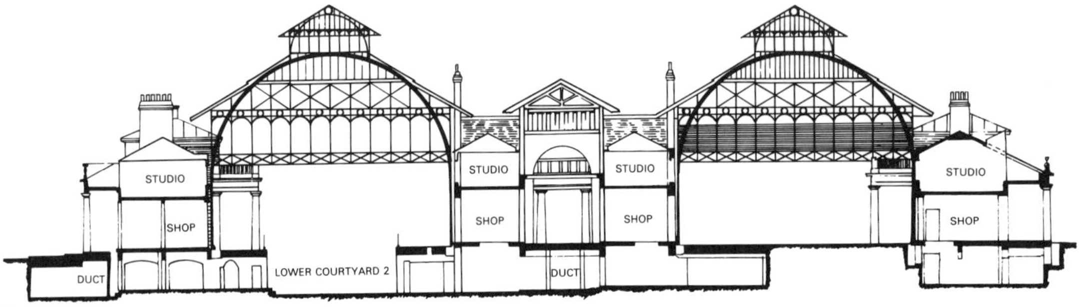

Section looking west

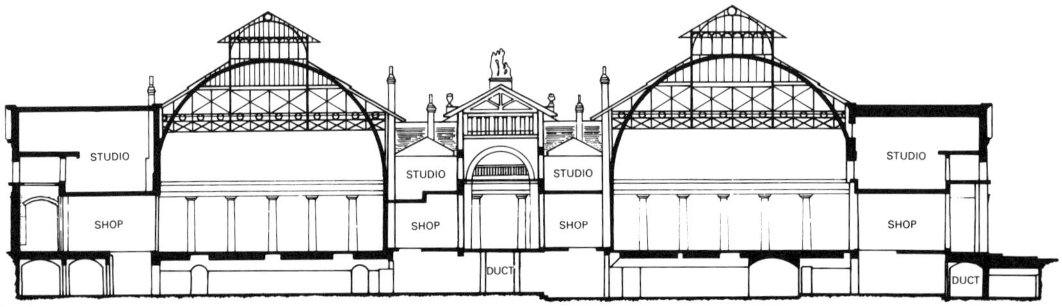

Section looking east

Basement plan

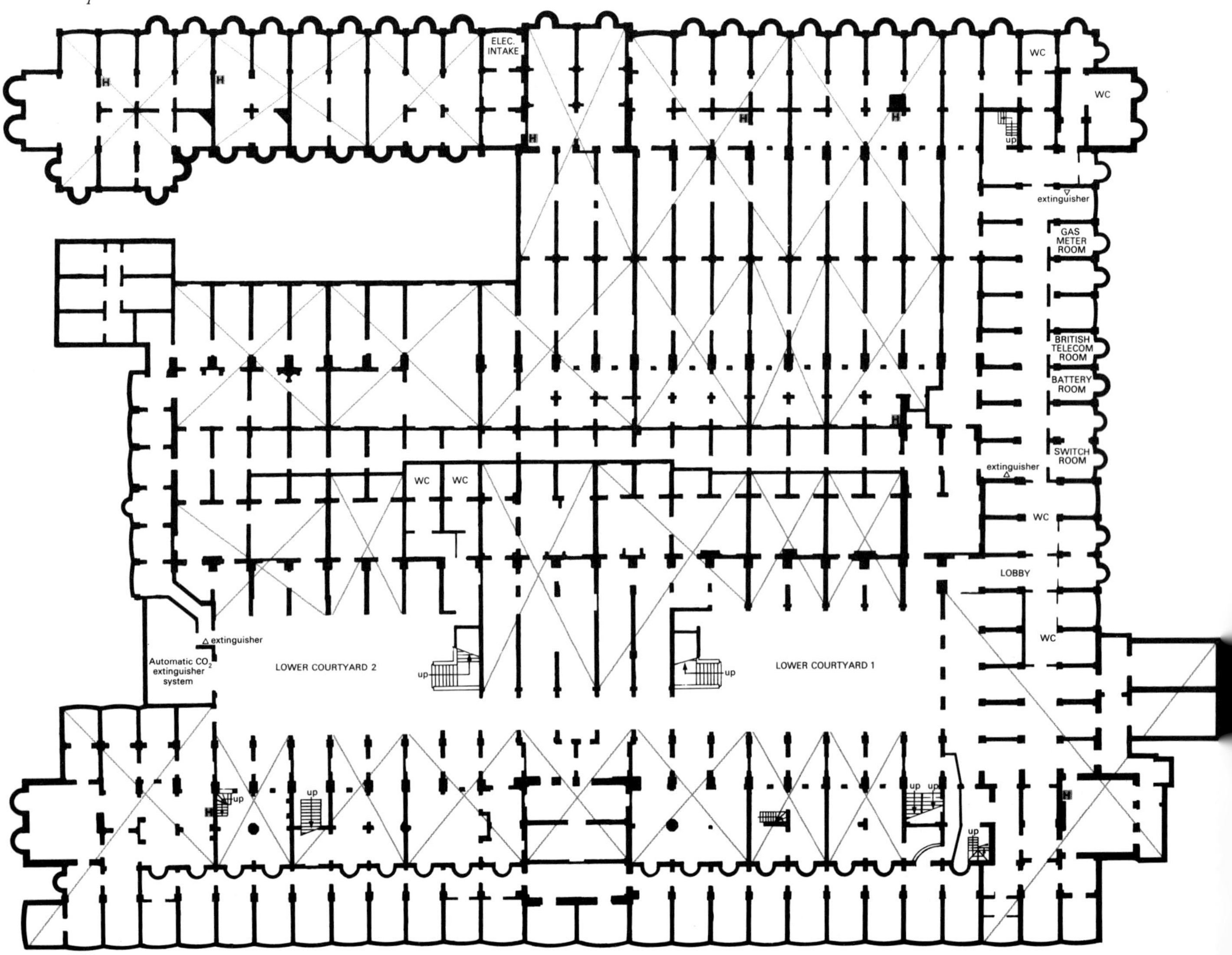

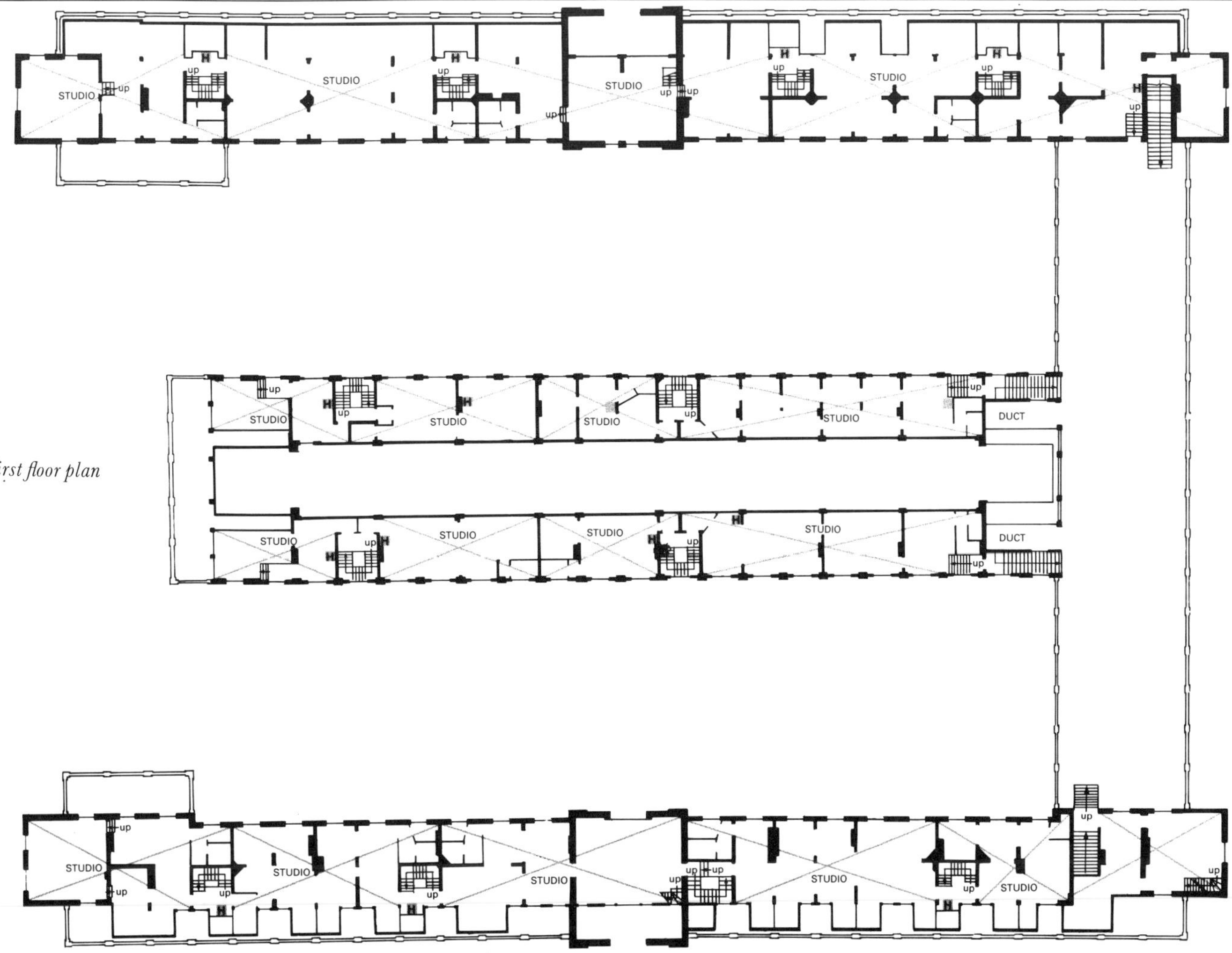

First floor plan

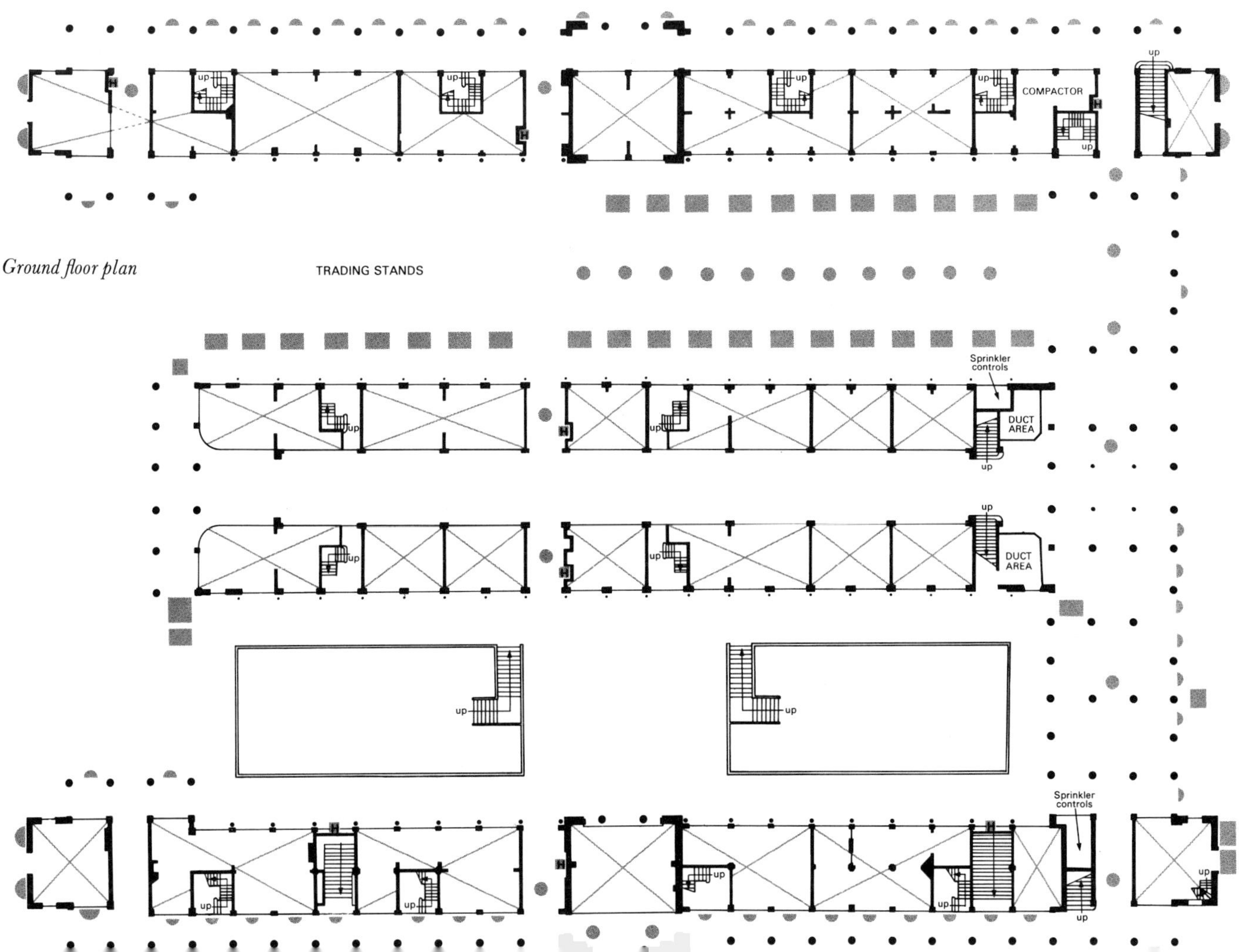

Ground floor plan

means of escape purposes, the new fronts have double doors, each leaf being approximately the width of the original.

The use of the first floor was also the subject of protracted debate. At the time of the approval given under the London Building Acts and By-laws (1976) it was to be a mixture of shops and artists' or craftsmen's studios. More emphasis was later placed on office uses, but the Building Regulations division accepted specialist shops where low customer density can reasonably be expected.

Sprinklers

Sprinklers were required throughout. It was considered that the cast-iron columns in the shops and first floor rooms required protection from fire. An external drencher system was avoided by positioning some of the sprinkler heads close to the windows.

Fire resistance

The 6 mm-thick intumescent coating required on the cast-iron columns has resulted in a certain loss of detail. The need for fire resistant partitions inside the building did not cause great difficulty because it was not considered necessary to preserve the original interiors.

The roof was glazed with wired glass and the timber boarding of the unglazed sections near the eaves was replaced with non-combustible material, at intervals, to form fire-breaks and prevent lateral fire spread.

Smoke control

Smoke vents were required from the basement and from the new stairways to the first floors. The pavement vents are breakout panels and the stair vents have been designed as openable rooflights. Neither type is visually intrusive.

References: Paras 2.2.8 and 2.4.5

5

Historic buildings as a special case

5.1 Establishing Standards for Historic Buildings

5.1.1 The creation and aims of standards

There are a number of different ways in which standards are created:

— established practice: the results of trial and error over many years are embodied in codes or regulations;
— expert consensus: similar to the above but more deliberate and on a shorter time-scale with experts discussing alternatives and agreeing on a suitable standard;
— recognised authority: differs from the above two points in that the expert passes judgement on each case through personal involvement (e.g. the building control officer's function when the regulation stipulates that matters are to be to the local authority's satisfaction);
— practical tests: experiments are carried out to find parameters of acceptable performance or establish acceptable 'type specifications';
— theory: mathematical theory, probably derived from practical experimentation, developed into a quantitative method of assessment (such as loadbearing properties of a structural section); and
— political: responding to public disquiet over a particular matter (e.g. furniture flammability regulations).

In practice most standards are set by more than one of these methods.

5.1.2 Subjectivity

One thing that they all have in common is subjectivity. Even such apparently objective topics as structural engineering are based on such subjective assessments as safety margins. One may, for example, design a structure to resist winds of up to, say, 120 mph, because the meteorological evidence is that winds in excess of this are unlikely to occur more than once in 150 years; but this does not rule out the possibility of the structure being blown down, it just makes that eventuality *reasonably* unlikely. In other instances we have only the most general notion of how safe or healthy a building, or feature of a building, may be and cannot 'rate' different solutions to legislative requirements in any precise way.

5.1.3 Recognition for historic buildings

If we consider this balance in the case of historic buildings, there are a number of patently subjective factors, such as aesthetics and historic interest, which favour doing as little as possible to change the building, its surroundings or its contents. When the standards were set in all these matters of health, safety, etc, it is unlikely that historic building factors were taken into account. Standards are concerned with the protection of people. People are considered to warrant the same protection whether they are in old buildings or new ones, and the fact that it is difficult, if not impossible, to achieve this protection in old buildings is not a consideration when the standard itself is set.

But as interest in historic buildings has become more widespread, various steps have been taken to add historic building considerations to the balance. There are planning and listed building controls which have power to stop standards being applied where they do harm in historic building terms, but these, of themselves, do not solve the problem where alteration, extension or change of use is required. However, there are also official pronouncements, such as DOE Circular 8/87, encouraging those who enforce legislation to take these special factors into consideration and, tacitly, to make *ad hoc* adjustments to the standards. And there are clauses in legislation permitting relaxations which may be interpreted as legitimate grounds for making special exceptions, such as where the particular application of a regulation could be considered to be 'unreasonable', or to 'vary the provisions'.

The kind of standards liable to affect historic buildings are set out in Table 9.

As all these standards are compromises between competing factors, it seems reasonable that, where there is no evidence of existing standards taking historic factors into consideration in the compromise, the relevant legislation should be amended to take into account the historic and architectural value of the buildings, and any representations made to the relevant authorities about that value.

5.1.4 The realisation of standards

Standards may be expressed in several ways. If expressed in performance terms, the designer has discretion to meet that performance in whichever way best suits the circumstances. The standard may be expressed as material specifications, such as the deemed-to-satisfy specifications and Approved Documents of the Building Regulations, which are rarely written with any thought to historic building construction. Or they may be imposed as rules of thumb, such as the need to provide a window area of at least one-tenth of the floor area to

Table 9. The legislative standards which most detrimentally affect historic buildings

Element of building affected	Type of harmful requirement	Type of harm done				
		Sub-divide	Extend	Conceal	Alter	Remove
Spatial quality	Fire compartmentation or means of escape enclosure		●			
	Structural strengthening		●			
Construction	Increase fire resistance			●	●	●
	Structural strengthening or repair		●		●	●
	Damp proofing		●	●	●	
	Seal for openings for compartmentation				●	
	Increase floor to ceiling heights				●	●
	Make construction non-combustible					●
	Accommodate new escape route	●				●
	Provide sprinkler system		●	●	●	
Components	Increase fire resistance of doors, floors, etc		●	●	●	●
	Safety guards to mechanisms (mills)			●	●	
	Reducing gaps between balusters		●	●	●	
	Increase window area				●	●
	Add handrails		●			
	Make stairways conform to regulations				●	●
	Seal window or door openings as part of compartmentation or escape protection			●	●	●
	Increase doorway height or width				●	●
	Hang door to open outwards				●	
	Timber fireplace lintel made non-combustible					●
	Structural strengthening		●		●	●
Finishes	Improve flame-spread properties			●	●	●
	Provide non-combustible finishes			●		●
	Increase fire resistance		●	●	●	●
	Make hygienic (foodstuff handling)		●	●	●	●
	Damp proofing			●		●
	Add equipment and fittings, e.g. fire bells		●		●	●
Exterior	Add external escape stairway		●	●	●	●
	Improve daylighting or ventilation		●		●	●
	Increase floor to ceiling height (e.g. attics)		●		●	●
	Damp proofing (reduce ground level)				●	
	Make windows fire resisting to protect external escape route		●	●	●	●
	Dangerous structure		●		●	●
	Provide sight line for highway				●	●
	Provide new access to highway				●	●
	Provide car parking space		●	●	●	●

ensure adequate daylight.

The weakness of specifying the performance rating is that there is considerable scope for disagreement as to whether a proposal will have the required performance. On the other hand, material or 'type' specifications suffer from inflexibility and may have to be rewritten to take account of new developments in knowledge or materials. They are very hard to write in such a way as to be appropriate to the wide variety of situations to be found in historic buildings. Rules of thumb are even more inflexible and can only be applied to very simple circumstances; even then, they can cause anomalies.

As flexibility is so important in designing for historic buildings, the performance type of standard seems better suited to these problems than the others. In order to prove that a particular solution satisfies the standard, the designer must call on test results or other precedents. Unfortunately there is a severe shortage of this sort of information relating to historic building construction and materials. Sometimes, there are no significant differences between old and new construction; for example, the use of BS CP 112: Part 2: 1971 is equally acceptable for the calculation of stability in old or new timber structures (although it does not necessarily resolve differences of opinion about load transfer and joint conditions). In some respects, historic buildings may provide a higher standard than modern ones, for instance in the reduction of noise transmission. In other areas, the standards they provide are inadequate because they were put up before the modern condition arose (for example, provision for motor vehicles). The most difficult problems arise in the large 'grey' areas where we do not know, other than in a general qualitative way, how old materials perform. Fire safety is the field where this shortage of information is most noticeable and most crucial. Any attempt to improve the situation for historic buildings should start with research into these aspects.

5.2 The Need for Further Research

5.2.1 Fire resistance

Various materials and structural elements are widely accepted as having x hours' fire resistance, either as a result of tests of proprietary fire resisting materials incorporated within traditional construction and published by manufacturers, or because they have been reported by the Fire Research Station and incorporated in guidance documents, such as BRE Digest 208 (Upgrading the Fire Resistance of Timber Floors). However, these tests represent few examples of historic building construction, and the expense of a BS 476: Part 8 fire resistance test is too great to be contemplated by most building owners. Therefore, the authorities are driven to assess the adequacy of existing or 'upgraded' construction by extrapolating the known behaviour of a material in different circumstances. It should be recognised that much 'fire resistance' is therefore notional, which is not very satisfactory when one considers the significant effects that such requirements can have on historic buildings.

With those elements which are most frequently affected and can be relatively easily tested, such as doors, efforts should be made at a national level to establish the actual performance of a representative selection of designs, materials and vintages, in terms of BS 476: Part 8. Our impression is that many such doors could be accepted for fire resisting duties (half hour or 30/20) with less radical alteration than is commonly required at present. Sheeting over an old door, for example, implies that it has no fire resistance at all since the sheeting on its own could satisfy the half-hour requirement. The effect of protective coatings of the intumescent type could also be examined in these tests in the hope that the uncertainties, which have lead to the widely varying attitudes of authorities, would be resolved.

Work in progress at the Fire Research Station on the fire behaviour of cast iron, and various techniques for its upgrading will be published at the earliest opportunity. Similarly, research papers on the performance of historic doors and frames should be made available. Information on types of fire resisting glass which could provide alternatives to the standard Georgian wired variety have been described in a 'draft for development' to be published by British Standards under the BS 5588 series; this includes assessments to tests under BS 476: Part 8.

5.2.2 Means of escape

There is a tremendous potential for research of a similar kind in the fire safety field, but unfortunately the basic information is more difficult to come by. Means of escape requirements have become more stringent, particularly in the last twenty years, and the fire statistics indicate that improvements in safety may have resulted. There are signs, for example, of a reduced injury rate in hotel fires which may reflect the now widespread implementation of the Fire Precautions Act. However, there are so many possible extraneous influences that one cannot draw conclusions from these figures about the particular effects in historic buildings. What effect has the upgrading or provision of fire doors on safety in an historic building fire? Does it delay discovery of the fire? Are the doors open when the fire occurs and do the occupants close them? Do they delay fire spread by an amount critical to life safety? Are occupants confused or even trapped by fire doors? Research into human behaviour in fires has attracted much interest in recent years; the Fire Research Station carried out a study of fires in modern school buildings based on post-fire surveys. A similar technique applied to fires in historic buildings might yield equally useful information, not only about fire doors but about all aspects of structural fire precautions, means of escape, detection, and human behaviour related to them.

5.2.3 Heat and smoke generation calculations

While all those involved with fire safety in buildings recognise that smoke and toxic products of the fire are the most common killers, none of the legislation is directly concerned with smoke control.

The provision of lobbies with fire doors and two-door protection to stairways are measures that should tend to reduce smoke spread, but it was only with the appearance of BS 5588: 1978 that an authoritative guide on means of positively controlling smoke movements in offices and shops became available. Instead of traditional space-dividing methods of fire precaution which can spoil historic buildings, the partial substitution of smoke control by pressurisation could be of considerable benefit. But, although this standard exists, there is as yet little sign of its use in historic buildings. At Worcester College, Oxford, the Oxfordshire Fire Service was most cooperative and open-minded in its approach to a novel proposal (Case Study No. 12A). It is to be hoped that other authorities take a similar position. The prime reason for the rarity of smoke control systems in historic buildings is that very few architects or engineers have either experience or knowledge of them.

5.2.4 Future developments in fire safety

A report commissioned by the Building Research Station and written by H. L. Malhotra, 'Fire Safety in Buildings',* may lead to the creation of a comprehensive package of fire safety requirements based on its recommendations which would involve a radical revision of Part B of the 1985 Building Regulations.

5.2.5 Accidents

There is a wealth of information on accidents in the home and elsewhere. An examination might show whether the pattern of accidents in old and new buildings reflected the benefit of such features as stairway design as controlled by Building Regulations.

5.2.6 Environmental health

We do not know if any work has been done on the health aspects of housing fitness standards in recent years, but none of the authorities who have shown reluctance to depart from a rigid enforcement policy has referred us to any such research in support of their attitude. It would be very interesting to have factual information on the occupants of those historic buildings that have been brought up to standard to see whether the health/housing fitness requirements benefited them significantly.

5.3 Relaxations

Table 9 sets out the kinds of requirements that were liable to harm particular features of historic buildings. The case studies illustrate ways around many of these problems, either within previous or existing standards or through their sympathetic or liberal interpretation. They also show that there have been persistent stumbling blocks. Given the change in balance with such clauses as 'varying the provisions' in the new Building Regulations, etc, and the extra scientific and research information that we have suggested, it should be possible to write supporting codes on historic buildings that enable performance standards to be applied in a more straightforward way. It will, however, never be possible to cover all contingencies in any written code or advice, and legislation will therefore need to have relaxation and appeal arrangements. A relaxation of the Building Regulations may be made where the effect of applying a regulation would be unreasonable. There is no definition of 'unreasonable' and there is thus uncertainty as to the intentions of the legislators. Because it is possible to solve most building problems if enough money is available, debate on what is 'unreasonable' often comes down to a question of money. This is especially so in historic buildings where both materials and craftsmen's labour are expensive and the uncertainties of radical alterations result in unpredictable additional costs to a contract.

See Case Study 12A, pp. 145-8

If authorities ignored the need for financial restraints, much more would be required to be done to promote health and safety in buildings. The need for some degree of cost effectiveness is recognised in legislation in that there are limits on the statutory requirements. The position in law has been stated by Lord Denning in the Court of Appeal in a case concerning an action brought by Kingston-

* 'Fire Safety in Buildings' is available from the BRE, Garston, Watford WD2 7JR, price £10.00.

upon-Hull City Council against the University of Hull under Section 16 of the Housing Act 1961. The university had been required to do fire precautions work in 147 houses which it let to its students; it estimated that the total cost of compliance would have been £114,000 and successfully appealed against two of the measures, the provision of heat detection systems throughout the houses and making cupboards under the stairs fire resisting enclosures. One of the points made to the Court of Appeal was that the matter should not be influenced by considerations of cost. Lord Denning, however, said of this:

Of course expense ought not to be spared when it is a question of saving lives: but it can be considered when it only goes in some way to reduce the risk. That was pointed out in an important report on old people's homes called the Fairfield Report. In that report it was clearly stated that whilst expense is absolutely justified when it is essential to save lives, there should not be excessive expense when it would only contribute in some way to reducing the risk.

From this it would appear that the test to be applied to any relaxation application where expense is an important factor is whether the matter to be relaxed is essential for saving life. It is hard to think of many building statutes where cause and effect can be so directly connected; structural failure and some aspects of fire safety are probably the only areas where this occurs. As far as other matters are concerned, a more generous attitude to relaxation may be justified in the eyes of the law, and any future arrangement for relaxations for historic buildings could start from the basis as to whether the matter to be relaxed is essential for saving life.

5.4 Exemptions

We should consider the possibility of not merely the relaxation of specific standards but also the exemption of historic buildings from certain legislative controls in the interests of retaining historic character. Partial and complete exemptions are allowed under Building Regulations at present but they affect only a minority of historic buildings, such as Ancient Monuments.

We consider that only the structural and fire requirements should be regarded as essential in most types of buildings, and that industrial safety and hygiene should only be enforced in special types of commercial premises. Otherwise historic buildings should be exempt if harmful alteration to the building or its contents would inevitably result from the application of requirements.

With regard to structural and fire requirements, there are many ways of reducing life risks. They need not be any more expensive than standard solutions and they may do less damage to historic features. The Thaxted Guildhall restoration (Case Study No. 4B) illustrates the skilful and inconspicuous application of structural improvements. Much greater use can be made of smoke control systems to replace structural fire precautions in historic buildings, as more recent case studies demonstrate. Mechanical systems such as that at Worcester College, Oxford, Hardwick Hall, Derbyshire and Cliveden Manor, Buckinghamshire (Case Studies Nos. 12A, 9C and 9D), carry the risk of system failure, which our authorities seem to fear more than patent shortcomings of innumerable fire doors and alternative superimposed routes of escape, but steps can be taken to make failure reasonably unlikely.

Case Study 9: Country Houses

Very few people nowadays can afford to maintain large country houses and new uses often have to be found to make them pay their way. There is a very wide range of possible uses and each has its own set of legislative consequences in terms of approvals needed and the alterations required to obtain them.

Opening a house to the public attracts comparatively few controls under building legislation. Means of escape requirements arise if the house is used for musical or other licensed entertainments or if liquor is intended to be sold in it, and Section 60 of the Public Health Act applies if sleeping accommodation is provided for, say, a caretaker on an upper floor.

Changes involving major alterations have tended to attract the more onerous provisions of the Building Regulations. Fire precautions are likely to be most onerous of all if a use designated under the Fire Precautions Act is proposed. Planning permission for a change of use from a single private dwelling has proved difficult to obtain in some cases involving isolated buildings being regarded as undesirable development in a rural area.

A. Brocket Hall, Hertfordshire

Brocket Hall was built to the design of James Paine (1716–89) between 1755 and 1780. There are magnificent state rooms on the ground floor around a top-lit stair well. The saloon rises through the height of two storeys to a fine painted ceiling. Planning permission was given for a change of use to a residential conference centre, but structural fire precautions required by the Building Regulations 1976 threatened the viability of the project. The problem was solved by a Determination from the Secretary of State.

Architects: Stone, Toms and Partners

Listed Grade I

Building Regulations

The local authority considered that the building would be used for two different purposes – assembly (the conference rooms) and residential (the bedrooms where conference members sleep) – and that compartment walls and floors were needed to separate them. The stairs were to become protected shafts, too, and there were several handsome doors that would have to be made fire resistant as a consequence. Investigation of the ceiling plaster revealed that its base was rush rather than lath so that, even where it was not too friable to take additional plaster, it was considered unlikely that sufficient fire resistance could be added to comply with Part E. The architects were reluctant to add fire resisting construction within the floor depth by lifting the floor-boards, because of the extra weight on the structure and because the flooring itself, which was parquet or wide boarding, was likely to be damaged.

An application for a blanket relaxation of E4, E5 and E9 of the 1976 Regulations was made and rejected. Further joint meetings were held with the local authority and fire authority, from which it emerged that life safety could be adequately ensured without complying with the Regulations' structural fire resistance requirements as then interpreted. To resolve the point about the purpose group interpretation, a Determination was sought. The Minister resolved that the whole building should be in purpose group III (other residential) and relaxations were obtained. Instead of the original hour and a half requirement, a modified half hour became acceptable so that a combustible timber secondary stair could be retained in view of the stone construction of the main stair, and the cavity barrier requirements of E14 for concealed voids in the ceilings were relaxed.

Means of escape

In order to separate and protect the two stairs, a number of new fire screens and doors were

Brocket Hall, Herts
Ground floor as first interpreted
Approximate scale 1:300

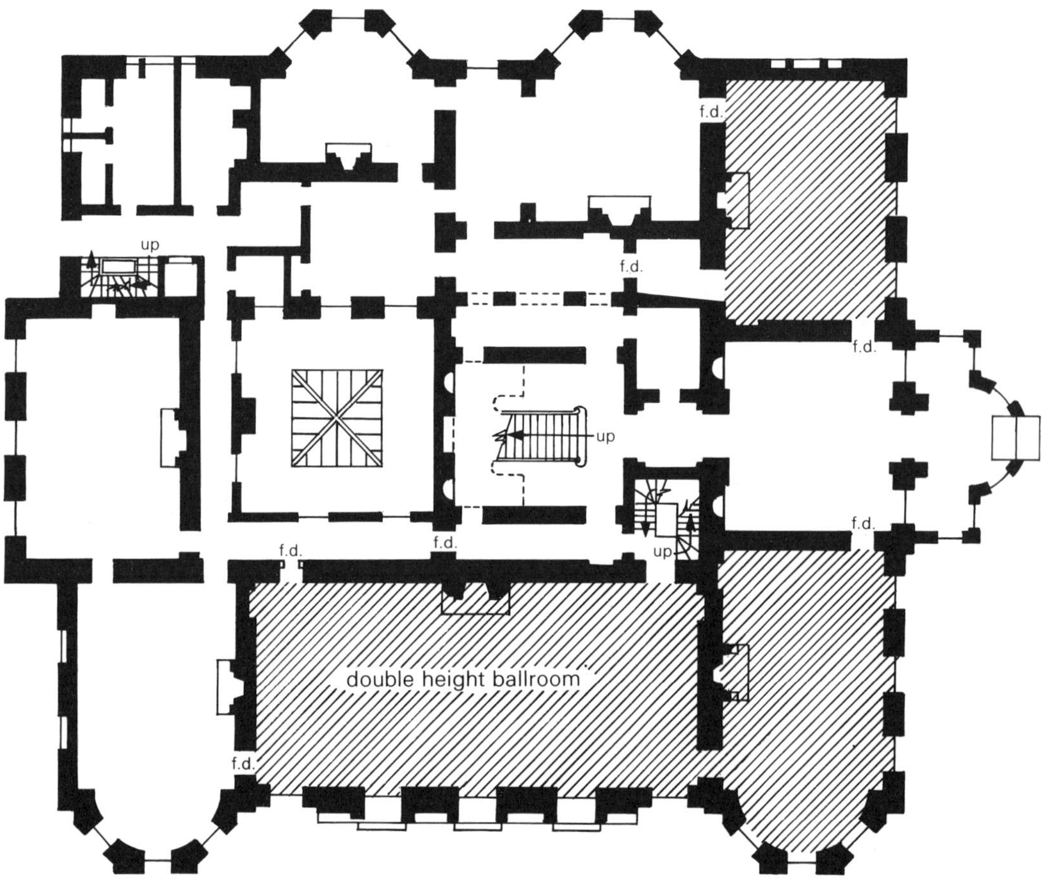

Hatched areas purpose group VII conference use
Remainder, purpose group III

Section through first floor
Approximate scale 1:25

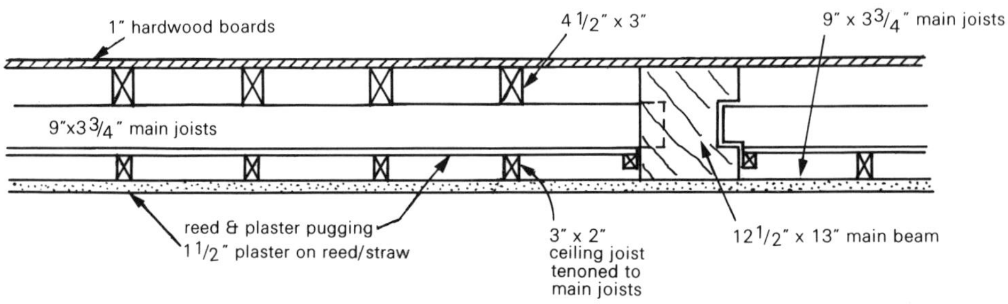

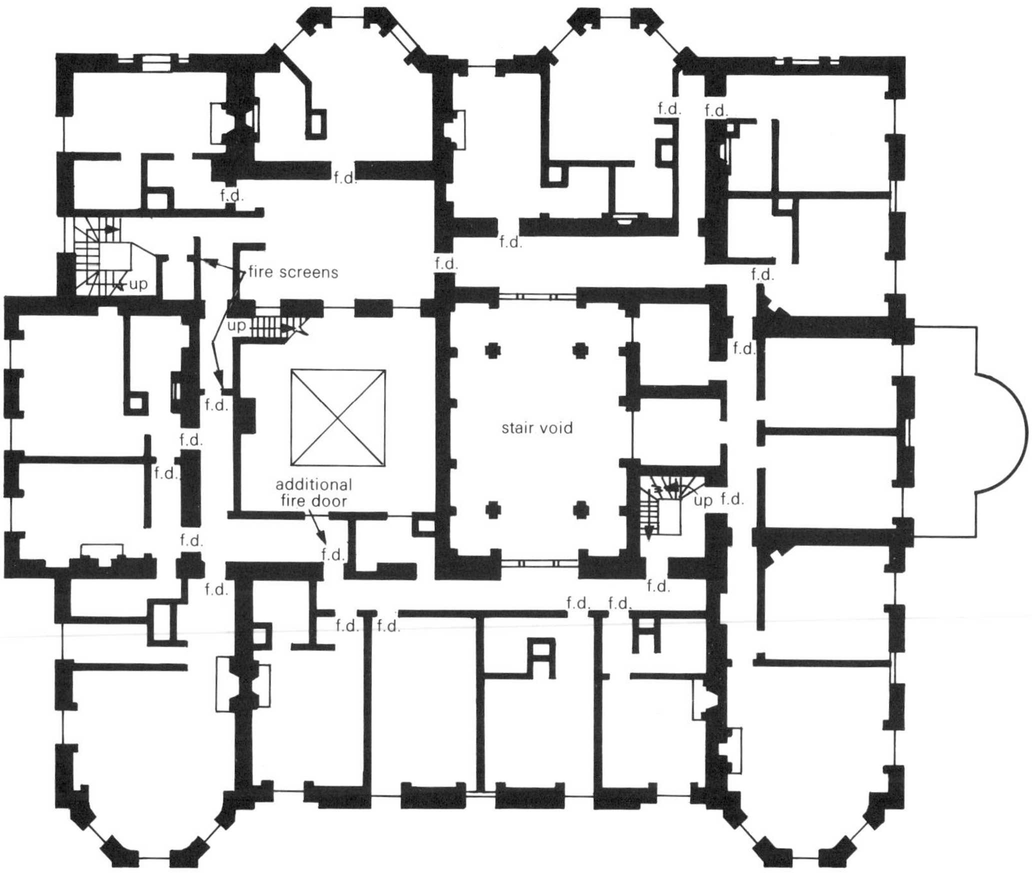

Second floor as finally agreed showing fire doors (bedrooms throughout)

needed. A new escape door had to be made in a former window opening from the lower ground floor. Initially, the fire officer asked for a number of doors to be rehung to open in the direction of escape, which would have resulted in some harm where the door head was higher than the soffit of the passage beyond. It was agreed that only the doors which could be rehung without architectural damage need be altered.

The cooperation of all concerned led to a satisfactory resolution of the legislative problems that avoided harm to the historic fabric and ensured a renewed lease of life for the building.

References: Paras 1.3.3, 2.2.9, 3.3.1 and 3.3.2C

B. Kenwood House, London NW3

At Kenwood the impact of legislation has been kept to an absolute minimum by ingenuity and careful development of alternative solutions with authorities who were prepared to be flexible.

Kenwood is a large house of two storeys, with an attic and basement, set in park land and built in about 1770 to an Adam design, with outbuildings and numerous later alterations. Adaptations and alterations were designed by the historic buildings section of the GLC's Department of Architecture and Civic Design. The house is now under the care of the Historic Buildings and Monuments Commission for England.

Listed Grade I

Legislation

The house and grounds were given to the former London County Council and are now run as a museum/art gallery, with ancillary offices and a curator's flat all within the main building. Recitals are given in the Orangery and Music Room. Fire precautions work was carried out over the last thirty years under Section 35 of The London Building Acts (Amendment Act) 1939 by virtue of the public use of the premises. There are insufficient office staff for a fire certificate to be required under the Fire Precautions Act 1971. A licence was needed for the recitals.

The need for fire prevention measures has been increased by the very valuable collection of paintings housed in the buildings. *It has been hard to define which measures were taken for statutory reasons and which were insurance and security requirements.*

Means of escape

There are three stairs, one of stone and two of timber. The soffits of the timber stairs were underdrawn with plaster. At the north-east end there is an open light well between ground and first floor and occupants of a first floor room must pass through the space containing the light well to reach a stairway. A smoke

Interior and exterior views of one of the emergency escape windows to the Music Room

Kenwood House, London NW3 Approximate scale 1:500

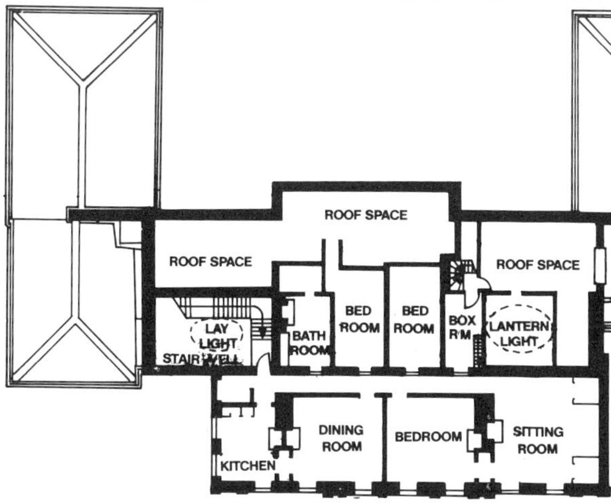

Second floor plan

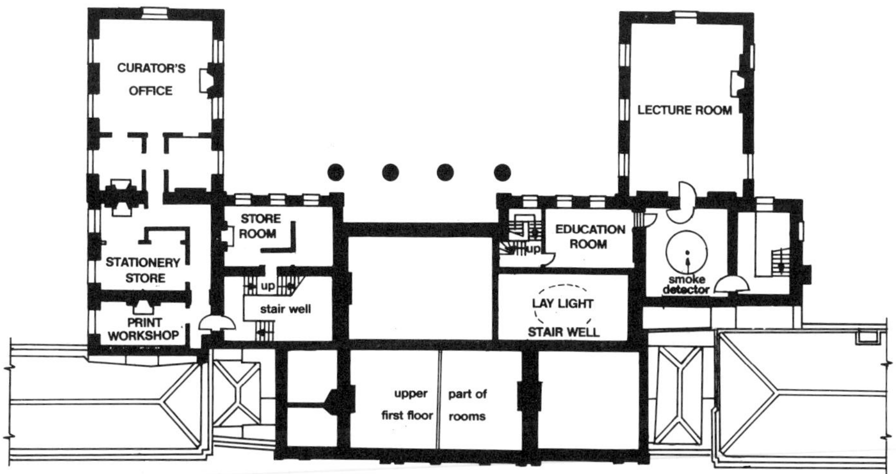

Mezzanine floor plan

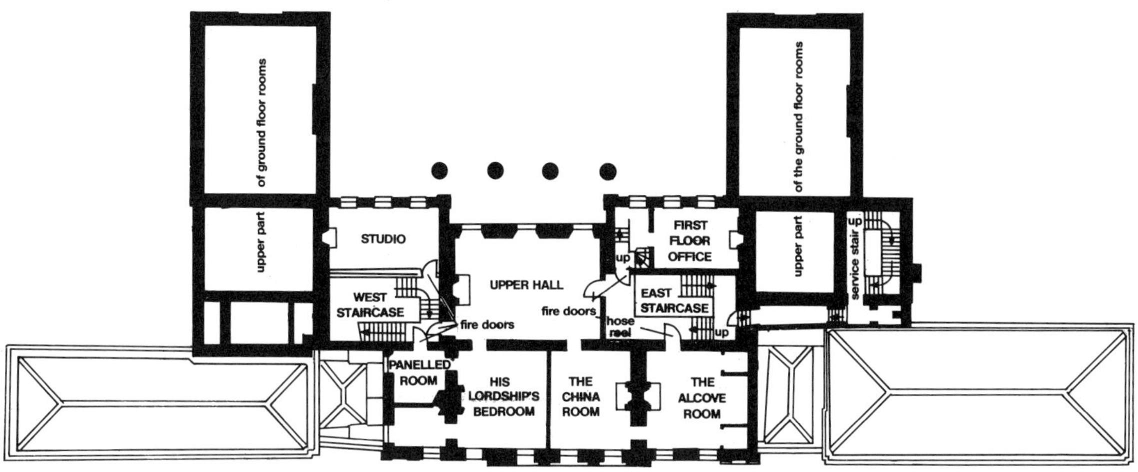

First floor plan

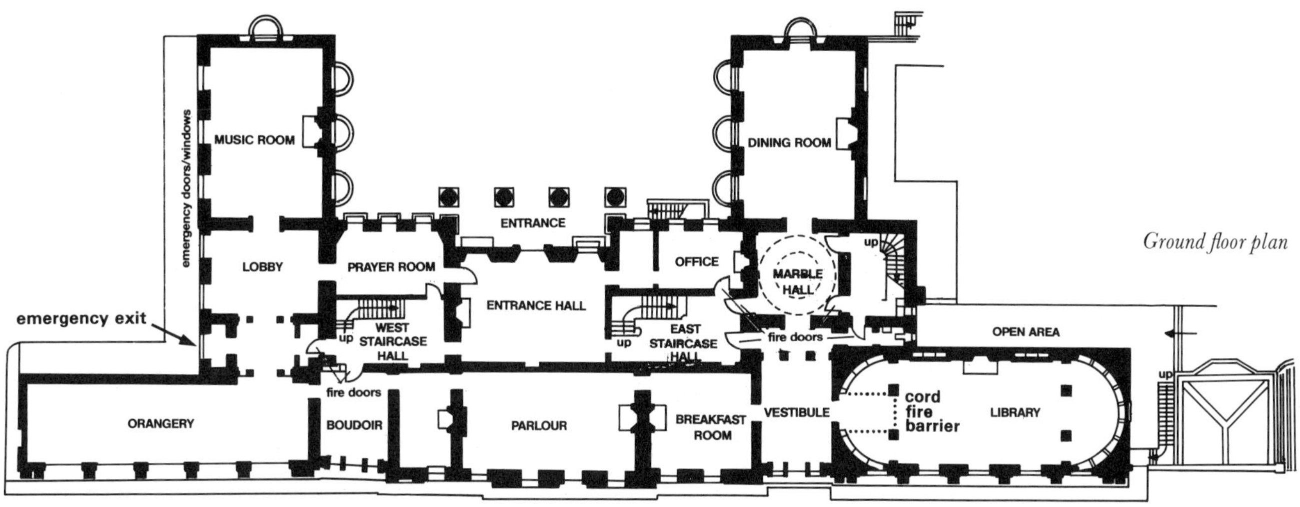

Ground floor plan

The Library, showing the cord barrier

detector is located above the well and the occupancy of the room is limited to seventy people.

Compartment walls separate the areas served by each stair. Doors in these walls and on the stair have been upgraded to be fire resisting by sheeting over and replanting mouldings on the new face. The deep reveals have been used to add second fire doors in compartment walls.

The need to permit public circulation has meant that the compartment doors and some stairway doors are held open during the day. However, this is permitted because there are attendants in every room. Similarly, security requires that all emergency exits should be kept locked at all times. Here again, there have to be attendants with keys in the rooms with the exits whenever the building is open to the public.

The distance from the far end of the ground floor library was considered to be excessive and so a simple rope cordon is placed across the room at the limit point.

To meet the licensing requirements for public recitals, emergency lighting and an additional exit were required. A sash window in one part of the recital room extends to floor level and this has been made specially available for escape; an attendant is stationed adjacent to the window while recitals are in progress. There are no permanent emergency light fittings, but a dedicated lighting circuit with mains and battery supply was installed, to which portable fittings can be connected by special plugs and sockets when required.

Fire prevention

There is automatic detection throughout and the alarm system is linked by landline to the fire service. For some heavy damask drapes which were required to be given a fire retardant treatment a borax solution of the type used for theatre stage drapes was accepted. A hose-reel, required in the south-west stairway for fire fighting, has been disguised by enclosing it in a low, glass-fronted cupboard on floor runners which can be rolled sideways for rapid access to the hose-reel.

References: Paras 1.7.4, 2.4.1A and 2.4.3E

A door on one of the escape routes

A glazed cupboard housing a hose reel on the south-west stairway

The well to the Marble Hall, which has a smoke detector above it

C. Hardwick Hall, Derbyshire

The main staircase

Edwin Smith/The National Trust Photographic Library

This three-storey house is one of the most splendid and least altered of all Elizabethan houses. It was built by Smythson for Bess of Hardwick between 1591 and 1597. Its design was revolutionary, comprising a compact H-plan and an exterior elevation in which the windows increase progressively in height from the ground upwards. This reflects the interior arrangement of the hall and servants' quarters on the ground, family apartments on the second and state rooms on the third floor, and gives a powerful vertical emphasis. The house contains the country's finest collection of Elizabethan embroideries, and tapestries dating from 1600.

The house was given to the National Trust in 1959 and is open to the public. Following the fire service's recommendations, the public are allowed on the ground, first and second floors only in limited numbers. The ground and first floors are divided into two halves separated by a large entrance hall some 8–9 m high. The second floor houses the long gallery, which also has a ceiling height of 9–10 m.

Legislation

This type of premises is not currently controlled by any Act of Parliament. In the past, the local fire authority has given advice on a 'goodwill' basis. However, the buildings can be designated under the Fire Precautions Act 1971 if the fire authorities consider that there is an excessive risk to persons from fire, by applying to prohibit or restrict the use of the building.

Fire detection

The house is provided with a comprehensive fire detection system comprising either a mix of ionization, smoke detector units or rate of rise heat detectors. In addition, there are manual 'break glass' fire alarms linked with the detection system. An 'auto dialer' is provided whereby a taped message is sent via the 999 telephone circuit to the fire service. The entire system is serviced and tested twice annually. Forty hand fire extinguishers and seven hose-reels are located within the building, which is surrounded by nine fire hydrants, and all the façades are accessible for ladders and fire appliances. These arrangements are supplemented by a detailed fire procedure, including the evacuation of visitors from the building and the prohibition of smoking except in the restaurant and shop areas.

Means of escape

Despite all these arrangements, the fire authority considered the means of escape inadequate because of the lack of separation between the two main staircases. The advice given by the fire authority was to separate completely the two halves of the building and to make every door on the route traversed by the public fire resisting and self-closing. This clearly posed considerable problems, particularly as some of the doors are important aspects of the house's historic character.

Fire engineering appraisal

Independent consultants were brought in to see if alternative ways could be found of ensuring that visitors and staff could escape from the premises without risk from fire or

Hardwick Hall

The National Trust Photographic Library

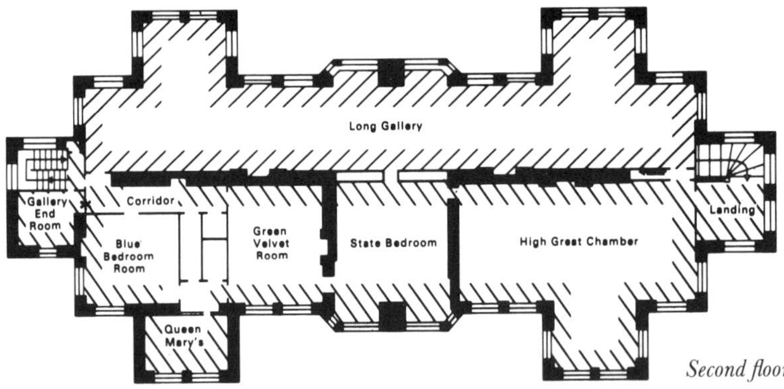

Second floor plan

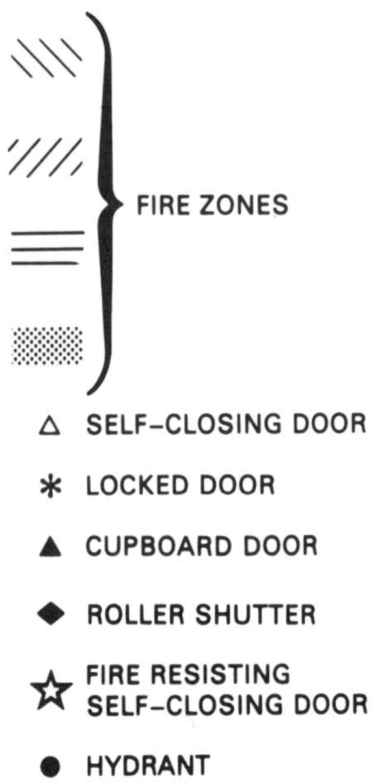

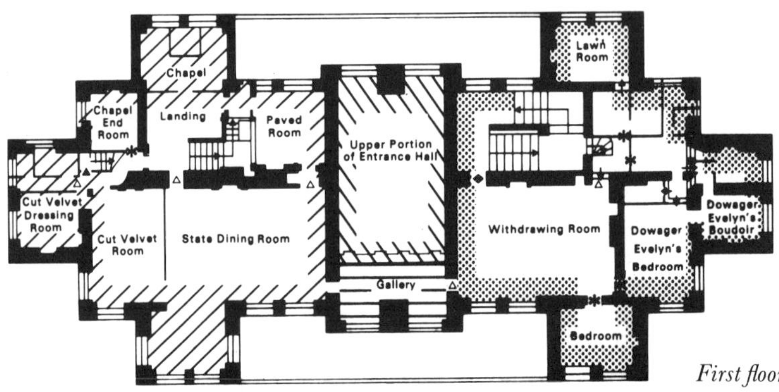

First floor plan

Site Plan

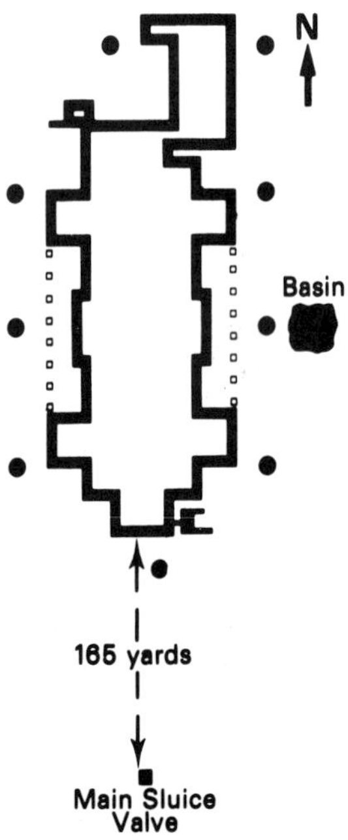

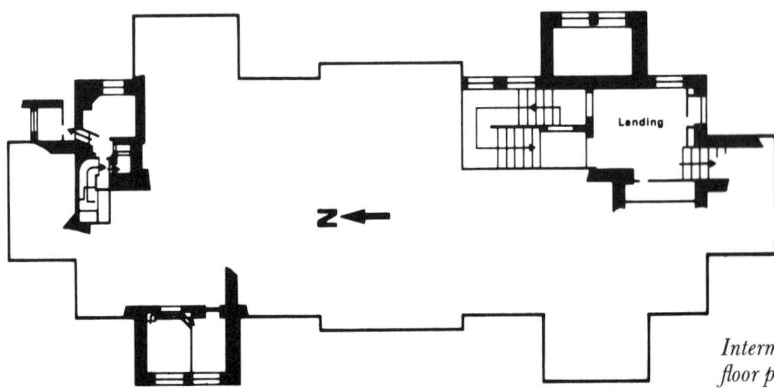

Intermediate floor plan

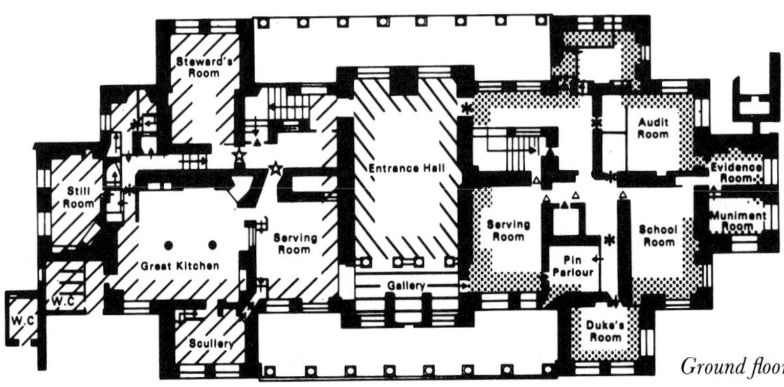

Ground floor plan

The Long Gallery

The National Trust Photographic Library

smoke, while maintaining the character of the interior.

Of the alternative approaches which can be adopted to achieve this objective, the most important is based on a comprehensive fire engineering appraisal. The aspects which have a bearing upon this approach include the fire load of the contents, surfaces and structure of the house, and the speed with which escape routes could become smoke logged.

In determining the fire load, two features were considered to reduce significantly the fire risk: the relatively low fire load of the contents and, probably more important, the height of the individual rooms, particularly those on the second floor and the entrance hall. As the ceilings are so high compared with the doorway openings, a deep smoke reservoir would be formed, delaying the spread of smoke to other areas of the house. It has been possible to indicate the potential fire size based on the type of furniture and furnishings within the building. This in turn has allowed an appreciation to be made of the smoke emission, the temperature and depth of the smoke layer. It has been possible to show how quickly conditions in individual rooms will become unsuitable for sustaining life due to the level of the smoke layer.

Fire prevention

The fire authority had requested that the house be divided into a series of fire zones and that the majority of the doors serving the route used by the public should be provided with self-closing doors, with a half hour standard of fire resistance, and the doors to any room or space other than those which are entered by the public kept locked shut. Locked doors might not have a full standard of fire resistance, but as the areas behind them are monitored by the automatic fire detection system, thereby ensuring an early warning of fire, this approach, taken in conjunction with the fire engineering analysis, would appear to be satisfactory for a building of this type. The layout of fire zones and door treatments are shown on the adjoining plans.

References: Paras 4.5, 5.4 and 6.2.2

D. Cliveden Manor, Buckinghamshire

Cliveden is one of England's great country houses, with a magnificent setting on the River Thames. The original house was designed by William Wind for the Duke of Buckingham in 1666. Unfortunately, a large part of the house was destroyed by fire in 1795 and in about 1850 the Duke of Sutherland employed Sir Charles Barry to design the present mansion.

The interior was transformed by the Duke of Westminster in the 1870s and contains handsome Brussels tapestries and Louis XV panelling in the dining room which came from Château d'Asruères, once used by Madame de Pompadour as a hunting box. The Astor family, who purchased the house in 1893, passed it on to the National Trust in 1942, after which it was occupied by Stanford University. In 1984 the Trust leased it to Blakeney Hotels who required considerable restoration and conversion work. The architects for this work are Messrs William Bertram and Fell.

The premises comprise a central mansion of three storeys 150 ft long with two wings of two storeys, united by a common basement and served by link corridors at ground and basement levels.

Legislation

The major legislation which applied was the Building Regulations 1985, and the Fire Precautions Act 1971.

Fire resistance

The fire separation within the premises did not comply with modern standards and appeared to be in conflict with the Building Regulations with regard to the fire resistance of elements of structure. There was also difficulty in meeting the restrictions on compartmentation and the surface finishes of walls and ceilings.

It was clearly apparent that it would be virtually impossible to comply with the Regulations in the normal way without destroying many of the historically or architecturally important elements in the building. To ensure that the structure of the building met the required standards of fire resistance would have involved removing virtually every ceiling and applying protection to the wrought-iron beams which support the upper floors. These

Cliveden Manor

The National Trust Photographic Library

floors are substantial and the voids between the ceilings and floors range from about one-third to half a metre or more. The beams are of heavy construction and, together with the timber floor and the ceiling beneath, would resist the effects of fire and heat for a long time. Other features which were clearly important were the height (about 3 m) and width (2.8–3 m) of the corridors on the upper floors. As with most great houses, the ceiling height on the ground floor, which includes all the main function rooms, is in excess of 6 m.

Fire engineering appraisal

This was clearly a case where a fire engineering approach was required and a detailed analysis of the fire load, possible fire development, temperature ratings and smoke propagation was prepared.

Although the distances from some of the bedrooms exceed that for hotels, the staircases are arranged in such a way that the problems associated with the means of escape in case of fire were, compared to most houses of this type, relatively simple to resolve.

Under the 1985 Building Regulations it was only necessary to show that the structure would survive fire long enough to allow persons to escape from the building.

The fire and building authorities agreed to a fire engineering appraisal, and it was found from the exercise that, if a combination of compensatory measures were introduced, it was possible to carry out the conversion without impairing the character of the house. These included:

— reducing the fire load on the premises by installing furniture and fittings which were incombustible to a degree compatible with hotel use, such as providing hardwood tables and chairs, and curtains and other hangings of inherently non-flammable or durable flame-proof fabric;
— providing separate storage facilities for spare furnishings and bedding;
— extending the fire detection system to include all bedrooms, suites and function rooms and connecting it directly to a central alarm depot;
— providing hose-reels on escape routes adjacent to staircase enclosures, and fire extinguishers in kitchens, boiler rooms, electrical intake rooms and other special risk areas;
— sealing up all openings where ventilation ducts, service piping and cables passed through walls, floors and ceilings;
— installing magnetic handles on many of the doors which would 'fail safe' when the fire alarm system operated; and
— ensuring that all staff received instruction in fire drill, keeping a log book and displaying plans of all floors at each ground floor entrance.

References: Paras 4.5, 5.4 and 6.2.2

John Bethell/The National Trust Photographic Library

Typical ornamental woodwork

The National Trust Photographic Library

Elaborate drapery in one of the bedrooms

Case Study 10: Country Cottages and Barns

Because cottages are generally small buildings, they are not often subject to sub-division (and thus the possibility of having to be compartmented) and only when there are three or more storeys does means of escape legislation start to apply. The only legislatively significant alterations that are likely to occur, therefore, are extensions or improvements.

Extending a cottage laterally is likely to involve architectural problems of scale, materials and character, but, without a material change of use, only the new work would be expected to attract Building Regulation requirements. The exception is the improvement grant, where a condition of the grant is that any building has to comply with the Regulations. This is not compulsory in the sense of the other statutory requirements referred to in this report, since the applicant can choose to withdraw his application for a grant and seek funds elsewhere. There are several examples of this, but in the main it seems that applicants do not have this option in practice and either comply with the conditions or abandon the project.

We have also included in this category reports on the conversion of field barns into overnight shelters for walkers. They are of interest as forerunners of a type of conversion we think may become quite common, and as illustrations of the way different authorities coped with cases to which they had not previously had to apply legislation.

A. Nos. 5 and 8 St John's Square, Wilton, Wiltshire

This case study concerns a domestic conversion involving an improvement grant, planning permission and listed building consent for buildings that date back to the fourteenth century.

Architects: Brandt Potter and Partners

Listed Grade II

Improvement Grant

To obtain a smooth, dry internal wall surface the ground floor was to be lined with a skin of blockwork. To provide a footing for this and to replace the existing damp floor a new concrete slab was to be laid with a finished surface 165 mm above external ground level. This was some 280 mm higher than the previous floor level and would have left only 2 m headroom. To avoid this the first floor was raised by about 300 mm.

In No. 8, the heights of all the doors had to be increased to 2040 mm with the exception of the front door. A condition of the grant was that the staircase was to be straight flight; this condition has been observed, but for a single step for the quarter-landing to the ground floor. Although the new stairs are not as steep as the original, they do not conform to the 1976 Regulations.

References: Paras 2.2.3 and 3.3.3E

St John's Square

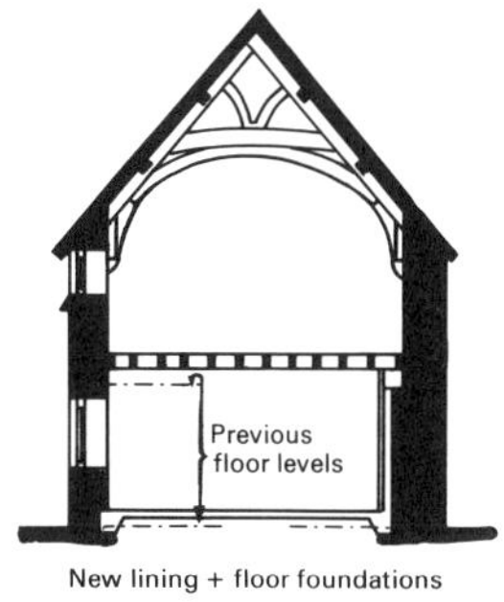

Nos. 5 and 8, St John's Square, Wilton, Wiltshire Approximate scale 1:200 Section A-A

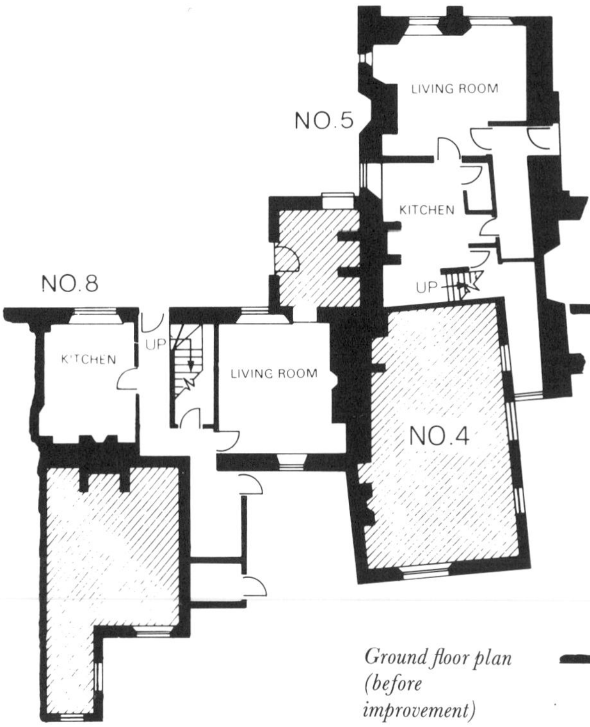

Ground floor plan (before improvement)

Ground floor plan (after improvement)

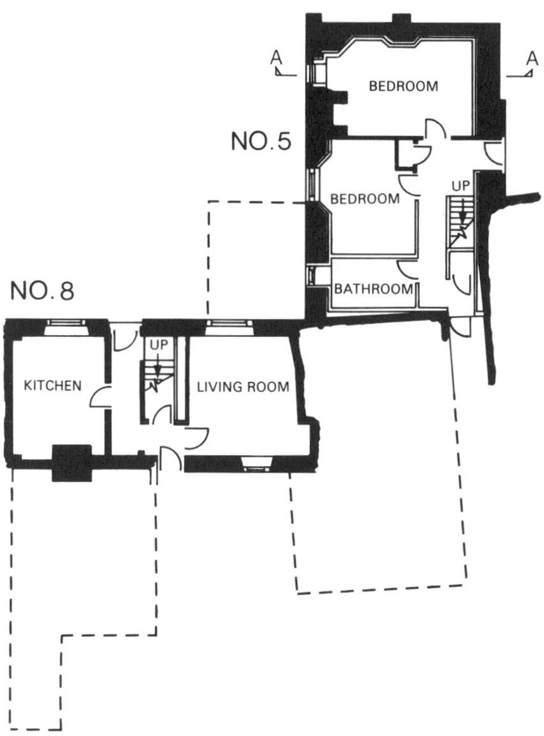

First floor plan (before improvement)

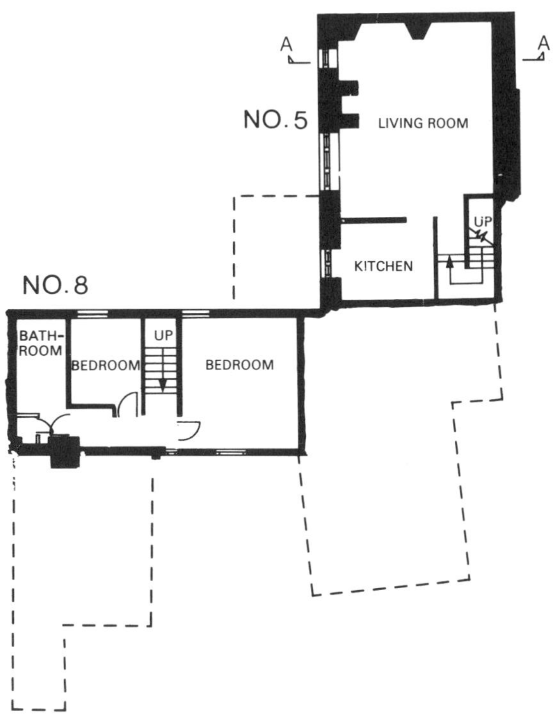

First floor plan (after improvement)

B. Old Manor Farm House, Torquay

Old Manor Farmhouse, Torquay showing proximity of roof to adjoining (newer) property Approximate scale 1:200

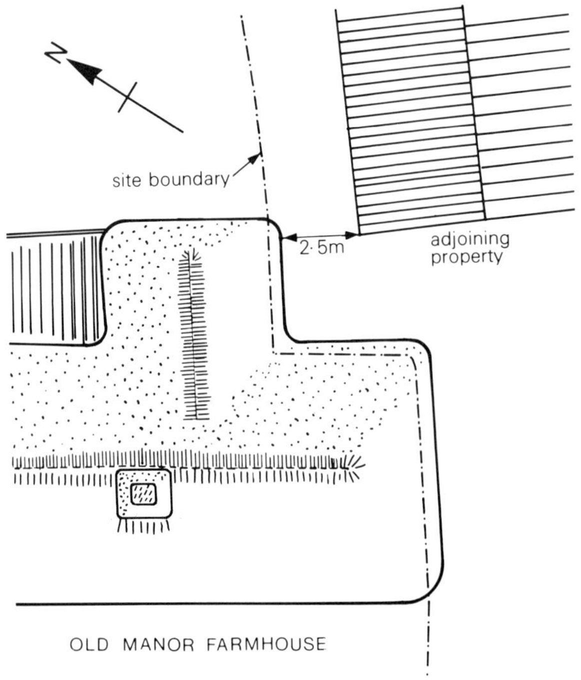

It is not unusual to find a historic building in a poor state of repair where totally inappropriate materials have been used to patch up some defect. In this case there was some difficulty in replacing the inappropriate material with the original because the performance of the traditional material did not perform so well in Building Regulations terms.

Architect: A. S. Taylor

*Listed Grade II**

When the architect bought this house it had a corrugated metal roof where once there had been thatch. This had to be replaced. Listed building consent was obtained, but the Building Regulations application was rejected, as was the appeal for a relaxation of E17. Under the 1976 Regulations, E17 controlled the minimum distance between the site boundary and a combustible roof finish, the dimensions being 6 m if the area of thatch was no more than 3 m^2 or, in any other case, 12 m. As the plan shows, 12 m was the appropriate figure in this case and the nearest adjoining property was about 3 m away. The building control officer felt that he did not have the discretion to recommend a relaxation, especially as the fire authority advised against it.

The Secretary of State considered that the regulation was unnecessarily onerous in this case and allowed the appeal.

Reference: Para 2.2.14

C. The Derbyshire Field Barns

A characteristic feature of the uplands of Derbyshire is the pattern of fields divided by stone walls and dotted with small stone barns. Changes in agricultural techniques have made many of these barns redundant and more and more are falling into a state of decay. Recognising the long-term effect of this change on the landscape, the Derbyshire Historic Buildings Trust, in conjunction with the Chatsworth Estate and the County Planning Department's conservation section, set up a pilot scheme for the re-use of three barns on an experimental basis. The idea was to make them into very simple overnight shelters for people using the countryside for recreational purposes, who would obtain a key and pay a small charge by contacting the neighbouring farmer in charge of the barn.

The barns were in need of repair and planning permission was required for the change of use. Slight alterations were needed: opening up blocked windows and doors and making raised timber floors for sleeping. Simple stone or slab shelves were put in for cooking and washing, and sanitation depended on simple or portable chemical WCs. Water was piped to a tap outside, and a little way from the barn a soakaway was provided.

The local authority had to decide which legislation applied to the barns and therefore what standard should be adopted on matters of building construction and environmental health. The project group wanted to keep the buildings as simple as possible to preserve their external appearance, because there was no money for more elaborate work, and because more luxurious facilities might attract too many people, causing problems of upkeep, security and over-development.

A typical field barn

The Derbyshire Field Barns Approximate scale 1:100

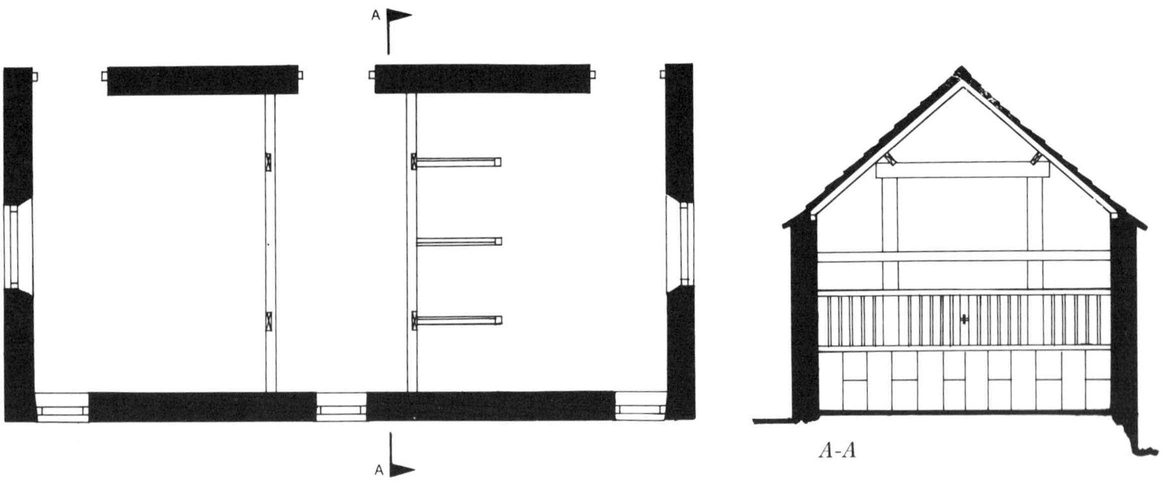

Before conversion

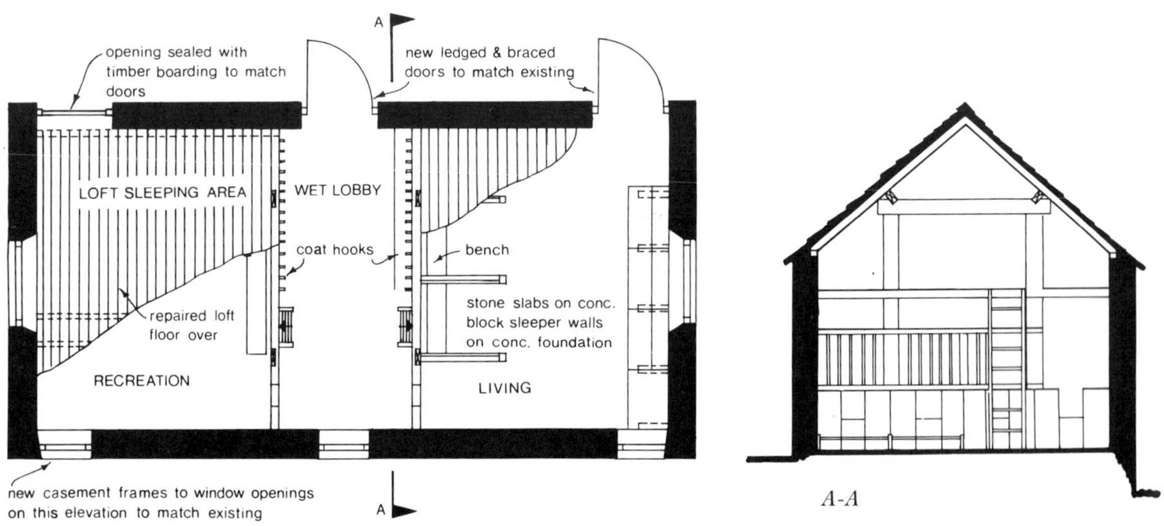

After conversion

If the Building Regulations 1976 were to be applied, various alterations would have been needed, such as the provision of stairs and handrails to the upper level, and headroom requirements would not have been met in places. Environmental health standards for residential buildings would have required separate WCs for males and females, plumbed-in water (possibly hot as well as cold), damp-proofing of floors and walls, cooking and food storage equipment, and so on.

However, the local authority decided to treat the barns as superior stone tents rather than inferior houses, and applied for a Camp Licence under Section 269 of the 1936 Public Health Act. If experience shows that adequate standards are not maintained this licence can be withdrawn.

Reference: Para 2.3.2

D. Barns at Buckden and Sedbergh, North Yorkshire

There is a shortage of convenient overnight accommodation on some stretches of the Pennine Way. The Yorkshire Dales National Park and the Countryside Commission implemented two projects at Sedbergh and at Buckden to convert barns into places for walkers to spend the night. Thc Commission provided grants of about 75 per cent as part of a pilot scheme to find alternative uses for agricultural buildings.

Fire precautions (Buckden)

The fire authorities were consulted. A Home Office ruling was obtained on the applicability of the Fire Precautions Act, as there was space for fifteen people and they might have been considered to be hostels. The Home Office ruled that the Act would not apply, so in Buckden fire precautions work was carried out on a voluntary basis. In practice, the standard of fire safety was much the same as it would have been if the Act had been applied. The concern was that the building was so remote that outside help from the fire brigade would not be available quickly.

Cam Houses barn is two storeys high and the original plan was to put the dormitories on the upper floor with the roof trusses exposed and partitions to head height only. The fire authority considered that, with such an arrangement, the danger of fire and smoke spread was so high that the dormitories would need alternative means of escape in the form of new external stairs. It was therefore decided to put the dormitories on the ground floor with 'half-hour' partitions between them. By permitting only daytime use of the top floor, the need for these stairs – which would have added to the cost and changed the barn's appearance – was removed.

Other precautions were recommended, including:

— automatic smoke/heat detectors and alarms (if mains power had not been available, battery powered units would have been required);
— fire exit signs (100 mm lettering) and procedure notices;
— a maximum travel distance of 9 m;
— fire fighting equipment (a garden hose was acceptable if the water pressure was adequate), with a fire blanket and dry powder extinguisher next to the cooker;
— half-hour fire resisting treatment to the timber beds;
— emergency lighting of at least one hour's duration;
— heating by electric, oil-filled type tubular convectors; and
— cooking by gas from a bottled supply in a secure store, with rigid supply pipework (no cooking on portable stoves of any kind was permitted).

Environmental health (Sedbergh)

In this instance the barn was regarded as a hostel and the sanitary accommodation was similar to that provided for the simplest youth hostels. The main problems concerned the size of the septic tank, and the provision of daylight and ventilation in a building with relatively few windows without upsetting its appearance. This was particularly hard at Sedbergh, where the only windows were narrow slits giving far less than a twentieth of the floor area – the minimum permitted under the 1976 Regulations. The authority accepted a mechanical ventilation system instead, which operated whenever the lights were switched on and, as the windows give little daylight, they are on most of the time. But this means that such a ventilation system does not work when it is most needed – at night when the room is full of sleeping people.

When we first discussed this case study, Cam Houses had been in use for over a year and appeared to be working well. However, there could be long-term maintenance problems with the fire protection equipment.

References: Paras 2.2.9 and 2.3.2

6

Conclusions and recommendations

6.1 Introduction

The undesirable effects of legislation which we have observed and described in this report are broadly as follows:

— the destruction of historically or architecturally important elements;
— additions to the cost of retaining historic buildings;
— the changes of character caused by additions or alterations;
— reduced usefulness or potential for use, as a result of planning consent conditions;
— delay in implementing work on proposals that would give the building a new lease of life; and
— inconvenience to people using the building, such as that caused by a multiplicity of self-closing doors.

These factors raise complex issues. There is a multiplicity of legislation that could be applied in whole or in part to works relating to alterations and extensions, to changes of use, or even to the basic occupancy of historic buildings. This is monitored through more than twenty central Government departments, and administered and enforced by local authorities at both county and district levels. This is not, of course, unique to historic buildings, but applies to all building processes.

Lord James of Rusholme, as Chairman of the Royal Fine Art Commission, may therefore have been expressing a general concern in his letter to *The Times* (8 September 1978) when he stated that many people felt that fire officers and other officials were doing more harm than good to our national heritage in requiring standards for historic buildings comparable to those required for new buildings. His letters were followed by others which likewise expressed disquiet; letters from such people as the President of the RIBA, the Chairman of the Historic Buildings Council, the Secretary of the Society for the Protection of Ancient Buildings and the Surveyor of the University of Oxford.

Such letters, from some of the most authoritative sources in the land, express the depth of the concern for a better deal for historic buildings. We indicated in the last chapter how such a deal might operate in practice. Briefly, where any question of measures to save life are concerned, in particular fire safety and structural measures, the emphasis should be on:

— requirements being expressed in terms of performance standards so as to allow flexibility in the ways whereby unavoidable needs may be met;
— research, including case studies of fires that have occurred in historic buildings to check the effects of upgrading to meet the requirements and the result of failing to take action;
— tests on historic building components to see how far they meet requirements;
— research into new techniques and, where these prove suitable, their recognition by the authorities concerned as a means of meeting specific requirements;
— preparation of a Code of Practice for historic buildings.

The same approach is relevant to other legislation affecting historic buildings except that, in the latter instance, greater emphasis should be placed on relaxation and exemptions.

Behind all this lies a need for new attitudes and greater understanding, and these imply better education and closer liaison between the officers concerned within local authorities.

6.2 Performance Standards

6.2.1 The Department of the Environment

The 1985 Building Regulations contrast with those of earlier years in expressing requirements in terms of performance standards in preference to specific controls. This should be greatly to the advantage of older buildings. Environmental matters such as those under the Public Health Act 1936, which relate to multiple occupation, residential care and licensed social services, would benefit from a similar approach.

6.2.2 The Home Office

In order to reduce the present burden of administration placed upon fire authorities by the certification provisions of the Fire Precautions Act 1971, and to enable control to be extended to a wider range of occupancies on a more selective basis than at present, proposals for a new system of fire precautions controls have been drawn up within the Home Office consultative machinery. A fundamental feature of this new system would be to place upon the owner or occupier of those premises put to a designated use a statutory duty to achieve and maintain a reasonable standard of fire precautions. The role of the fire authority would be to give advice, inspect and, where necessary, take enforcement action. This would be comparable to the existing system of responsibility under the Health and Safety at Work, etc Act 1974.

Again, the emphasis would be on performance standards and guidance documents. Already this change of emphasis is occurring: for example, fire authorities are now more sympathetic towards 'active' fire protection measures in addition to 'passive', that is, structural requirements. Far greater recognition is now being given to the contribution that such techniques as smoke control, pressurisation and the use of automatic systems of detection and extinguishment can make, and the way these reduce the need to change the structural or decorative qualities of these buildings as the recent work at Hardwick Hall and Cliveden Manor shows (Case Studies Nos. 9C and 9D).

6.3 Research and Codes of Practice

There is no doubt that the local authorities generally recognise the special needs of our historic buildings and are often prepared to accept alternative techniques for protection which avoid structural or decorative disfigurement. These new and alternative techniques, along with the more traditional solutions, should be consolidated and rationalised into a common Code of Practice for older buildings. However, such a Code cannot reasonably be produced without the benefit of research.

Research is needed into such matters as the design of systems for detection, communication, alarm and extinguishment, and systems of smoke controls. Research is also needed into the ability of historic building elements such as panelled doors, partitions, structural framing, etc, to meet the requirements of the established fire test, BS 476, etc. The results of research on cast-iron structures would likewise need to be completed before a Code of Practice could be produced. Further work should be done on the value of the various intumescent coatings; these can do much to improve the fire resistance of traditional materials and structures, and intumescent paints can reduce the surface spread of flame.

The object of this research would be to enable the guidance documents, implicit in any control based on performance standards, to be prepared. These would assist owners and occupiers by showing how the necessary standard could be met in particular circumstances. Such an arrangement would help to produce a uniform standard throughout the country. No code could hope to cover every possible situation, but compliance in appropriate cases would be deemed to satisfy the statutory requirement. Although it is envisaged that such codes would be related to particular uses, such as shops, factories or hotels, it might be possible to produce a separate code for historic buildings or to include in codes prepared for each type of occupancy a section dealing with the special problems of historic buildings which are put to that use.

6.4 Relaxation and Exemptions

We have found that some authorities are more ready than others to consider relaxations and exemptions; we have seen that more experienced officers are less hidebound and generally more ready to use their own judgement in particular instances. Despite this, we have found a reluctance on the part of some authorities to grant relaxations because of the legal liability which authorities carry for health and safety with regard to buildings whose design has been approved by them. This situation applies especially to historic buildings. It could perhaps be resolved by the introduction of a national scheme of cover for matters relating to building control.

See Case Studies 9C and 9D, pp. 124-7 and 128-9

6.5 Education

Changes in legislation and administration on the wider front could do much to free historic buildings from inappropriate requirements but the need will still remain for specialist advice to ensure that they can meet the required standard of performance in terms of health and safety. The choice of solutions will become wider, and professionals working in the field will have to discriminate between these alternatives.

Professionals, both in the private and the public sectors, will therefore need to acquire a firm grasp not only of the new legislation but also of the performance of historic buildings elements. This implies a great deal of new knowledge which goes beyond even that currently available to the few specialists in this area. A programme of education is therefore required which uses every available means – mid-career courses, summer schools, seminars, exhibitions, specialist publications and centres of advice and information such as the

Building Research Station, Fire Research Station, Building Conservation Trust, etc. Professional bodies should take part in developing this programme.

6.6 A New Coordinating Role for Conservation Officers

In all discussions it is vital that the conservation issues should be carefully considered. This may occur if specialists in the private sector are appointed to certify work, and develop solutions which meet requirements without destroying historic fabric or the character of buildings of merit. But in perhaps the vast majority of cases there is a need for a strong voice within the authority to emphasise the conservation aspect. The obvious focus for such a voice will be the section of the district planning department responsible for controlling works involving the demolition, alteration or extension of listed buildings. For this purpose some authorities have a conservation section; others may employ a single conservation or 'historic buildings' officer. Even if there is no officer with this title, an officer within the planning authority should be nominated and identified as the focus for coordinating historic building matters.

The key work is *coordination*. There are many examples of a lack of communication between the various administrative departments involved; as a result, works were liable to be carried out without the knowledge of those responsible for administering listed building control.

In addition to having an officer or section responsible for coordinating matters relating to historic buildings, suitable administrative arrangements should be organised to enable a more common and sympathetic understanding to be gained. Matters such as Dangerous Structures Notices, and all matters relating to building alterations, fire safety and health should be channelled through the listed building section in order to maintain a sympathetic and comprehensive control. The resurvey to update the lists of buildings of special architectural or historic interest in England has created the need for coordinated action even in many authorities which were not previously endowed with large numbers of listed buildings.

The same historic buildings offices would be expected to liaise with owners of properties in need of repair. This would not only provide an early warning system but enable them to bring to the notice of property owners the best ways of tackling and financing the work.

The new role will call for a programme of specialist education for historic buildings officers. This is because effective liaison calls for a positive rather than a negative stance; one geared to the development of acceptable and suitable solutions rather than the application of specialised control mechanisms.

6.7 Recommendations

The measures discussed above, all of which we consider to be necessary, can be summarised under the following recommendations:

— the reassessment of those remaining controls concerned with amenity and convenience rather than health or safety;

— the completion, publication and dissemination of recent research relating to fire in historic buildings and the immediate development of a programme of further research in this field;

— the preparation of a Code of Practice dealing with new techniques relating to fire protection and means of escape and their application to historic buildings;

— the creation of a national scheme of cover in connection with any liability risks taken by individual local authorities: this cover would be made available subject to expert advice in each case from an independent or central source;

— the preparation and implementation of a programme of education and the setting up of a specialist committee to assist in this. Membership of the committee would be drawn from the bodies most concerned and include specialists from the private sector;

— the nomination within each district of at least one suitably qualified member of staff to coordinate historic buildings matters. The officer would have a duty to liaise with other officers at district, county and national levels and a right to report cases to his or her parent committee before a decision is taken by any other department. He or she would have the title of historic buildings officer.

Case Study 11: Schools

Given the comparatively short history of State education in this country, it is natural that most historic school buildings are in the private sector. Many are housed in buildings which were not constructed as schools. Since there has been little retrospective legislation affecting schools, they are able to retain their features unaltered for tradition's sake and meet their development requirements with new buildings or alterations to non-historic parts. The historic buildings affected by legislation in this sector are only those which have come into educational use relatively recently. In these cases, Building Regulations and Section 60 of the Public Health Act appear to be the two most influential pieces of legislation.

In the private sector it has sometimes been difficult to establish whether fire precautions work has been done voluntarily or by statute under the Education Act as a requirement of registration with the Department of Education and Science. When a school applies for registration, the DES obtains reports from the local fire authority on the standard of fire precautions and from appropriate authorities on building safety and environmental health. The DES passes on the fire authority's recommendations to the school's proprietors, and thereafter, from time to time, asks the school whether the work has been done and requests the fire authority to revisit the premises. Quite frequently, the advice of the fire authority is specifically requested.

Large houses lend themselves to conversion into schools, but they often carry high maintenance costs. Having to comply with legislation superimposes another financial burden and, as a consequence, the work has to be done as cheaply as possible. This is sometimes to the detriment of the architectural or historic character of the building such as when surface wiring and such materials as hardboard or plasterboard are used next to original finishes of higher quality.

A. Leadenhall School, Salisbury

The school occupies a three-storey building that was originally a private house. Now a girls' preparatory school, it has dormitories on the top floor for about thirty children. The means of escape from this level was seriously inadequate, and the school had been carrying out a programme of fire precautions work on their own initiative when they ran into planning and Building Regulations difficulties over a new external escape recommended by the fire authority. They engaged architects who were able to find a better solution to this problem, although they have not been able to eradicate some of the undesirable visual effects of the work done before their appointment.

Architects: Brandt Potter and Partners

Listed Grade I

The external stair

The dormitories were served by only one stair, which was not protected, and reached ground level in the centre of the building. There was also a hatch in the floor with a vertical ladder down to a classroom on the first floor. The fire authority called for a new enclosed stair either inside or outside at one end of the building. The planning officers indicated that the authority would not entertain the addition of a stair tower to the building, although it was generally recognised that an alternative means of escape was required in the general position proposed. The architects made a very careful survey and were able to find a route for an internal stair from second to first floor that would not affect the external appearance. An external spiral stair leading from an existing, though modified, window balcony was needed to reach the ground. Enclosure was not necessary for this stair under the Building Regulations 1976 because its height was less than 6 m, and planning approval was obtained.

A door in the escape route

Other fire precautions

The fire authority took considerable pains to give comprehensive advice to the school. Their plans showed which items of equipment, notices, smoke and heat detectors were required, together with doors that needed upgrading to a fire resisting standard, and this was backed up with a five-page schedule of works. The unfortunate effect of such comprehensive advice in this case was that the school was able simply to pass it to a contractor to carry out the work. They did not feel the need to take professional advice to safeguard the character of the building at this advanced stage.

Reference: Para 1.7.1

Leadenhall School, Salisbury Approximate scale 1:200

Section with new stair

South elevation with new stair

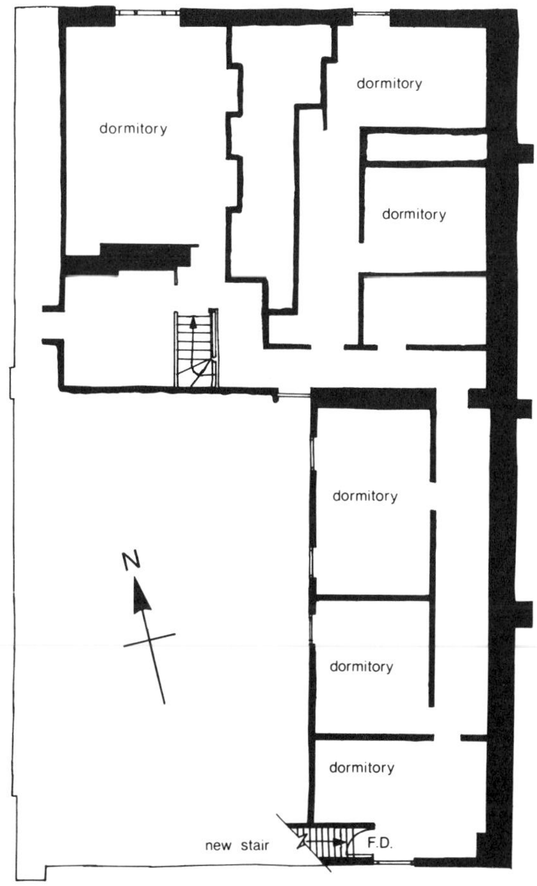

Second floor plan

Ground floor plan

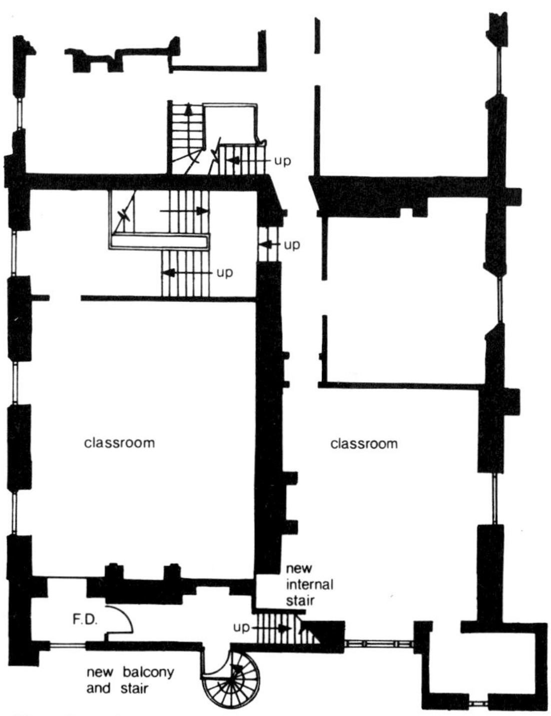

First floor plan

B. Bootham School, York

This case study illustrates the conflicting requirements that can arise in historic buildings of high quality. They were centred around proposals to provide fire protection to a main staircase, the final nature of which was determined by listed building considerations.

Architects: Colin Rowntree and Partners

Listed Grade I

The proposed changes resulted from fire service advice on means of escape improvements following the conversion of some dormitory space into staff flatlets. They recommended that the main stair, which only serves the ground and first floors, should be separated from the first floor accommodation and circulation to limit fire and smoke spread and improve the availability of the second stairway as an alternative escape route. Connecting doors and corridors were required to give a by-passing route round the main stair well. The stair landing was connected to the corridor around the stair through two arched openings, and in August 1978 an application was made for planning permission to enclose the stair with new fire doors in these openings. Permission was refused in November 1978.

The grounds for refusal were that the design of the new doors was not of sufficiently high quality in the context of the handsome staircase, and the planning officer recommended that either a new location for fire doors be found, or that the design of the doors should be improved and the possibility of using a 'heavy grade of clear glass' in the arched heads of the opening considered.

The lobby system, which was acceptable to the fire and planning interests, was disliked by the school. The corridor is used by the pupils and can be very busy. The school felt the doors would obstruct the traffic and might cause injuries. However, they felt that they had to accept the arrangement as a compromise between fire safety and architectural considerations. Planning and listed building approval was given in April 1979 and work began in summer 1980.

The school has in fact discovered that their misgivings about restricted circulation were unfounded. The stairway and main entrance hall below are now also noticeably warmer because the doors restrict the flow of warm air from the head of the stair.

References: Paras 1.7.1 and 3.3.1

Bootham School, York
Approximate scale 1:200 and 1:50

Elevation

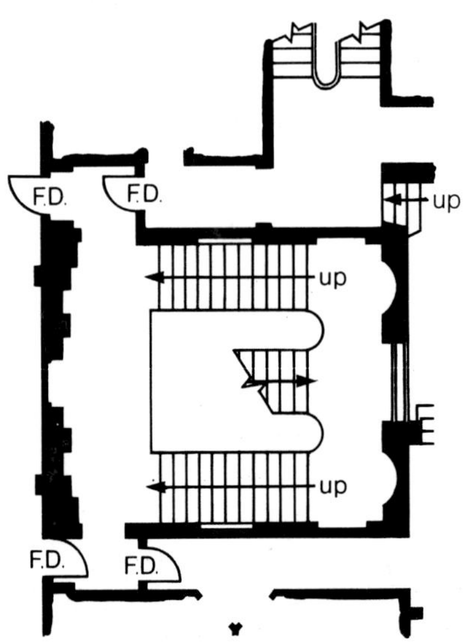

Accepted plan

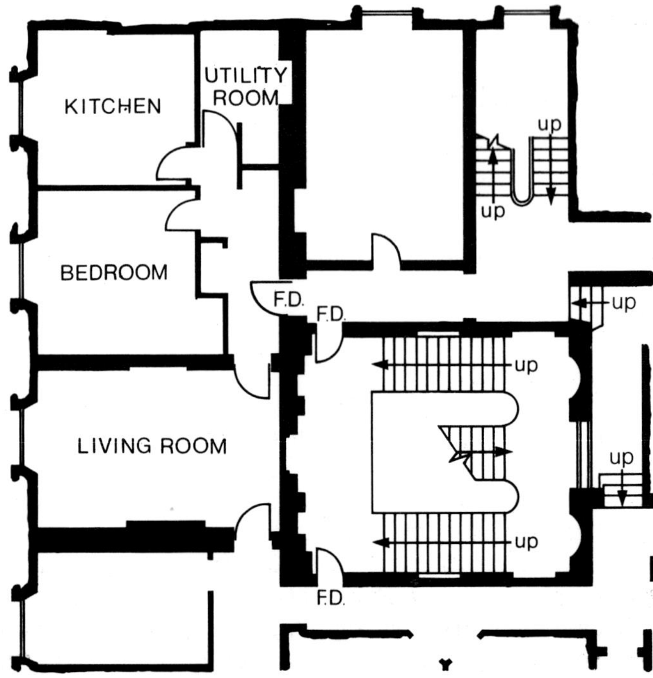

Rejected plan

Case Study 12: University Buildings

Although universities are mainly supported by public funds, they do not have the special building legislation status enjoyed by maintained schools. They have therefore been subject, wherever appropriate, to Building Regulations and the full spectrum of fire, health and safety legislation.

However, we have found that problems of interpretation occur quite often. The general rule when deciding how a building should be categorised for regulatory purposes, such as the appropriate purpose group in the Regulations or a use designated under the Fire Precautions Act, is that the relevant use is the principal one to which the premises are put.

For example, offices are designated under the Fire Precautions Act, and although a great deal of the work of university academic staff is carried out under office-type conditions, the purpose of the work comes under the description in section 1(2)(d) of the Fire Precautions Act 'for purposes of teaching, training or research'. This class of use has not been designated under the Act, so that a fire certificate is not automatically required. The question still arises for the university's administrative staff: is a professor's secretary performing an administrative function or an educational one. And what about a computer operator? The distinctions become blurred.

A similar problem may occur in student hostels. We have included in para 5.2.3 details of an important appeal case in which legislation for means of escape in houses in multiple occupation was applied to one type of student residence. Again, if halls of residence are let to 'outsiders' in vacations, they may be subject to the Fire Precautions Act for means of escape as though they were hotels. Some universities have resisted this strongly, arguing that rooms are only let to people on vacation courses at the university and hence the 'education' status is maintained. Other universities have decided that the standard should be improved, and have worked out phased programmes with the fire authority so that income from the holiday lettings is used to pay for the alterations as it comes in.

A. Worcester College, Oxford

The College has recently carried out fire precautions measures in two stages: the first was to improve the means of escape in the Terrace building, which has residential accommodation on the upper floors and offices at ground level; the second was to provide adequate means of escape from the extended library within the roof space.

Architects: Godfrey Macfadyen and Sturgis

Listed Grade I

The Terrace building

The College had approached the fire authority to specify the work necessary to bring the means of escape in the Terrace building up to fire certificate standard so that the premises would comply in advance with any forthcoming requirements. The work cost about £100,000 and included rewiring, upgrading of doors to stairways, the formation of protected routes and lobbies from some offices and the provision of crawl-hatches between some upper floor rooms; the hatches would allow occupants of rooms affected by fire in their own stair to reach another stair. Considerable practical problems arose in implementing this last arrangement as the occupants demanded very high standards of sound insulation. In order to retain the appearance of the old doors, whose battered attractions were more traditional than aesthetic, they were sectioned and a new insulating layer incorporated down the centre.

The library

The drawings show the rather complicated layout of the new stack area above the main library. Fire service advice had been to provide an alternative escape stair from the north end near the Pottinger room. The problem was to find an acceptable path down through or past the chapel below. The first proposal faced very strong opposition from the Victor-

Worcester College, Oxford
Approximate scale 1:250
First proposal

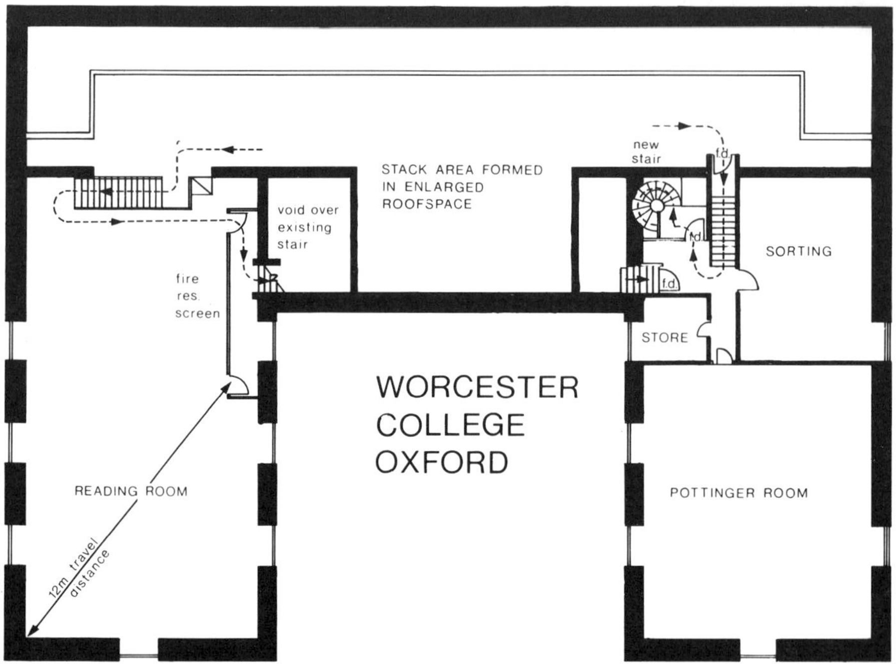

Second floor

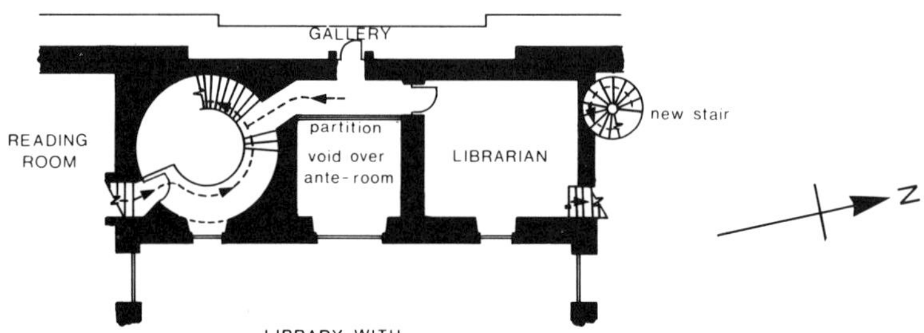

Mezzanine above first floor

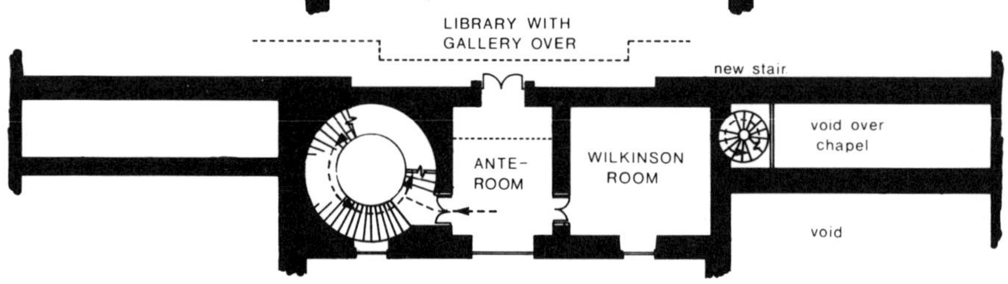

First floor

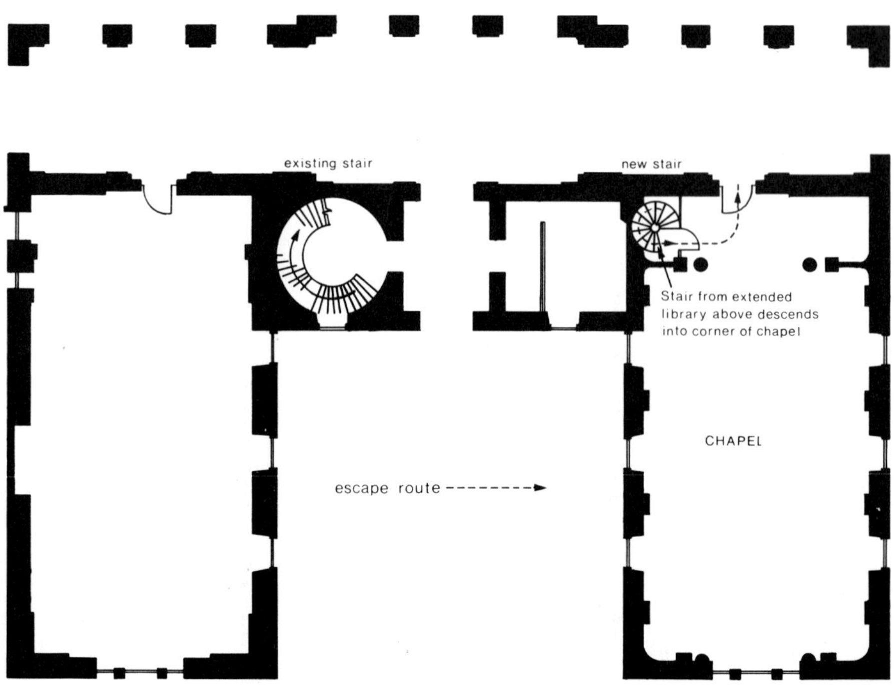

Ground floor

Approximate scale 1:250
Final scheme using pressurisation

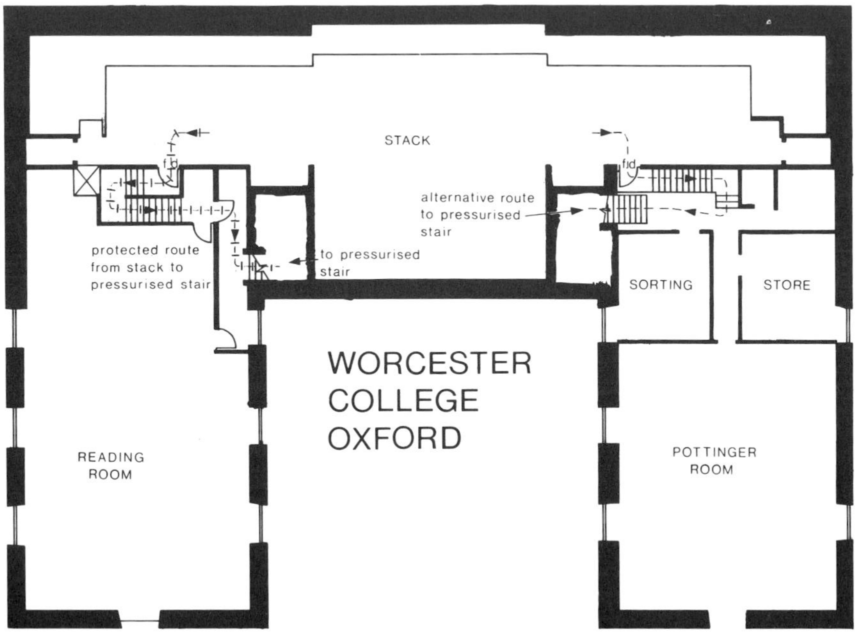

Second floor

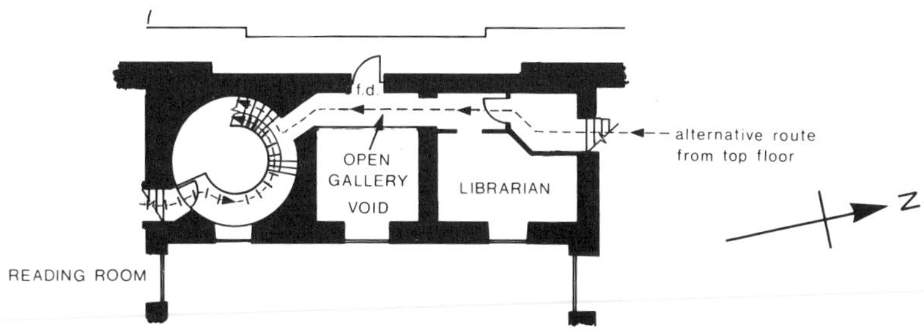

Mezzanine above first floor

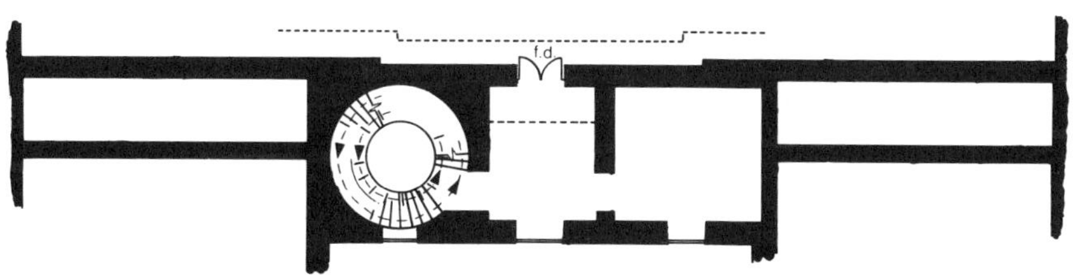

First floor

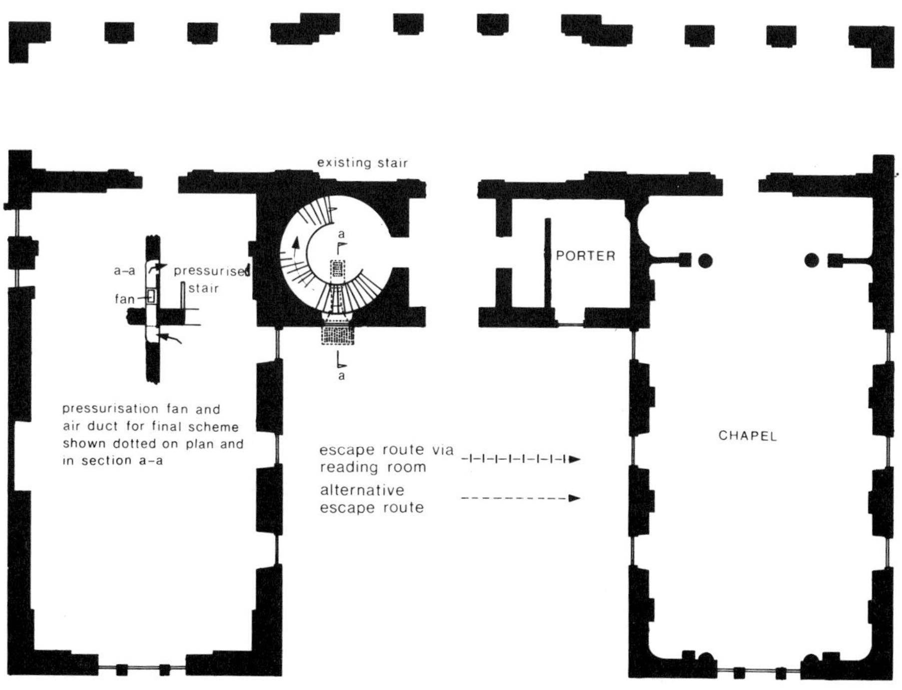

Ground floor

ian Society, because of the damage it would have done to the chapel's internal decorations.

Therefore a specialist fire engineering consultancy, Fire Check Consultants, was engaged, and, with the cooperation of the fire service, demonstrated that an air pressurisation system could be used to prevent fire or smoke spread into the existing spiral stair. The fan and motor for the pressurisation system are in a pit below the spiral stair and the only visible sign of their existence is a grille in the ground floor of the stair. A stair through the chapel was not required because, as a result of the use of pressurisation, the independent routes from the second floor could be brought together at first floor mezzanine level and permitted to share the single staircase.

Reference: Para 5.2.3

The concept of fire resistance is central to structural fire precautions. The degree of resistance is measured by the time taken for an element of building construction to withstand the effects of a fire.

This ability depends among other things on the severity of the fire – how fast it develops, the maximum heat output, maximum temperature, duration, etc. To enable comparisons between different types of construction, standard test conditions were devised and set out in the relevant parts of BS 476.

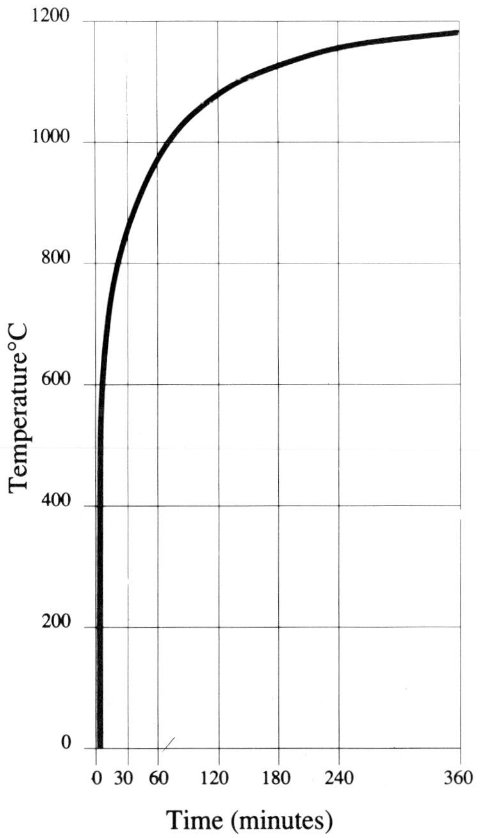

The test specifies three criteria:

'Stability': the ability of the element under test to resist collapse either during the test or afterwards.

'Integrity': its tendency to develop cracks or openings developed during the test, through which flames or hot gas can pass.

'Insulation': where the element separates a space containing a fire from some other space (e.g. an escape route), it must not spread fire by transmitting heat to combustible materials on the non-fire side.

The element to be tested is either placed within the test furnace or it is built into one side of the furnace (a free-standing column would go inside, a door would be fitted in a side wall, a floor would be fitted into the top of the furnace). The furnace is controlled so that a standard time–temperature curve is followed (see graph) and the fire resistance of the element is given as the time it takes for failure to occur. Thus a 30/20 fire door is one which maintains stability for 30 minutes and integrity for 20 minutes (insulation is not a criterion normally applied to fire doors).

However, if the occupants of a building are protected by a 30-minute door they are not necessarily assured of a 30-minute safe escape period. According to the severity of the fire, the door may fail much sooner or much later and, whether it fails or not, it is quite likely that the escape period will depend on the rate of smoke leakage around the door.

Quite minor changes in the test specimen can have a significant effect on performance in the test. It is therefore difficult to estimate the behaviour of a design. The 'notional' fire resistance period given by such an estimate is very approximate.